My old friend from many years ago. So glad to see that the Lord has blessed you with a great family!

Rev. 21:1-4

Your fried in christ,

A WALK THROUGH THE MARKET

- SECOND EDITION -

WADE J. CAREY

CROSSBOOKS
PUBLISHING

CrossBooks™
A Division of LifeWay
1663 Liberty Drive
Bloomington, IN 47403
www.crossbooks.com
Phone: 1-866-879-0502

Cover Artwork By: Robert Chadwick
Portrait of Mick by: Alfred Jones

Second Edition

First published by CrossBooks 6/28/2012

ISBN: 978-1-6150-7312-2 (sc)
ISBN: 978-1-6150-7539-3 (e)

Library of Congress Control Number: 2010939406

Printed in the United States of America

Photographic images in the following chapter headings are used by permission granted from
Madelyn A. Bloom, www.theviewfromrighthere.com: Title page, chapters 2 thru 16, 18, & 19

Certain stock imagery for the following chapter headings are used by permission from
www.bigstockphoto.com: Prologue, chapters 1, 17, & 20, Epilogue,
The Mythology Found in A Walk Through The Market Angels, Demons, &
The Flaming Sword, Prayer of Salvation, & Biblical Verses Used or Referenced.

FACT VS. FICTION

Just a quick note, before you begin reading . . . .

As a novel, this book is fictional by its very nature. However, its real purpose is to demonstrate essential biblical concepts within the context of a story. Admittedly, this can be a very slippery slope, indeed. So please . . . let me make this abundantly clear, right up front—*the Bible is the holy, inerrant Word of God.* There is absolutely no question in my mind about that. I also believe it to be the unquestioned authority in all matters.

Since the writing of novels can be a challenging way to draw someone towards biblical truth—which is the unambiguous goal of this book—I cannot recommend strongly enough that you read the "Mythology" section at the end of the story. It explains the major concepts being used throughout the book, and separates biblical fact, from biblical speculation (fiction). It also outlines the approach for this; the first in our *biblical teaching novels.*

Personally, for those of us who love Jesus Christ, I feel very strongly that the exploration of some of God's wonderful mysteries to be a healthy and natural endeavor. To me, it only shows that we wish to know more about Him. However, we must be cautious as we do so. Therefore, as you read this story, I ask you to please consider my reverence towards the Bible, and the critically important role I believe it plays in our walk with the Lord.

All glory goes to Jesus Christ, who died for our sins. I hope that you enjoy your *walk through the market!*

Wade

A Letter From Mick . . .

Howdy there, dudes! My name is Mick.

Oh by the way, I'm an angel. Not only that, but I'm also a *warrior* for Jesus Christ. Anyways, before you begin this story, I wanted to give you a little bit of a "heads up," before you get started . . . .

Early on, you'll learn much about God's holy angels (those who didn't follow Satan), and how we serve Jesus Christ, the Savior of the world. During the process, you'll also learn about our evil counterparts; i.e., demons. You see, ever since Adam and Eve were booted out of the Garden of Eden, the Earth has been the arena for an epic war between good & evil, and all human beings are born smack dab in the middle of it.

Anyways, I'm fixing to turn the floor over to a good buddy, who I call *The Storyteller.* His job is to tell you about an interesting experience I had with a friend named Wyatt Hunter, in the autumn of 2009. You see, prior to my mission to go see him, Wyatt had undergone some hard times in his life. So . . . when Jesus determined that the time was right, I was sent to teach Wyatt a few things that would help him with his troubles.

You wanna know something? I remember that day so very well. It was a gorgeous October day in Seattle, and the coffee was outstanding (actually, the coffee in Seattle is *always* outstanding!). Anyways, ole Wyatt and I chatted at-length as I taught him the basics about spiritual warfare. But alas, I'm getting ahead of myself . . . .

So grab yourself a cup of joe and hop aboard! I think you'll enjoy hearing about our interesting talk that fateful day. During the process, I hope you'll also learn a few things about angels, demons, and how things work in battling the forces of evil. Please believe me when I tell you this last, *very* important thing—the war between God and Satan exists all around you, whether you realize it or not.

All glory to the Lord Jesus Christ!

Your eternal friend,
Mick

PROLOGUE

Athens, Georgia
August, 2008

The early evening in north Georgia was hot and sticky that night, as a now distant, rumbling summer rainstorm continued its unruly march towards the northeast. Following in the storm's aftermath was a landscape covered in puddles, soaked roadways, and an almost suffocating squall of humidity. Under a semi-dark sky, intermittent sparkles of distant lightning now joined the chirping crickets in the resumption of their nighttime symphony. Faded purple rain clouds on the horizon noisily moved away in the disappearing light.

Mick-the-angel stood on a grassy promontory above Atlanta Highway, watching the grisly scene below. Unlike most of his assignments to deliver holy missions, this one was a quick trip to Earth to oversee something that made him very sad—the grief-stricken Wyatt Hunter, getting into a vehicle that would take him home. Unfortunately, he would be alone.

Just a short time before, Wyatt's wife, Vanessa, had been killed in a car accident. Due to his family's importance in the affairs of God's kingdom, the angel knew that he would return one day soon to visit Wyatt, so that he could help him with his future work. However, he had no idea when that would happen.

Mick was very pleased to have met Vanessa Hunter as she passed into her eternal home in Heaven, just a short while earlier. Although the angel had much to discuss with Vanessa, he was quickly called to duty and dispatched to Earth to check-in on Wyatt. Mick promised Vanessa that he would visit her once again, upon his return to Paradise. He then descended to Earth to oversee the situation.

There were many local officials finishing up their business at the accident scene now, and the traffic was just starting to get back to normal; the roadway was now cleared. Mick knew very well that there was a sinister and evil element involved in Vanessa's death, and that some time later on, its truth would be revealed.

But for now, the angel sadly gazed down at the passenger side of the car where Wyatt was sitting. The officer in the driver's seat of the unmarked police car was busily discussing several matters with one of the EMT's; obviously wrapping things up. As Wyatt sat there, his look of shock framed a river of tears rolling down his face. This really made Mick's heart ache.

However, at that moment, the angel was unable to do anything about it. You see, angels are messengers of God, and are therefore not worthy of worship—only the Lord is worthy of worship—and only the Lord can call all the shots. As a holy angel, Mick knew that he would simply have to observe and wait. However, his emotions were to run down and tell Wyatt:

"Vanessa is doing wonderfully in Heaven my friend – I promise!
I just met her Wyatt, and trust me –
she'll never have any pain or suffering ever again!
That's what Heaven is all about –
giving praise to God, and being with those who you love,
who also know Jesus as their Savior!"

But alas, that would have to wait for another day . . . .

PART 1

IN THE BEGINNING . . . .

A NEW MISSION

Heaven
October, 2009
- Today -

The "locker room" at the edge of Heaven was unusually quiet that morning, as three angels found themselves sitting around their old wooden table, reviewing reports and awaiting their next assignments. Of course, there weren't any locks or lockers; that was just the current nickname of this place, which was their home base.

These angels were not your ordinary, pink-cheeked cherubs. But rather, they were hard-working, lunch pail toting, blue collar angels, who were among the proletariat; not the "pretty boys," who have garnered so much artistic and literary attention throughout the ages.

All three of these angels comprised part of a special operating unit under the command of the powerful arch-angel, Michael. Their particular unit was assigned to the United States, a country with not only an alarming growth of secular tendencies, but also a burgeoning emphasis on evangelism. Both of these ideals are clearly at odds with each other, and are at the forefront of a huge cultural battle in America; one which continues to rage on, every day. This battle is representative of the age-old war between good and evil, and the chasm between these two camps continues to grow.

The "dirty dozen" was one of the current nicknames of this group of angels, which was partially coined from the 1960's movie about a group of misfits who had a tough assignment against a formidable enemy. That, and because these angels had to get their hands "dirty" on missions to Earth, by travelling from their heavenly abode to the fallen land.

Because these angels have had centuries of missions behind enemy lines, they are considered very special envoys from God; ones who were normally only called upon when the Lord needed to send a special message or mission to someone on Earth. On that particular day, there were only three members of the dozen in Heaven. The rest of the members of their team were all out on various assignments.

Back some time ago, an original member of dozen was banished for pride and vanity; an event which the remaining eleven angels continued to mourn. All of the angels in the dozen didn't care for talking about that issue very often, because their types of duties put them squarely in the middle of the battle between God and Satan.

In Heaven, it's a well-known fact that there are dire consequences for not serving the Lord. Even though there have only been eleven of these angels for most of their existence, they recently dubbed themselves the "dirty dozen," as a reminder of the grave consequences of any compromise before the throne of God.

All angels have a specific purpose for the King of kings, but not all of them are permitted to travel through the flaming sword portal to enter into the current Earth's realm—often referred to in the locker room as "the enemy's" territory. The "enemy" is the first fallen angel Lucifer, now called Satan. Satan has been the tempter and destroyer of humans for a long time now, and he is known to have a real penchant for doing anything he can to corrupt the Lord's creation. It all started way back in the beginning with Adam and Eve, and unfortunately, Satan's folly has continued up to current times.

The Bible states in *Genesis 3:24* there is a flaming sword wielded by mighty angels called cherubim, which is also a special angel task force. Similar to the dirty dozen, they are under the authority of Michael as well. Michael, who has been in charge of this critical gateway since the fall of mankind, keeps a constant watch on the events which take place on Earth. Since Michael's gateway responsibilities also include special missions against Satan and his demons, he helped to create *the dozen* in an attempt to offset their attacks, and to make occasional reparations for some of God's people who were harmed in the process of the enemy's mayhem. Michael's battles with the enemy are briefly described in *Revelation 12:7*, but that's only the tip of the iceberg. These battles are actually raging on during the present day, and one day soon, they will culminate in the final battle and victory for the Lord, Jesus Christ.

When you really got down to the nitty-gritty, not many angels were designed for front line assignments behind enemy lines, in a temporary physical body. Although the Lord designed His heavenly host for various reasons for service unto Him, only certain angels were actually designed to deal with the fallen world attributes which one sees when venturing away from Heaven.

Indeed, God made all of his angels differently and for specific purposes, just like His image-bearing human creations. The dozen all well understood that the human misconception which says that angels are clone-like, wimpy, and have no specific purpose, was utterly absurd. Satan wants the world to think that he and his minions are powerful and that the angels in Heaven are impotent. Of course, this is completely untrue. This false image was created by none other than Satan himself, who is the chief refugee on the fallen Earth.

As the angels sat sipping coffee—the most incredible coffee anyone could possibly imagine—the lead angel named Mick asked the other two, "So . . . what are your prospects for a new mission these days? Has the boss said anything directly to you?" The other angels were both reading over their reports, and hesitated for a moment before responding.

The second angel named Jimmy said, "I'm actually still waiting on that return assignment to the Los Angeles area. You know, the things that happen in that city never cease to amaze me."

The third angel named Ruth quipped, "The city of *angels*, huh? *Better you than me."* Jimmy and Ruth often gave each other a hard time, but they truly respected each other and often had to get the other's back during their often dangerous assignments. Ironically, they usually worked together as a team.

"Alright, how about you guys knock that off," Mick said, but not in serious tone. They all went back to their comfortable silence for a few minutes. Mick was surprised that the dozen was still not quite the same since the loss of one of their members, some time ago.

You see, angels had a choice whether to serve God or not, just like their human counterparts now do. However, unlike humans who are created in the image of God, any angel who rebelled does not have the chance for redemption.

For any angel, not serving God meant banishment from Heaven. In a manner similar to Lucifer, who was once a holy angel and is now called Satan, pride was the driving force behind an angel's dismissal and banishment. Damon, the "fallen name" for this former member of Mick's team, was originally member number four in the dozen. Unfortunately, Damon fell into pride and was banished from Heaven, along with the rest of those who aligned with Satan. He was then converted into a demon, and continues to roam the Earth, creating trouble for God's people.

"Well guys," Mick said, closing a file folder. "My report tells me that the new mission in the Pacific Northwest is now ready for me to deploy."

"Is it *finally* ready?" Ruth asked.

"Yep," Mick said. "It sure is. I've been waiting a long time for this."

"Indeed you have," Jimmy agreed.

Mick nodded, "Interestingly, my orders say that I have to first make a stop in Minneapolis."

"Hmmm . . . that doesn't sound so bad," Jimmy said.

"When do you leave?" Ruth asked.

"Very soon," Mick said, sounding eager, "and by *very soon,* I mean *right now."* Jimmy and Ruth both nodded their understanding.

Mick got up from the table and walked down the hall to his personal room. He then prayed for a few minutes or so, asking for God's continuing guidance on what he sensed was an important mission. Since Mick was the chosen leader of the dozen, he often drew the responsibility of being the first contact with the people on Earth who were chosen by the Lord to either receive a message, or an offer of a holy mission. Sometimes, it was both.

Little did Mick know that his impending mission would be just the beginning of an enormous battle that would ultimately lead to his needing help from several other members of the dozen, as well as many other angels. "See you guys later," Mick said, returning to the table where Jimmy and Ruth were seated.

"Serve Jesus well my friend," Jimmy said. "And feel free to stomp on a few demons while you're at it . . . ."

Mick winked at Jimmy, then exited the locker room and walked the short distance over to the massive terminus that was the flaming sword.

He took a moment to look at the incredibly beautiful tree of life to his left; a tree that was once on Earth, but after the fall of mankind, was then moved to its temporary home in Heaven.

As Mick stood before the magnificent flaming sword portal, he gazed over and gave a big thumbs-up to his boss Michael, as well as the in-charge members of the cherubim. As usual, Michael was intently watching events on Earth unfold, while the cherubim were guarding the way to the tree of life—as was their ardent duty.

When he arrived at his special portal passageway, Mick thought that he must look like a paratrooper getting ready to jump out of an airplane and into enemy territory to do battle, just like so many human soldiers have done in war time on Earth. A fellow angel and good friend named Bob, greeted Mick before he opened the special doorway at the east end of the flaming sword. Mick often used this doorway to travel back and forth to Earth, to carry out his God-commanded duties. Bob nodded at Mick and asked, "Headed back down, huh?"

"Yep . . . and it looks like the Lord has an *extra special* mission for me this time. I've been eagerly waiting for this one."

Bob nodded, "Go git-em, my friend."

"*You got it,* bud-dro," Mick said. He then entered through the portal doorway and passed into the fallen land, descending to Earth.

Back in the locker room, Jimmy said to Ruth, "I've got a funny feeling that you and I will be getting our marching orders to join him before this new mission is over."

"I'm with you," Ruth agreed. "But I think some of the others are already involved."

"Actually, I think you're right."

"Hey Jimmy . . . ." Ruth said slowly. "Isn't it your turn to make coffee?"

"I suppose it is."

"Well by now, you certainly know how I take mine."

"You got it," Jimmy said, getting up from his chair.

It was indeed, another spectacular day in Heaven.

2

FIRST CUP

Seattle WA

Emerging amber beams of sunlight slowly shuffled away the starry-filled sky, as dawn greeted a typical Seattle autumn morning with a kaleidoscope of colors. Following suit, the ancient downtown waterfront began to awaken, greeting forty three year old Wyatt Hunter as he prepared to make another visit to his favorite place on Earth—the nearby, world famous, Pike Place Market. The October morning was seasonally crisp, and he very much looked forward to a relaxing day.

Wyatt had moved to Seattle just ten months before, in January. It was an unusual confluence of events which precipitated his move, and life was just beginning to settle down from all of the turmoil from the previous year or so. Wyatt had always dreamed of relocating to Seattle, and before making the permanent move, he had often visited the city for nearly twenty years, on both business and leisure trips.

Contrary to mainstream thinking, Wyatt truly loved the Seattle area weather. After having spent most of his life on the outskirts of Atlanta, Georgia, he found himself still getting accustomed to living in the northwest, where many homes don't have air conditioning. *We only need it for a couple of weeks during the summer, so we just tough it out,* Seattleites often say, and at no point would you ever have the need to put away your jackets for the season. These things were unheard of in Atlanta.

Wyatt often laughed to himself about the false rainfall paradigm which most people in the country had about the Emerald City. Although Seattle averages rain during more days per year than Atlanta does, the peach capital usually experiences more annual inches of rainfall by a fairly comfortable margin. The same comparison was true for many other major cities throughout the country. Actually, the current rainfall leader among the top one-hundred largest cities in the United States is none other than Mobile, Alabama. Seattle is further down the list.

The driving forces behind Wyatt's westward trek was the allure of the overcast, foggy, and cool weather, coupled with his love of Pike Place Market. Although he was completely oblivious to this fact over the years, his many trips to Seattle had slowly forged an island of peace and contentment within him; ultimately it drew him to the Emerald City like the North Pole's silent magnetic pull to a compass needle.

Although the past year had been an extremely difficult one to endure, Wyatt felt both fortunate and very blessed to have landed in such a comfortable situation. Right before his move from Georgia ten months before, he purchased a condo along the Seattle waterfront on Alaskan Way. Seattle was definitely not the cheapest place to live, and condos along the waterfront were at a premium. However, Wyatt had enjoyed the guiding hand of the Lord during the entire process.

Were it not for the unexpected financial blessings after the turmoil from the previous year, he would never have been able to afford such a place. Through his life's experiences, he now had firsthand knowledge that life on the current, fallen Earth, consisted of both great joy, as well as terrible sadness. Wyatt knew of many people who only counted their blessings as the positive things in life. However, through his ongoing Bible studies, he discovered the truth that both your good and bad experiences should bring you closer to the Lord. He often struggled with how to share this incredibly ironic concept with others—especially non-believers.

Wyatt stood over the kitchen sink and soaked in the peaceful morning air, gazing out the slightly ajar window. The view offered a glimpse of the parking area near the bottom of Pike Place Hill Climb, his soon-to-be gateway to Pike Place Market. He was almost ready for his uphill hike, but not quite yet. As Wyatt continued to survey the overcast morning, he savored the view of the Seattle Aquarium to his right. Using his annual pass, he frequented the quaint-but-enjoyable aquarium, where he often found a quiet bench to sit down, read, and relax.

Wyatt's sense of oneness with the Lord was curiously at its strongest near his home in this older part of Seattle, which was on the waterfront and just down hill from the market. Although he never understood how a "southern boy" from Georgia could have found such happiness in a faraway place like Seattle, he was grateful to have moved there, nonetheless. Wyatt sighed as a feeling of tranquility passed through his entire body, like a gentle wave, calmly gliding towards the shore.

Because the temperature had dropped into the high forties that morning, Wyatt decided to don his favorite cool-weather gear—a faded black Pittsburgh Steelers sweat shirt. To complete his comfort-driven ensemble, he added some old, worn khaki pants, and comfortable cross-training sneakers; the latter of which were black and gray, highlighted by neon yellow striping.

At this stage of his life, Wyatt enjoyed dressing more for comfort than for looks. A few years before, he had come to believe that the old cliché, "the clothes make the man," was nothing but a bunch of hogwash. While he had no issue with dressing nicely for appropriate occasions—like work and certain social events—in his true leisure time, he wasn't interested in trying to impress anyone. He had long ago lost the phony pretense that clothes, money, and possessions made you better than anyone else. He figured this new thought process was part of maturing into your forties. That, and spiritually growing with a Christ-centered outlook on life.

Walking was so much easier for him these days since he had lost most of the weight which had plagued him for the past twenty years. Wyatt's weight had ballooned upward during that time, but he ultimately decided to get rid of the excess pounds for good. He well understood that ninety-nine percent of beating any kind of adversity or challenge was mental, and the biggest part of that ninety-nine percent was using the power of the Lord.

Due to his troubles from the previous year, he also came to realize that dealing with tragic losses usually points a person towards one of two directions—it either gives you the strength and determination you didn't know that you had, or it can destroy you. *It's up to each person to decide whether or not to use their resolve and faith to forge ahead,* he thought. *The Lord is always willing to lend a significant helping hand—if people will simply reach out to Him.* It always made Wyatt very sad when he saw instances where people encountered difficulties, then turned away from their faith in an effort to take on their troubles in a solo fashion. He knew this was always a road to nowhere.

It was 6:30 am, and Wyatt had already gone through his morning routine of showering and getting dressed. Since he had long ago lost most of his hair, he now shaved his head once a week, to compliment his short, gray-streaked goatee. The lack of hair treatment had thankfully cut a lot of time out of his morning routine, and Wyatt relished this simple pleasure. *The simpler life is—the better,* he thought.

Out of all of life's simple pleasures, Wyatt's first cup of coffee each morning was his absolute favorite. This was something he cherished very highly. He continued to stand over the sink, taking the final sip of his first cup of the day. He was just about ready to leave his condo as he savored the peaceful feeling provided by the morning's solitude, along with that first taste of java heaven.

Coffee was another fringe benefit that Wyatt loved about Seattle, often referred to as the "coffee capital of the world." While he didn't go as far as drinking several pots of coffee each day, like some of his colleagues in the trucking business, he usually enjoyed three or four daily cups. It was actually hard to find many spots in Seattle which didn't have a coffee cart or shop nearby. This allows both Seattleites and its visitors have a minimal chance of missing out on a caffeine fix, whenever the urge presents itself.

As he rinsed out his *Mall of America* coffee mug, Wyatt remembered that he had to pick up a few letters to drop in the mailbox for his neighbor and friend, Charlene Harris, from down the hall. Miss Charlene was often a "life saver" when it came to having a good friend close by. She was actually very much like a family member to Wyatt. Charlene was a widowed, sixty-eight-year-old woman who embodied genuine Christ-like kindness and giving.

Wyatt always admired Miss Charlene's incredibly bright demeanor, despite some of the previous challenges in her life. Charlene was an African-American who had lived through the thankfully extinct, "back of the bus" days, which was a very difficult time in her life. Losing her husband of almost forty years also could have made Charlene a bitter person, but somehow it didn't. Actually, that "somehow" was quite clear to Wyatt now—Charlene Harris was one of the warmest Christian people who he had ever met. Her faith was at once steady, strong, and completely unwavering.

Charlene's late husband Robert had been in the aerospace business in southern California, and had made a nice living. After he passed away ten years before of an apparent heart attack, Charlene sold their home for a bundle, then relocated to her home town of Seattle. Actually, Miss Charlene was originally from the Yakima area, and grew up on an apple farm as a young girl. Her family later moved to West Seattle, and she and Robert moved to southern California after marrying.

Today, Miss Charlene dearly loved living on the Seattle waterfront. Her condo sported a fabulous view facing Elliott Bay, and in the evenings when the sun was slipping into the mountains to the west, her view was nothing less than stunning. Wyatt and Charlene would often have dinner together on her terrace, while enjoying discussions on their favorite topic of discussion—the Bible and its teachings.

While Charlene apparently didn't have a large bank account, she certainly didn't have to worry about paying her electric bill either. Both she and Robert had lived a good life in California, raising three children and putting them through college. Charlene was now a grandmother of seven, and a great grandmother of one. Her children and grandchildren were scattered all over the country, and her closest living relative was actually her youngest sister Candace, who lives in Boise, Idaho.

After Wyatt had moved to Seattle earlier in the year, the unwitting combination of his depleted emotional situation, his need for a real friendship, and his growing faith in God, quickly evolved into his becoming a de facto part of Charlene's family. Charlene still maintained strong mothering instincts, and Wyatt needed a friend who could support him during the difficult transition in his life. The result was that their relationship naturally evolved post haste, and was now equally cherished by both parties.

Wyatt left his kitchen and began to move towards the front door. He picked up his well-worn backpack from the chair where it was perched, swinging his arms through the straps and flipping it onto his back. He then locked the door behind himself, departing his condo. After only a short walk down the hallway, he arrived at Charlene's front door.

The hallway was cool from the overnight temperature, and the carpeted floor muffled his footsteps. Just as Wyatt was about to knock, Miss Charlene opened the door, "Good morning, dear!" she said. "How're you feeling this morning?" When addressing you, Miss Charlene had a certain way of making someone feel like they were the most important person in the world. Her effervescent smile and loving warmth was absolutely contagious.

"I'm fine, Miss Charlene," Wyatt said in a slightly sheepish voice. He was slightly taken aback, because she had opened the door, right as he was about to knock. It was almost as if some inner sense told her he was standing there. "Where's the little stinker?" he asked, quickly regaining his composure.

The "little stinker" was his five year old female Boston terrier named "Baby." Wyatt had to face it—Baby was Charlene's dog, just as much as she was his own. To evenly divide their joint responsibilities, Baby often spent the night with Charlene. Truly, Wyatt couldn't have picked a better dog sitter than his wonderful spiritual companion from down the hall.

On occasions when Wyatt would do any traveling, Charlene would be almost ecstatic about the chance to care for their canine companion. So, whenever he could find the time to break away, Wyatt enjoyed taking overnight trips to the San Juan Islands and the Olympic Peninsula—both destinations only a short ferry ride away. The state parks and natural scenic beauty in western Washington are among the most spectacular in the entire world. Wyatt often utilized the nearby Washington State ferry terminal to take these jaunts. This was just another one of the many fringe benefits of his new locale.

Charlene had enjoyed many dogs over the years, and Baby really seemed to help fill a void in her life, which was created by her husband's passing. *"Our furry friends are gifts from the Father, dontcha know,"* she often said. In the past, Wyatt had fallen victim to the human-centered opinion that since human beings are God's crowning achievement in creation—and are therefore "superior" to animals—the Lord's "lesser" creations weren't important, and ceased to exist at death. After a review of some of his favorite Scripture passages, this school of thought now seemed utterly absurd, and completely contrary to the nature of the loving God of Genesis, who declared that His entire creation was "very good."

Wyatt was always saddened when people espoused biblical "truths," which weren't necessarily rooted in Scripture—whether it was animals in Heaven, or any other subject. After both his wife, Vanessa, and his other dog, Scout, moved on to be with the Lord the previous year, Wyatt only found true solace in the word of God—not in the opinions of man.

Subsequent to Vanessa's funeral, and even after his unexpected estrangement from his only son Danny, Wyatt discovered that nothing can make you feel better when your heart aches, except the love and hope of Jesus Christ and God's plan of redemption. Regardless of how many things that you possess, accumulate, or accomplish during your lifetime on Earth, nothing can surpass the Lord's truly wonderful gift of Hope.

As Wyatt's path towards the Lord continued to accelerate with each passing day, he came to realize that the thing which his heart yearned for the most, was to be with the Lord, who was his best friend and Creator. If everything in the Bible was really true as Wyatt believed it to be, logically, he had to release his anxiety over being separated from Vanessa. Wyatt realized that she was unquestionably in that place which Jesus had prepared for her, as spoken of in *John 14:1-3;* however, his heart still ached for his beloved wife.

Wyatt also strongly felt that you can't just be a believer for an hour in church on Sunday, then go out into the real world—which is full of tribulations and strife—without using God's Holy Word and its hope as the antidote to one's troubles. The Bible is a real, living thing, and Wyatt tried very hard to concentrate on his blessings, instead of his sorrows. After all, it was a beautiful autumn morning in Seattle that day, and he was indeed glad to be alive.

"Baby went back to sleep after her morning meal and walk," Charlene said. "You know how routine oriented she is."

"Yeah, I suppose she is . . . ." Wyatt trailed off. "Hey Miss Charlene, would you mind keeping her for a little while longer today? I'm kicking around an idea for a new article, and I'd like to spend some extra time up in the market this morning. I'm thinking that it should be a little slow up there, and it'll give me some time to think."

Along with his job as a ground transportation manager for a large, downtown Seattle worldwide logistics provider, Wyatt wrote some occasional freelance articles for a couple of small, contemporary Christian magazines. While it was true that he wasn't widely published yet, he did have enough articles in print to show off to his family and friends. His regular job had him usually working Thursday through Monday, often on the second shift.

"That's perfectly fine, dear," Charlene beamed. "I'll call your cell if I need anything. You just take your time and enjoy yourself . . . oh, and please try to relax a little bit dear, would you?"

Wyatt nodded, smiling at her covert attempt at mothering. He gave Miss Charlene a reassuring hug and kiss on the cheek, before saying, "Okay then, I'll see you later. Hey, if it's okay with you, I'll wrestle up something fresh from the market to cook us up a nice dinner tonight. How does that sound?"

"That sounds *great* dear—whatever you like," Charlene said. "We'll see you in a little bit." *Her enthusiasm over the simplest things is something to be admired,* Wyatt thought, as Charlene continued, "You go now, and don't you worry about a *thing.* I'll look after Baby when she gets up from her beauty rest."

Wyatt nodded, "Thanks, Miss Charlene."

"Oh, I almost forgot. Here are the three letters I need you to mail for me."

Wyatt hated long good-byes, so he quickly took the letters and left the second floor of the condo. After arriving on the first floor landing, he walked out of the nearby exit door. As he made his way out into the open, a rush of cool air and mist swooped around him like a new skin, instantly spreading across his entire body. He then blurted out an inadvertent "ahhh," and stood still for a moment, taking in the glorious morning. Wyatt then made his way south towards the hill climb.

3
AN INTERESTING STRANGER

As he approached the bottom of Pike Place hill climb, Wyatt wondered what its official name really was. It's often referred to as "Pike Street" hill climb, "Pike Place" hill climb, and "Market" hill climb, among others. Just as he got to the bottom of the steps, he looked to his right at the vacant space that used to be a pretty neat furniture store, several years ago. He thought for a moment about how things changed in this world, whether you liked it or not. It seemed to Wyatt that the older he got, the more his heart longed for a place where negative changes didn't occur, and where everyone was friendly and knew who you were. No, not "Cheers"— Heaven. Cheers would be a distant second . . . .

Wyatt started up the stairs and hiked up past the Zig Zag Café, a hip and trendy bar where the bartenders mixed some pretty exotic drinks. Wyatt was fairly boring when it came to alcohol consumption, because unlike many others, he didn't like getting drunk anymore. He knew from his Bible studies that God has a proper purpose for alcohol, just as He does for sex, money, and all other *double-edged swords*.

Wyatt also knew that, much to the delight of Satan, people often didn't follow true biblical teaching on these double-edged swords, and often ignored the Bible's warnings about them. Because of mankind's propensity towards sin, he knew that alcohol, sex, and money were very dangerous, if not used according to the Bible. He felt like these things should be approached from a biblical perspective—and a biblical perspective only.

As it related to alcohol, Wyatt often read *Ephesians 5:18,* which was his go-to passage on this subject . . .*"Do not get drunk on wine, which leads to debauchery. Instead, be filled with the Spirit."* Although Wyatt understood that some Christians choose to not drink alcohol as a positive witness to others, he also felt that those who do drink alcohol, should do so in moderation. *If someone can't do it in moderation, then it should be avoided altogether,* he thought. Wyatt also felt that if someone does choose to drink, it should be done in a way which would never cause their witness to the world to become questioned. In other words, it should never cause their brother or sister to stumble.

On occasion, Wyatt enjoyed venturing up to Woodinville, WA, to visit the wineries and take in the ambience of the quaint town. Woodinville was about a half-hour drive north of Seattle, and there were many excellent wineries and restaurants to explore. Vanessa and Wyatt had often visited Woodinville on several of their vacations in the past, and he still enjoyed driving up there a few times a year. The restaurants and wines were very good, and Woodinville reminded him of great memories and better times.

Even though he desperately tried to avoid it, Wyatt's anxiety over losing Vanessa the year before often flooded into his head. It was almost like a game of mental dexterity—that is, trying to keep out the pain, and maintain a positive outlook. These remorseful thoughts often came rushing at him like an attacking infantry unit, which he regrettably referred to as the "pain brigade." Sometimes, he simply had to engage his painful thoughts, so his feelings of remorse from the previous year's turmoil could run their course. Essentially, the pain brigade couldn't be kept at bay all of the time.

No matter how mentally strong one may be, you're bound to lose a battle to invasions of painful memories on occasion. Ironically, the loss of this kind of battle can often lead you to greater strength. In other words, dealing with your pain is often better than hiding from it. When the pain brigade crossed Wyatt's battle line and had their way for a while, he always retreated into his faith in God—his only true solace. He often wondered how people who didn't have this sanctuary, coped with the inevitable tribulations which life on this fallen Earth has in store for everyone.

Wyatt crossed the bridge over Western Avenue and continued his upward climb. He was huffing and puffing by now, but he enjoyed the exercise. Plus, it wasn't ninety-five degrees and humid outside, something that the weather in Georgia had often heaped upon his unwilling shoulders. He could still see his breath in the cool, early morning air as he continued his ascent.

Wyatt often felt that the effort it took to climb the stairs and ramps up to the market was similar to a person's upward struggle through tribulations, before arriving at Heaven's gate. He always felt like the prize in both cases was worth the struggle—especially the Heaven part.

Once inside the lower levels of the Main Arcade, Wyatt continued his march through the ancient wooden ramps and old, concrete steps, until he passed the restrooms on his right hand side. After one more short flight of stairs up, he was standing in what might be the most heavily foot-trafficked area in all of Seattle—the heart of the world famous Pike Place Market. Right near where he stood was Pike Place Fish Market, home of the fishmongers and the phenomenon of the "flying fish," a Seattle tradition known to most people throughout the country.

Wyatt stopped for a minute to catch his breath. On any Saturday morning and three hours later in the day, this place would be mobbed. However, it was a little before 7:00 am, and it was still pretty quiet. Several of the vendors were beginning to stir, but this normally vibrant place was not awake quite yet.

For several reasons, the early morning was definitely Wyatt's favorite time to go to the market. In those early stages of the day, although it was still very peaceful, you could also sense the impending onslaught of lively commerce about to take place. Wyatt stood there for a few moments to take it all in.

After a minute or so, he hooked a left to see what the ladies at the Pike Place Bakery were offering that day. As usual, they had some unbelievably gorgeous—but probably not very healthy—pastries and baked goods. *Perfect,* he thought. *After all, bakeries aren't supposed to serve alfalfa sprouts.* There were some gigantic donuts in the case around the side, and Wyatt was always tempted to buy one, because they looked so delicious.

Slowly proceeding past the bakery through the Main Arcade, Wyatt approached the Athenian restaurant on his left. As he did so, he thought about having some breakfast later that morning. From his many previous visits, he knew that the Athenian had some wonderful views of Elliott Bay. This served as a wonderful accompaniment to its excellent menu.

However, breakfast was for later. Right now, it was time to go to his favorite coffee bar in the entire world—the Seattle's Best café on Post Alley.

He veered right, passing through one of the vendor hallways and out onto Pike Place, which is the main road through the market.

The brick road felt uneven under his feet as he crossed over the ancient street. Once on the other side, he turned diagonally off of Pike Place and onto Post Alley—a quaint area with many shops. A couple of the fruit and vegetable vendors were already setting up for the day, and as usual, the produce was absolutely beautiful. A waft of fresh seafood assaulted him from his right, but this was not a good thing for Wyatt Hunter—he hated seafood, pure and simple. Yes, the man who loved the Pike Place market like no other place, hated eating seafood. Ironically, watching it fly through the air, much to the delight of tourists, was something he enjoyed very much.

As Wyatt passed by the *Made in Washington* store to his right, he picked up the welcoming scent of freshly brewed coffee and espresso. It was obvious to him that the baristas at Seattle's Best were busily brewing-up an array of delicious beverages. He was convinced that the aromatic trail this created was most assuredly designed to ensnare any passersby. Wyatt then suddenly felt a tractor beam lock onto his nose, drawing him towards the front door of the café. Seemingly beyond his control, when he arrived at their doorway, he eagerly opened it and stepped down into his ambrosial destination.

On warmer mornings, the sliding doors to his right which faced Post Alley would be open, and Wyatt would have preferred it that way. However, that morning was apparently a little too chilly for most people, so he would have to deal with balmy temperature and intense coffee aroma inside. As it was, the bench table and seats facing Post Alley were empty, save for the remnants of a newspaper. He continued into the café, noticing only a few other patrons.

There was a couple sitting at a table across from the register, and one older, hippie-looking guy, who sat near the corner of the red-tiled bar, to his left. This pony-tailed gentleman sipped away at a large coffee, apparently pleased with his morning libation. The two baristas were the only other people in the store, so Wyatt quickly bellied up to the register to order his usual.

"Good morning, sir!" the genuinely chipper twenty-something girl at the register said. "What can we getcha this morning?" Wyatt observed her curious face piercings and slightly gothic makeup. He had long ago given up trying to figure out why people did what they did, and now accepted most people at face value. As long as they are genuinely polite, he really didn't care how someone dressed—or pierced for that matter. By this point in his life, Wyatt knew that God's children often came in non-stereotypical packages. Because of this, he had learned to train his personal radar towards discerning where someone was with their faith in God, instead of why they may have a butterfly tattoo on their ankle.

Curiously enough, for his fortieth birthday a few years earlier, Wyatt decided to go way outside of his comfort zone, and had gotten a beautiful medieval cross tattooed on his upper left arm. You might be able to just see the bottom of the cross when he wore short sleeved shirts. Wyatt didn't do it for a "hey, look at me—I'm forty" kind of attention getter; he simply wanted to remind himself of Who he belonged to. When he showered each day, his tattoo reminded him that his personal mission was to help God guide His children home to Heaven, and that his current life on Earth was only temporary. Somehow, the new tattoo really did the trick.

Out of nowhere, the pain brigade launched another assault at Wyatt. Although this irritated him, he fought off them off and focused on ordering his coffee. "Yes, I'll have double tall, no whip, extra hot, soy mocha," Wyatt said. Admittedly, this was not a very masculine sounding drink, but it tasted fantastic. *Soy is good for you, and it really cuts down on the calories,* he thought.

"Comin' right up," she said. Her name tag said, "Sally."

"Thanks, Sally," Wyatt said. He recognized her from his many previous visits to the café. But before today, he had never noticed what her name was.

Wyatt moved down the bar to his left, passing the Star Wars looking espresso machine and sat down, two seats to the right of the ponytailed gentleman. He then set his backpack on the vacant chair to his right, opened up the front zipper, and pulled out his Bible, a notepad, and a pen. He also pulled out his reading glasses for the small print. "Getting old is a bummer" he would often say, and by using the term "bummer," he knew that he was already there.

Wyatt often used his quiet time like this to review Scriptures from the previous week. Each day, he received emails from various faith based sources, all of which helped him to learn more about the Word of God. *Technology is amazing, and the Christian faith seems to be keeping up with the times,* he thought.

Wyatt received daily emails from LifeWay, and periodic ones from EPM and Randy Alcorn, Lee Strobel, Got Questions.org, and several others. He often used these emails to do biblical research. Admittedly,

Wyatt usually did his Scripture research on the computer at home, utilizing Biblegateway.com, which contains numerous biblical translations. To him, this was easier than flipping pages. He found this method to be a kind of modern-but-effective way to read the Bible. However, when doing research outside of his home, Wyatt always opted for his well-used "travel Bible."

Sally's co-worker was also an early twenty-something youngster named Ryan, who sported dirty blonde, spiked hair. This served to compliment his engaging personality. As he began to work on Wyatt's coffee, Ryan looked like a pilot who was preparing to guide a starship through hyperspace; he manipulated the espresso machine with skill and confidence. *This young man is obviously in great shape—he probably spends four hours a day working out,* Wyatt thought. The younger man asked the elder, "So where are you from, sir?"

Wyatt sighed, quietly. Although the use of the word "sir" was very polite, he always preferred much less formal terminology. *Well, at least this kid has manners,* he thought. "I'm a local now," Wyatt said.

"Oh, cool," Ryan said, nodding. The young man proceeded to ramble-on about some local band's triumphant return to the stage at a local club. Wyatt nodded, while not taking his eyes off of his note pad. He continued to survey his Bible passages for the day. After a minute or so, Ryan placed the foamy mocha in front of Wyatt on the red tiled bar. The barista then said, "Wait a sec." He then placed the traditional small stick of chocolate on top of the paper cup, like it was a ruler measuring the diameter. "Now you're all set, chief," Ryan said.

"Thanks buddy," Wyatt said. He then dropped the chocolate into the mocha to melt, before continuing his Bible study.

The cafe remained quiet for a few minutes until the hippie-looking, ponytailed guy two seats to his left piped up and said, "I'll have another one when you have a minute, Ryan."

The stranger had an oddly comforting sound to his voice, and Wyatt instantly felt foolish. In the back of his mind, he thought this peculiar guy might sound like an edgy, homeless person when he spoke. He was wrong. Seattle certainly had its share of homeless people and vagrants, but many of them stayed several blocks south in the Pioneer Square area. Nearby Victor Steinbrueck Park, with its incredible views of downtown Seattle and the waterfront, was another gathering place for both the eclectic and the destitute.

No matter how much you try to eliminate the pre-judging of people based on appearance, prejudices can still rear their ugly head and prove you to be foolish. Now was definitely one of those moments for Wyatt. The interesting stranger was dressed in tired old blue jeans and well-worn sneakers. He still had his jacket on, which was made of brown leather; it looked neither spiffy nor shoddy. He was wearing a faded black Krispy Kreme tee shirt which appeared to be very comfortable, although it had certainly seen its better days.

Wyatt could just barely see the red glow of the "Hot Now" signature logo on the stranger's shirt, but he tried to avoid thinking about those deliciously delightful hot donuts, which originated back in the southeast U.S. *If you have one Hot Now donut, you have to have six,* he thought. Although there were a few Krispy Kreme stores in the Seattle area, Wyatt waited to go on an occasional "Hot Now" bender when he visited friends back in his home town of Jefferson, Georgia. He always made sure to walk extra laps on those days, when he and his buddies ventured into nearby Athens to partake in the sweet sensations at the seemingly pearly gates of Krispy Kreme.

The interesting stranger perched two seats over from Wyatt looked like an odd combination of a biker, a surfer, and an old soldier. He had long, grayish blonde hair in a pony-tail, and a short goatee style beard. Although his complexion had some wrinkles, he looked more like a tough war veteran than an aging geezer; his manner appeared to be firm-yet-gentle.

The stranger continued to look into his coffee cup, apparently deep in thought. Wyatt wondered what travails this tattered looking stranger had gone through. Was he an old sailor? A biker? A construction worker? What was he like, and more importantly, did he believe in the Lord? Wyatt's mind was on a tangent pondering these things, when Ryan brought the stranger his new coffee.

"Here ya go, Mick," Ryan beamed, handing him a new cup. So, the stranger had a name—"Mick." Wyatt wondered what it was short for, or if it was just an arbitrary nickname given to him when he grew up in some rough neighborhood. *Oops, there goes the stereotyping again,* he thought.

"Are you okay for now, sir?" Ryan asked, his question interrupting Wyatt's trance.

"Oh—I'm fine, thanks," Wyatt replied, taking a sip of his mocha. His thoughts instantly returned to Mick, and he wondered what would be a good topic to start a conversation with him. Being friendly certainly wouldn't hurt, and maybe—*just maybe*—this Mick fellow was a nice guy.

As Wyatt ruminated for a minute or so over this, Ryan and Sally disappeared into the back room of the store, due to the lull in business. The couple sitting at the table across from the register had already disappeared via the back entrance of the shop, into the Sanitary Market building. The ambient sounds of the cafe and the early morning vendor setup in all directions was still present, but all else was quiet in the store. It was just Mick and Wyatt, sitting with two empty chairs in-between them.

The room took on an odd ambience; odd because it was a little eerie with anticipation, but also rather intriguing. Wyatt had a strange-but-unidentifiable sense of expectation as he prepared to address the interesting stranger. However, before he could say a word, Mick said something to him that would forever change his life. No day after today would be the same, no matter how much he might want it to be. Although these five words would instantly re-route the river of his future, and ultimately lay out the path towards mending his broken heart, they initially hit him like a raging linebacker sacking an opposing quarterback.

"Vanessa is okay, you know," Mick said, and those five simple words started everything in motion that was destined to happen that fateful day.

4
CROSS EXAMINATION

The Earth stood still. All thoughts and sounds evaporated into a vacuum, as Wyatt's mind swiftly focused on the man before him. His first thought was one of wonder—how could a seemingly innocent thing like getting a cup of coffee, suddenly turn into an episode of *The Twilight Zone*? He found himself temporarily paralyzed from Mick's lightning strike from out of nowhere, and for a few moments, he had no idea what to say or do. *How can this jerk possibly know anything about Vanessa?* he wondered.

Mentally, Wyatt felt like he was being pummeled against the ropes in his emotional boxing ring. However, his instincts quickly rebounded and his thoughts naturally turned to the offensive. Within a few moments, his mind pushed back the pain brigade, and a wave of outrage almost seemed to pour out of him. *Who is this rude guy, anyway???* he thought.

Still though, Wyatt also felt a simultaneous curiosity about where this interesting stranger was coming from. Before he was able to verbalize his response, he felt an oddly reassuring twinge in the back of his mind regarding Mick, giving him an unexpected feeling of comfort with the stranger. This was due in part to Mick's laid-back voice, which was a fused combination of three-fourths cowboy, and one-fourth surfer; it was masculine and deep like Sam Elliott the actor, but also very casual, with no pretense.

"Come again???" Wyatt asked, regaining his composure.

"Vanessa is okay, dude. I just wanted to let you know."

Wyatt quickly began his counter-offensive, "Look sport, I don't know what kind of game you're playing here, but it sure isn't funny. I was just trying to—"

Quickly interrupting, Mick held up his hands in a benign, defensive gesture, "I know what you were trying to do, and I appreciate that. I just wanted to let you know that Vanessa is okay."

"How did you—?" Wyatt's voice trailed off as curiosity began to replace his irritation.

"Look partner, you may not believe me right now, but today will end up being an absolute *landmark* day in your life."

"What are you talking about???"

"Let me put it to you like this," Mick said. "Although there's no way you could have possibly known it, we've actually been watching you from above for quite some time now."

"Once again—*what in the world are you talking about?* Are you some kind of space alien—or are you just nuts or something?"

Ignoring Wyatt's question, Mick continued, "Now then, please listen to me *closely.* You've been chosen for a mission. And along with that, the Father wants to give you some gifts. I'm simply your messenger."

Very unexpectedly, a cloudbank of calmness appeared on the horizon of Wyatt's irritation, and began slowly drifting towards him. The diverse and eclectic nature of the market will almost certainly ensure that you'll meet all kinds of interesting individuals; including misfits, and people with strange personalities. In that regard, the market was no different than any other public locale.

However, Wyatt's instincts told him that something was different with this guy. Most of the time, people make instantaneous decisions as to whether they click with someone or not; likely because the majority of human feelings and communication happen in the world of the unspoken. Despite his shocking opening salvo, Wyatt couldn't quite pinpoint why Mick seemed so unthreatening. He leveled in a calmer voice, "Look Mick, I don't know what your deal is, but you're playing a *very* dangerous game here."

"What do you mean by that?"

"You can't just hit people with comments about their dead spouse, then expect them to be all playful and happy. Furthermore, you—"

"Please take it easy my friend," Mick said. "What's it gonna hurt to hear me out?"

"Because you picked a helluva difficult subject for me to be all *friendly* about," Wyatt said. "And by the way, how in the world do you know anything about me *or* Vanessa?"

"Scout's okay too," Mick replied calmly, not answering his question.

Wyatt sighed in frustration. "You also know about my dog that died last year?"

"I sure do. Listen, it's sad when anybody or anything dies a physical death here on Earth. However, it's beautiful beyond words when they experience redemption through Jesus Christ, just beyond what you can see. Our Lord is awesome, my friend."

Geez, that was pretty profound, for a psycho, Wyatt thought. "Why are you here?" he asked, resuming his interrogation.

"I've already told you—because you've been chosen for a mission. Not only that, but—"

"Mister, I have *enough* work already," Wyatt interrupted. "I don't need any new burdens."

"Believe me, you'll like this gig," Mick said. "Actually, I mean, this *mission.*"

"You sure are persistent," Wyatt said.

Mick chuckled, "Well, I suppose this isn't the first time I've been accused of *that.*"

By now, a sense of calm had enveloped and quelled most of Wyatt's anger, like a steady rainstorm cooling down a hot summer afternoon. *Talking about the LORD was a wise tactical move by this potential kook,* Wyatt thought; it piqued his curiosity. *Maybe this old guy isn't so crazy after all,* he thought. However, Wyatt decided to follow his instincts, continuing with a lawyer-like mental focus. If Mick was indeed a phony, he wanted to quickly expose him, so he could resume his Bible study. "Okay sport, I'll play—who sent you?"

"My boss man, Michael."

"Michael who?"

"Michael is a singular name, like 'Sting' or 'Madonna'."

Wyatt made a loud, buzzer noise, then said, "Oh, c'mon! That's cheating and a cop-out."

"No it's not," Mick replied coolly.

"Okay then, who do you and Michael work for?"

"Yahweh," Mick countered.

"Very funny. Now seriously, who do you work for, and why are you here?"

"I already answered those questions. Look—let's try this thing another way. Go ahead and ask me something about the Lord."

Ratcheting up his questions, Wyatt said, "Fine, then. If God truly loves us, then why do we experience pain and suffering—then die?" The intonation in Wyatt's voice sounded like he was in a courtroom, beginning a cross examination.

"Don't you wanna ask me how I know about Vanessa and Scout?" Mick asked.

"Sure I do. But before we get into all of that, you're gonna have to prove to me that you're *not* a psycho."

"Fair enough."

"So . . . are you gonna answer my question?"

"That's actually a pretty simple question to answer, dude. I was just thinking that you're starting me off *way* too easy."

"Is it, now?!?!" Wyatt asked.

"Yep. You don't have to handle me with kid-gloves. I can pretty much handle anything that you can throw at me."

"That's a pretty bold statement. But you need to know this—I'm just getting fired up big boy—*just you wait.*" Wyatt aimed a penetrating glare squarely into Mick's eyes. Mick retained Wyatt's gaze, returning a benign and warm look. This unexpected benevolence knocked a chip off of Wyatt's stony exterior.

Mick shrugged and said, "To be honest, I don't quite understand why you people think the question of why an all-powerful God allows evil to be so hard to answer—it's really quite simple. All you have to do is R-Y-B."

"RYB?"

"Yessiree—*Read Your Bible.*"

"That's cute," Wyatt said, a smirk slipping onto his face. *I like that expression–RYB. At least this guy has moxie*, he thought. *I have to at least give him that.*

Mick began his explanation, "Listen to me now—there's a lot more to the book of *Genesis* than the *In-the-beginning* thing. Have you ever read the first three chapters of *Genesis*—I mean *really* read them?"

Although Wyatt had known of the story of creation since he was very young, it wasn't until he had begun walking briskly towards the Lord that he truly understood it for the very first time. *Genesis 1, 2, and 3* had amazingly sprung to life in his heart and mind, and he was fascinated at what God revealed to him through His Holy Word. "Yeah, I really began to understand a lot about the 'why are we here?' thing when I studied those chapters while reading 'Heaven' by Randy Alcorn." Alcorn was Wyatt's favorite contemporary theologian.

"Yeah, Alcorn's the man, for sure," Mick said, then continued, "So you understand that our Father made everything in six days, and then rested on the seventh. He made the heavens, the Earth, and the animals. Next, He made Adam—then He made Eve for Adam; they had a perfect life in total communion with the Father, in a perfect paradise. You understand all of that—right?"

"Yes, but there's so much *more,*" Wyatt said.

"You bet there is, partner," Mick agreed. "Then Adam and Eve rebelled and broke the only rule they couldn't break by eating from the forbidden tree. We watched in absolute horror as our former compadre tempted Eve, and as they both made a terrible choice."

"Your former, *compadre?*" Wyatt asked.

"Lucifer—fallen angel—serpent—duh!" Mick snapped back.

"So, let me guess—you're a demon?"

"Are you kidding me? Gimme a break, man—I'm just the opposite."

"You're an *angel?*"

Mick shook his head in disappointment, "Oh, c'mon. I told you I was a messenger. What do you think an angel is?"

"Well, I suppose I haven't really thought about it too much. Besides, you sure don't look like any angel I've ever seen before—no offense."

Mick chuckled, "None taken. But please; don't try to stuff me into some wimpy stereotype about a weak, girly-man with wings, who can only play a harp and fly around with no purpose. To use the human expression, my boss man Michael is the 'General in charge of God's Army'. That's a pretty serious job, and we deal with some pretty serious stuff."

Wyatt was starting to enjoy their conversation, so his questions began to naturally shift from that of a courtroom interrogation, into an interview. "So . . . I suppose this *Michael* you speak of is the archangel Michael?"

"The very one."

"Okay, Mick. I hear what you're saying. For argument's sake, let's just suppose that you're not a nut job—which I still think you are. I well understand the story in *Genesis 3,* which is basically the story of mankind . . . ."

"Go on."

"Well, we-humans—the descendants of Adam and Eve—inherited this misery because of their terrible mistake. An all-powerful God who didn't punish disobedience would be uncaring, apathetic, and aloof. To the contrary, God loves us so much *more* than we realize, because He made us in His image, which is a pretty tall order to fill. Basically, Adam and Eve failed Him due to their disobedience, and all of the death and destruction since that simple act has been the result of mankind's first sin against God—the original sin."

"Keep on going, partner—you're on a roll."

"That's it, Mick. There was no pain and suffering until the curse was laid on mankind. Now, we all have to surrender to Christ and go through pain and physical death, before we're allowed back into Paradise with God."

"That's correct. You now can't have fellowship with the Father, until you accept the work of His Son on the Cross as your only hope. Oh, and when you get to Heaven, you'll also get to hang out with a bunch of us angels, who serve God and his incredible creation. I have to say though, right now, you people tend to keep us *pretty busy.*"

"You can't be all that crazy if you understand the curse on mankind," Wyatt admitted. "Many people are so inwardly focused, they forget who made them—they can only see the world from their own, selfish point of view. In my opinion, that's why some people rant about, *how can a loving God let babies die*, etc. The problem is—"

"The *problem* is their assumption is flawed."

"Hmmm . . . what do you mean by that?" Wyatt asked.

"Their mistake is that the life that they currently live is their *real* life. It's absolutely not, but it does carry with it a lot of critical, eternal choices. Believe me, your short lives on Earth under this curse are really only like boot camp for eternity. I'm pretty old my friend, trust me on this."

"You're preaching to the choir, bubba," Wyatt said. He just couldn't shake his southern roots . . . not that he wanted to. "And if your looks are any indication of your age, then—"

"Easy there partner, even angels have feelings," Mick said, laughing heartily for the first time. They both had a sip of their coffee as a few moments of silence between them settled in.

The Seattle's Best café was still quiet as well. However, Sally and Ryan were now stirring about at the east end of the counter. They began slowly moving back towards their stations, but Wyatt barely noticed. He was now fully engaged in his conversation with Mick, and was surprised at how much he was enjoying himself. Because of this, Mick's comments about Vanessa and Scout had crept silently into the background.

"By the way, how many angels have you ever seen before?" Mick asked.

"Huh?"

"A minute ago, you said I didn't look like any angels you've ever seen before. So tell me . . . how many others have you seen?"

"And *you* used the term 'girly man'!" Wyatt countered, not answering his question.

Mick grinned and nodded, "Touché, dude. I'll admit; I do like to take in one of the old-school Schwarzenegger movies when I get a chance."

"And I suppose I'll have to admit—you're the first angel who I've ever personally met—at least as far as I know," Wyatt said. "I'm still not sure about all of this angel stuff, yet."

"I see . . . so will you at least admit that I'm not some crazy old fool?"

Wyatt nodded, "You're passing the test so far, but we still have a ways to go. You still might be a psycho for all I know." Just then, three people entered Seattle's Best from the front entrance, meandering over towards the register, where Sally eagerly awaited.

Mick simply shrugged in retaliation, "Okay my friend, I've had enough coffee for now. How's about you and I take a little walk? The market is still pretty quiet, and I'd like it very much if we can finish up this discussion. It's really getting interesting."

"I suppose it is . . . and that's fine with me, but you're not gonna go all *serial-killer* on me, are you?" Wyatt chided.

Mick's expression fell into a smirk as he said, "Only if you call me a *psycho* again." They both had another chuckle. And thus began Mick and Wyatt's eventful walk through the market.

PART 2

COFFEE ANYONE?

5
MAN'S BEST FRIEND

I n preparation for their departure, Wyatt donned his backpack and deposited their empty coffee cups in the trash can. As he did so, Mick shook hands with Ryan, bidding both he and Sally a hearty goodbye. The baristas were obviously saddened to see Mick leave. This only added to the surreal nature of what was thus far, a very unusual rendezvous.

Wyatt shook his head. His weekly jaunt to the market had taken an unexpected turn, and thus far, he found himself feeling ambivalent about the whole experience. He was at once skeptical about Mick's claim of being an angel, but he was also immediately comfortable with this laid back fellow, who was so easy to talk to. Deciding to plunge ahead through his forest of doubt, he looked back at Mick and asked, "Okay Mick—where to?"

"Let's head this way," the angel said, nodding towards the café's back entrance, which opened into the Sanitary Market building. After leaving Seattle's Best, they began a relaxed stroll towards the south end of the building.

Pleasant smells from some of the ethnic food restaurants were already beginning to entice Wyatt's nose, and he instinctively thought about getting some breakfast. Pike Place Market is truly an enchanting place, which provides several concurrent sensory joys—the sights, smells, tastes, sounds, and old feel to the ancient pantheon of commerce had an almost living feel to it. *Sometimes,* Wyatt thought, *Pike Place Market almost seems like it's alive.* "Are you hungry?" he asked.

Mick nodded, "Yeah, I could use a bite to eat. Whatcha got in mind?"

"Well, the Athenian in the Main Arcade has an excellent breakfast menu."

"Cool, let's head that way. But before we get there, I'd like to have a little chat about dogs."

The angel intentionally let this sink in for a few moments as they slowly walked in silence. Wyatt's thoughts gravitated towards his pain over the passing of his dog, Scout, the year before. This was one of many painful events in a very difficult year for him. His mind then naturally drifted back to the age-old debate on whether pets go to Heaven.

He knew in his heart that it was absolutely not a coincidence when his furry pal entered his life several years before, and that the loving hand of God had certainly been behind it. Wyatt first found Scout roaming aimlessly around a park, so he took him home and cared for him. After posting several "dog found" notices to no avail, he kept him.

Scout was a mutt, and unfortunately, due to a myriad of health issues, he had to be put down the year before. Wyatt felt a huge loss at Scout's passing, but he was even more disturbed with the lack of consensus within the Christian community concerning what happens to a person's pet when they die.

Wyatt recalled the exhaustive research on animals in Scripture he had done the year before. It simply didn't make any sense to him for a loving God who called his creation "very good" in *Genesis 1:31* to simply allow the meaningful companionship of our animals to cease to exist at death. By taking the steps forward to investigate this issue, Wyatt found many interesting things in the Bible, relating to God and His animals.

From the mention of "good" regarding the creation of animals in *Genesis 1;* to the giving of them as companions for Adam to name in *Genesis 2:19;* to their first death in *Genesis 3:21;* to their being saved by God before the flood in Noah's ark in *Genesis 8;* and finally, as an integral part of creation—their eager awaiting for the children of God to be revealed as per *Romans 8:19-22*-it was apparent to him that animals are very dear to God's heart. As the Holy Spirit grew within Wyatt, he realized even further how much God desires for His people to appreciate and give glory to His magnificent creation, which absolutely includes His animals. Although Wyatt had no inkling of it at that moment, throughout the day, this topic would be one of the centerpieces which Mick would use to demonstrate the Lord's great kindness to His entire creation.

The Sanitary Market had several openings onto Pike Place, so the hallways were cool inside. Wyatt's deep thoughts quickly retreated after Mick noticed his semi-trance. The angel then gently nudged him back to reality with a friendly pat on the shoulder. Wyatt smiled at this, and they engaged in some small talk about some of their favorite places in the market. Ultimately, they arrived near the entrance to the Dog Alley store, on their left.

Wyatt noticed that the store wasn't open yet, which put a halt on any potential shopping. However, he decided to go ahead and probe Mick about his dogs comment from a few minutes previous. "So, what do you have to say about dogs?" Wyatt asked. "I'll have to admit, you've piqued my curiosity." He thought they might delve into the meaning of life, or some other deep subject. Little did he know what was in store . . . .

"Ah yes—dogs," Mick began. "Well, you humans have this topic so twisted around, it actually makes me sad . . . and that's saying a lot for an angel. Don't forget where I live—you know, happiness and joy, etc."

"Okay, so where *do* you live?"

"In Heaven, of course," Mick said. "Listen, I'll tell you more about that later on."

"No problem," Wyatt said. "So again, what do you have to say about dogs?"

"That God is omnipresent, and He speaks to you not only through His Holy Spirit, but also through the specific circumstances of your life. Believe it or not, some of your tragedies from last year fall into this category." Wyatt's countenance visibly sunk for a moment, as the pain brigade fired a shot at his heart, and the reality of his losses came swarming towards him once again.

In the case of Scout, due to his illnesses, *it was actually a blessing when he passed-on,* Wyatt thought. However, he knew that it's always your head talking when people say things like that. The heart was another matter altogether. Mick continued, "In your case, a few years before Scout passed, God sent Baby to you; He obviously knew ahead of time that you'd only be able to bear a certain amount of pain last year. So . . . even in the midst of your troubles, there actually were blessings from the Holy Spirit."

Wyatt was quiet for a few moments as he pondered this. "You know, I'm not sure that I really understand the Holy Spirit very well," he admitted. "He seems so mysterious."

"That's understandable. However, I need to once again say—*RYB dude.* Do you have a Bible handy?"

Wyatt chuckled, "Sure I do. I have a copy of—"

"I gotcha," the angel interrupted. "We've watched you read it before, and were quite happy every time you did. Of course, I know it backwards and forwards, and in dozens of languages."

"Geez, that's a little creepy."

"What is?" Mick asked.

"The watching part. Anyway, you must be smarter than you look," Wyatt quipped.

"You're pretty funny, dude. I'll have to admit," Mick said dryly. "But looks ain't everything, ya know."

"Ha-ha, a funny angel." Wyatt said, grinning.

"What else did you expect?" Mick asked. The angel knew the odd combination of their discussion centered on the Lord, combined with some jocularity, was an excellent ice-breaker, and an effective way for two strangers to get to know one another in a unique scenario such as this.

"I have no idea—this is all new to me. Furthermore, I'm not entirely sure I'm awake right now. This could be a dream, or it could be a *nightmare,*" Wyatt joked. "Okay, so what do you want me to look up?"

"You probably should pull out your reading glasses," Mick said.

"Fine." Wyatt pulled out his glasses. "Shoot," he said.

"Please look up *John 20:22.*"

"Okay." Wyatt quickly found the passage and read . . ."*And with that He breathed on them and said, Receive the Holy Spirit.*"

"Yep. This was near the end of the gospel of John. Not long after that, Jesus ascended into Heaven. Let me tell you; I remember that event *very well*—we had an incredible celebration that day."

"I'll bet," Wyatt agreed. "That is, if you're really an angel."

Mick shook his head, admonishingly, "Anyways, the point I'm trying to make here is this—the sacrifice of Jesus Christ was God's ultimate gift of mercy for mankind. God had endured many centuries of disobedience from His children, but Christ washed all of that away and gave mankind the chance at redemption. Since then, only select angels from Heaven have had any direct contact with humans . . . and only a few of us get to do that."

"So tell me this—what does all of this have do with dogs?"

"Stay with me, dude. Dogs are only one of the many gifts your Father gives to His children. For some people, its horses, cats, a special place to live, good friends, a beautiful view of the mountains or beach—pretty much everything in His creation. He only wants for His children to recognize that it's out of *His* bounty and provision that you receive *everything*. I'm afraid that all too often, many people don't get this."

"So, what are you saying here? I'm still not getting it myself."

"It's obvious, isn't it? Jesus completed the Old Testament prophesies. Essentially, He was the ultimate gift of love, mercy, and grace from the Father—He became flesh, suffered, and died for your sins."

"He did, indeed," Wyatt agreed.

"And remember, sins are essentially acts of disobedience. Failing to obey your Father and Creator is a bad idea, no matter what the sin is."

"I'm pretty much tracking with you. Keep on going dude, now *you're* on a roll."

"I'm glad you're paying attention . . . oops, where were we?"

"Sin."

"Oh yeah. Well, I was through with sin. My point here is that God gave you the ultimate gift of grace by sending His Son to die for your sins. If He would do a magnanimous thing like that, doing the little things are really pretty easy. Essentially, the Lord wants to save you, lead you, and bring you joy—both in the big things, and in the small things."

"I suppose you're right."

"Trust me—I am. Anyways, in this passage, Jesus reminded the apostles that the Holy Spirit would be with them. Essentially, God has given all people the tools which you need to make the right choices—His Holy Word, His Son's blood, and His Holy Spirit."

"And this relates to dogs—how???"

"I'm circling back to that. The Lord has given you the ability to sense His ways through the Holy Spirit, and has provided you with the ultimate *survival manual* in the Bible. I just can't stress enough to you how important it is to remember these wonderful gifts. Essentially, they can help you live successfully during your brief life on this fallen Earth; that is, if you'll simply use them."

"Okay—?"

"In addition to these gifts, the Lord also speaks to you through the circumstances of your life by sending you blessings, like the companionship of your pets—dogs, dude! Your life has been blessed by Scout and Baby because God is your Father and He loves you . . . get it now?"

"Hmmm . . . I'm starting to. I've always tried to be grateful for all of the blessings in my life. Admittedly though, I guess I've struggled with the concept that God would be so deeply involved in my life that He would provide the companionship I needed, by sending me a pet."

"It's a big mistake to short-sell how incredible the Father is," Mick said. "Unfortunately, a lot of folks do that. I can guarantee you that God is involved in *all things* in His kingdom—both big and small."

"That's good to hear. I've always known that the Lord is awesome, but it's hard to imagine a God who is *that* involved in my life. However, it does make sense that He would communicate with me through circumstances and blessings. I guess what I'm saying is, I've never really put it all together."

"I'm glad you get it now. People often use the expression, *everything happens for a reason,* but that's not quite accurate—though it's close. What they should actually say is, *God makes things happen for a reason.*"

"So . . . the Lord really sent Baby and Scout to me, huh?"

"Exactly. Scout was sent to you to help you deal with everyday stress, and to help you enjoy your life. His time was always going to be up at some point, and the Father knew when that would be. In the meantime, He wanted to give you another blessing. So, a few years ago, in anticipation of Scout's passing later on, God made sure that Baby came into your life."

"Like I said, I've honestly had a hard time imagining a God so powerful, that He can actually be involved among even the minutest details of my life . . . I also don't think that I'm the *Lone Ranger* on this issue."

"Believe me, you're not. Listen, I've been around humans long enough to understand that the majority of Christians clearly underestimate the greatness of Jesus—they actually tend to put human limitations on Him. Don't forget, although I'm quite different from you, I understand my clientele pretty well. But still, I'm gonna have to drop another *RYB, dude* on you."

"What now?"

"Matthew 10:29."

"Oh, I know that one," Wyatt said. "It speaks of the sparrow not hitting the ground without the Father's knowledge. It even says in the next verse that the hairs on our heads are numbered."

"Well . . . perhaps you're an exception to the rule in the latter scenario," Mick quipped, commenting on Wyatt's shaved head.

"If you keep on with those kinds of cracks, I'm afraid I won't be buying you breakfast," Wyatt retorted.

"Whoa there! I'm afraid you're gonna have to—I'm not carrying a lot of cash with me today. You see, we don't need it where I live."

"Why is that?"

"Because everything in Heaven is free! Why else?"

Wyatt sighed, "Quit bragging."

"I'm *not* bragging, Wyatt. Anyways, do you understand what I'm saying about dogs now?"

"Of course. God's merciful hand is behind all blessings—including dogs."

"*Especially* dogs," Mick said. "Cats and other animals too. However, I believe that He created dogs especially for mankind. The ironic thing is that most dogs embody so many of God's loving attributes."

"Let me guess . . . loyalty, enthusiasm, unconditional love . . . ."

"Bingo. He also left many clues behind for His children to figure out. Are you familiar with *Romans 1:20?*"

"Perhaps . . . let's look it up." Wyatt paged over and read aloud . . ."*For since the creation of the world, God's invisible qualities, His eternal power and divine nature, have been clearly seen, being understood from what has been made, so that men are without excuse.*"

"That about says it all, doesn't it?"

"Yeah, I suppose it does," Wyatt agreed. "If people become so self-absorbed that they can't see the obvious hand of God, then—"

"Then they're just not *looking,*" Mick said.

"I suppose you're right. Anyway, let's keep walking."

Mick and Wyatt wound their way past the Pike Place Market Creamery on their right, and then meandered around a bit as they enjoyed some light chit-chat. Ultimately, they made their way down a hallway which led back onto Pike Place. Mick stopped for a moment and looked at the beautiful assortment of breads at the Three Girls Bakery. He was almost mesmerized.

"What are you thinking about, Mick?" Wyatt asked.

The angel sighed, coming out of his semi-trance, "That God gives you your *daily bread.* Why should you worry about anything else?"

Wyatt shook his head, "That's actually an unfair question. Since humans are clearly different than the angels, it's virtually impossible for you to put yourself in our shoes."

"I suppose you're right. I live in Heaven, and have direct access to the proof which mankind has always longed to know since the banishment of Adam and Eve. Once that flaming sword was established in *Genesis 3:24* to guard the way to the tree of life—"

"Then we have to die a physical death before we can once again have access to that life-sustaining tree. Oh, and of course, we now must surrender to Jesus Christ as our Savior."

"That last thing ain't a small detail!" Mick said. "That, my friend, is the purpose of a human's life—to get through your temporary lifetime on Earth with your future secure. If you receive the gift of eternal life in Heaven with the Lord—*you win.* But, if you refuse God's free gift offered to mankind—*you lose,* because you get eternal separation from the King . . . just as you wished for. Christ is the one who made the decision to die for your salvation. Your decision is to stop trying to do it for yourself."

"I see. So, the meaning of life is—?"

"Ah-ha!" Mick said. "The *meaning of life* is to get to your *real* life with God in Heaven for eternity, and to guide as many others towards the Cross as you can." The angel's voice had an almost melodic timbre to it.

"Well . . . I'm sure glad we solved *that* issue—and we even did it *before* breakfast. Not bad, for a couple of old guys, huh?"

"Old? *You have no idea!"* Mick said, smiling.

"Time for some grub!" Wyatt declared. With that, they left the Sanitary Market to cross Pike Place, heading towards the Main Arcade for a nice breakfast and the continuation of their growing conversation. Although Wyatt couldn't have possibly known it at the time, he and Mick were really just getting started for the day.

6

ANGEL'S FOOD

In a decidedly relaxed pace, Mick and Wyatt slowly crossed Pike Place in the cool morning mist. By this time, the main road through the market had many delivery vans unloading their goods for the day, bringing with them an abundance of fresh fruits and vegetables. The variety of stunningly beautiful natural foods was beyond compare.

The activity on Pike Place was steadily increasing as the market continued to awake from its nighttime slumber. Interestingly, Mick and Wyatt's interaction was following a similar path, as their discussion continued to grow and evolve. After crossing the street, they passed through one of the vendor entry portals and into the Main Arcade, trekking towards their morning repast.

After a quick right in the main hallway, they walked the short distance to the Athenian restaurant on their left. A majestic, ancient neon sign greeted them as they entered the eatery. As they did so, Mick readied Wyatt for their next topic, "Well, have you noticed that we haven't really talked a whole lot about angels yet? You know, all of our dos-and-don'ts?"

"I suppose you're right, but you seem to be leading this parade—*so lead on.*"

Before Mick could respond, a waitress spotted the two new customers and told them to "pick any table you like." There were only a few occupied tables in the entire restaurant, and no one was at the counter. The corner of one of the counters was a famous spot filmed in the movie, "Sleepless in Seattle," where the Rob Reiner and Tom Hanks characters sat having lunch. The film came out back in 1993, and several items of memorabilia on the wall commemorated that particular scene.

Because of its extraordinary view, Mick and Wyatt selected a booth against the back wall. Their newfound perch overlooked the back of the market, which bordered on Western Avenue. The back of the Athenian restaurant was far enough uphill from the waterfront to have a beautiful view of Elliott Bay, Puget Sound, and the mountains on the Olympic Peninsula in the distance. As they took a seat, Wyatt noticed that a Washington State ferry had just left the dock, which was only a few piers south on the waterfront. He wondered if the ferry was going to Bainbridge Island or to Bremerton . . . .

"Hey dude, that 'Sleepless in Seattle' movie was a major *chick flick*, huh?" Mick asked, almost as if he was reading Wyatt's mind.

"I didn't know that you heavenly-types were so colloquial," Wyatt said.

"So what's *that* supposed to mean?"

"Well, you seem to be a pretty regular guy for an angel."

"C'mon dude—show some love."

"See what I mean?"

"Alright, if you want to get into this, let's go," Mick said, changing directions. "Instead of me pontificating; once again, why don't you ask me some questions to get us started?"

"Pontificating? Geez, that's a pretty big word for a *dude!"* Wyatt chided.

"A question?" Mick asked, trying to hide a grin.

"Fair enough. How old are you?"

"Very old."

"Oh, c'mon—you're gonna have to do better than that," Wyatt said.

"Okay, the Bible doesn't say, and to be honest with you, I really can't answer that question."

"That's not very helpful, Mick."

"No, you don't get it. I'm gonna have to pull out the 'DP card'."

"I'll bite, what does 'DP' stand for, Diet Pepsi?"

"How about Divine Privilege?"

"Go on . . . ." Wyatt said wearily.

"Well . . . how can I say this?"

"How can you say *what?"*

"Just this—we-angels have rules which absolutely must be adhered to. In this case, we have certain things about God that we're not permitted to discuss with humans."

"Why is that?"

"It's because there's a strict set of rules in the dirty dozen."

"The 'Dirty Dozen'? You mean the movie with Lee Marvin?"

"Yeah, but it's also one of the current nicknames of my group."

"You're part of a group?"

"Yep, I sure am."

"So what's your group's purpose?"

"You mean now, or overall?"

"Uhmmm . . . ." Wyatt stammered. "How about both?"

"About now—we'll get into that later. Overall, we're like . . . well, we're often like a Special Forces group which does missions behind enemy lines. Whenever Michael dispatches us, we show up here to try to fix whatever Satan and his minions have really messed up. However, most of the time we're simply charged with delivering holy missions."

"And to think I was just about to give up on the idea that you were a whacko."

"C'mon man—let's keep talking, and you'll see. Anyways, we're not permitted to divulge certain things."

"Like how old angels are?"

"Exactly."

"Why is that?"

"DP rules . . . like I just said. However, it'll probably help you to know that God wants it that way, so that when you get to Heaven, He can share many of His mysterious ways with you, Himself. Remember, the Bible doesn't tell you everything there is to know—it merely tells you what you *need* to know—at least for now. It's very much like a survival manual, like we discussed a little while ago. I *will* tell you that I've witnessed most of human history . . . perhaps all of it."

"All kidding aside, that almost makes sense . . . about the Bible and God wanting to surprise us, I mean. I'm not quite sure about all of the other stuff, yet."

"It makes a *lot* of sense. Listen, you folks need to show a little patience, and quit trying to be the center of the universe. In other words, you need to let God be God. No offense dude, but sometimes you people act like petulant children."

Just as Mick was finishing his statement, a waitress named Ruth came up to their table and asked, "What can I get for you fine gentlemen this morning?" Her voice was very cheerful, but not obnoxious. She seemed vaguely familiar to Wyatt, but he was fully engaged with Mick, so he didn't give it any further thought.

Mick quickly blurted out, "I'll have a coffee, and the *lady,* here," he motioned towards Wyatt, "will have a coffee and a glass of water." Wyatt couldn't help himself and vaulted into a hearty chuckle.

"You'll have to please excuse my friend, Ruth. He's pretty sarcastic for an ang—" Wyatt trailed off and thought better of finishing his sentence. Perhaps he would be considered the crazy one if he had said *angel.* "Never mind."

Ruth smiled at this and said she would be right back with their drinks. In the meantime, Mick looked out at the beautiful view from their booth. He seemed to be ruminating on something serious, when he surprisingly said, "You know, I *love* movies . . . in case you can't tell."

"Actually, I can tell—so do I," Wyatt said. He continued, "I must say, though, I'm a little surprised that a Heaven-sent angel like yourself is into movies; you know, with all of the violence and whatnot."

"Good point. However, I'm afraid you haven't really thought it through," Mick said.

"Please—pray tell."

"Well, in many cases, art imitates life. If you think about it, most movies have a common theme—good guys versus bad guys. In the old westerns, you could tell who the good guys were by their white hats. The baddies wore black hats. Nowadays, it's not much different, except the good guys and bad guys don't usually get identified by something as overt as hats. Most movies—and most stories for that matter—would be a lot less entertaining if the good guys didn't defeat the bad guys after a lot of battling and drama. Think about it—good triumphs over evil."

Wyatt chewed on that for a moment, then said, "I can't argue with that. Are you saying that most stories revolve around the fundamental good versus evil theme?"

"Yep—that's *exactly* what I am saying. For example, consider the *Terminator* movies. Arnold started out as a bad guy. They changed his direction in subsequent movies to be a good guy; albeit still a terminator. It's sort of like when one of you people move off of Satan's path and accept the truth of Christ—then *bingo*, you become a good guy, because you're washed in the blood of the Lord."

"That's a stretch Mick, but an interesting thought, nonetheless." Wyatt began to think about the analogy, and for some reason, it started to make some sense. Then he completely changed the subject and asked, "So tell me . . . what's your all-time favorite war movie?"

"That's easy dude, *The Longest Day*. How about you?"

"Hands down, it's *Where Eagles Dare.*"

"Oooo, that's a good choice—I love that one, too. Hey, with Richard Burton, Clint Eastwood, a cool-looking castle, lots of snow—"

"*And* guns," Wyatt challenged.

Mick shrugged, "True enough, but in the end, the good guys beat the bad guys. That's art imitating life, dontcha think? By the way, did you notice how great the music in that movie was?"

"I sure did," Wyatt agreed.

Right on cue, Ruth brought their beverages on a tray. "Are you ready to order?" she asked. Ruth had dyed red hair, was somewhat full figured, and *probably in her mid-forties*, Wyatt thought.

Before Mick could say anything, Wyatt jumped in and said, "Yes, I'll have the classic eggs benedict with extra crispy hash browns."

After a few moments Mick announced, "Make mine the smoked salmon benedict Ruth—the same on the hash browns. Thanks dear." Ruth smiled at Mick's order and moved back towards the kitchen. Wyatt was beginning to admire Mick's uncanny ability to make people feel at ease.

Both of them looked out the window at the beautiful waters of Elliott Bay and Puget Sound for a moment, before Wyatt said, "Mick, I'm sitting here *dying* to ask you about the whole wings-thing."

"I don't like Buffalo wings, if that's what you're gonna ask about."

"No—"

"Let me guess," Mick interrupted. *"Do all angels have wings?"*

"You're quite the mind reader."

"No—not all angels have wings. How stupid would I look walking around Seattle with feathered flippers?"

Wyatt chuckled, "Well then, what's the deal?"

"Actually, only two kinds of angels have wings—cherubim and seraphim. They actually only have wings because of their status and job duties. Us front line grunts have to be able to blend in, so it's ix-nay on the ings-way for members of the dozen . . . among others."

"Wow! Did you just whip out some Pig-Latin?"

The angel winked at Wyatt, *"But of course."*

"Anyway," Wyatt sighed. "I guess all of those Renaissance frescos threw me off."

"That's understandable. Actually, that reminds me why I'm here today. And before you ask—*no* I'm not ready to tell you your mission yet." At hearing this, the pain brigade quickly launched an offensive at Wyatt. Unfortunately, it made some headway this time. He remembered how their whole conversation started about Vanessa, and something about a gift and a mission, or an assignment of some sort. The market was a special place for Vanessa as well, and she and Wyatt had often enjoyed breakfast at the Athenian on their many trips to Seattle. Mick sensed Wyatt's building anguish, so he quickly continued, "Trust me, dude. Later today, you'll feel like a weight has been lifted off of your shoulders."

"That remains to be seen. Anyway, we were talking about wings, frescos, and your bad pig-Latin. What point were you trying to make?"

"Just this—the enemy has launched many misconceptions about faith in God, the Bible, and belief in Jesus Christ. That's one of the reasons why I'm here today—to discuss these things with you. It seems that we have some lies which simply must be cleared up. Listen, we'll get into all of that later today, okay?" Before Wyatt could respond, Mick continued "But, as it relates to Divine Privilege overall, I'll refer you to *2 Corinthians 12:3-4*. Only God can decide what He wants communicated and what will be a surprise. To effectively live with the Lord, you only have a few rules to live by. It's really not that hard."

"That's fine with me," Wyatt said, going with the flow. "I'll let you tell me whatever you want to tell me, *whenever* you want to tell me. I'm also okay with DP. It makes perfect sense . . . assuming you're for real and all."

In the meantime, Ruth stopped by to freshen up their coffee. "Your breakfast will be right up, guys," she said. Wyatt was glad, because he had gotten pretty hungry.

"Next angel question Mick," Wyatt said. "If you're so heavenly, how come you eat?"

"That's actually a good question. Let me ask you this—do you think there's eating in Heaven?"

"RYB, dude!" Wyatt said. "Of course there's feasting in Heaven . . . and ultimately on the new Earth." Wyatt's favorite passage of Scripture was *Revelation 21:1-4*, where John talks about a new Heaven and a new Earth. *God living with His people sure sounds good to me,* he thought.

"Do you mind pulling that Bible out of your backpack again?"

Wyatt had previously placed his backpack in the booth to his left, against the wall. "Sure," he said. He pulled out his Bible, "Fire away, my crazy old friend."

"Awww, that's cute," Mick teased. "You called me your 'friend'. I suppose I can put my chainsaw away for now, huh?"

The point was not lost on Wyatt, "Alright, what's first?" he asked.

"*Hebrews 1:13-14.*"

Wyatt read aloud . . ."*To which of the angels did God ever say, 'sit at my right hand until I make your enemies a footstool for your feet'? Are not all angels ministering spirits sent to serve those who will inherit salvation?*"

"So tell me, what does that mean to you?" Mick asked.

"To me, it means that although angels are created beings just like humans, y'all are very different from us, because we're made in God's image. It also indicates that angels are servants of humans. It seems to me that angels were made to do God's bidding in serving His creation—*especially* humans."

"I couldn't have said it better myself," Mick chortled.

"Wait a minute now . . . let's not get off track, here. So, tell me about food and angels," Wyatt said.

"Well, I can tell you that the biblical passages about feasting in Heaven are, of course, true. Meals are different in Heaven though. First off, I hate to tell you this, but nothing has to die to have a meal in Heaven."

"Really?"

"Yep. Many humans can't relate to that, because you're all born under the curse on mankind, which was *not* God's original plan. Animals actually started dying in *Genesis 3,* and later became acceptable for food. All of this time later, mankind has become very accustomed to killing in order to eat. However, when both *Isaiah 65* and *Revelation 21* speak of the new Earth, the Lord will have wiped away all pain and death."

"Tell me then . . . what do you put on a pizza in Heaven if you can't have Italian sausage and pepperoni?" Wyatt joked.

"My friend, you can't even *imagine* how good the food is in Heaven. I promise you this—you've never had food and drink so good." Mick's eyes lit up as he spoke. "The only thing close to heavenly food here on Earth is coffee, especially in Seattle," the angel added, not kidding one single bit. "Now then, about not eating meat in Heaven—*RYB, dude.*"

"Oh geez," Wyatt bemoaned. "Another RYB???"

"I'm afraid so," Mick said.

"Anyway, allow me help you out with this one," Wyatt said. "Before the fall of mankind, *Genesis 1:30* speaks of only *plant food* for all living creatures. And as I understand the Bible, we're headed back to life similar to how it was in Eden. Except this time, we'll have had our sins forever washed away by the blood of Christ."

"Right on, man," Mick agreed.

Just then, Ruth brought out their food. She placed the plates in front of each of them, asking, "Anything else sweetheart?" She was clearly talking to Mick. *If he wasn't an angel, he might be quite the ladies-man,* Wyatt thought.

"That'll do for now, darlin'," Mick said. "Oh, and do you have any ketchup?"

"It's right there," she said, pointing to the end of the table.

"Sorry babe, my eyes are getting old."

"Wave at me if you need anything," Ruth said. She then headed over to check on her other tables.

"Let's pray," Mick said, and continued as they both bowed their heads. "Father we thank you for this food and chance to fellowship with each other. Please be present with us as we talk today, and please bless this food for the nourishment of our bodies. Amen."

"Short and sweet—just the way I like pre-meal prayers," Wyatt said. "The same goes for the National Anthem before ball games."

"I heard that," Mick agreed. They both began eating.

After a couple of quiet minutes, Wyatt said, "Now then, let's not lose track of our discussion."

"We won't—no worries. By the way, this salmon and eggs combo is outstanding."

"Mine is really good, too," Wyatt said.

"Okay, I suppose we should get back to the feasting discussion as *we* feast!"

"That'll work for me," Wyatt agreed, chewing.

"Well dude, you were right on track with the return to Eden concept, except the Lord's redemption is even greater than that. Remember—although *Revelation 21* says there will be a 'new earth,' that doesn't mean God is creating a *brand* new Earth; He's redeeming the fallen one and restoring it, according to His original plan."

"Why is that?"

"It's because God wouldn't be truly omnipotent if He lost His original creation and started a brand new Earth, would He? Of course not! That means God would've lost to Satan—the Lord can't lose, dude."

"So, there's no salmon in Heaven, huh?" Wyatt asked.

"Not on a plate. There are umpteen gazillions in the rivers and waterways, though. You need to remember this—in Genesis, God said His creation was *very good.* That's not something to be taken lightly."

"I'm sure there are a lot of folks here on Earth who would be awfully disappointed to hear that you don't eat meat in Heaven."

"Not if they knew about the other incredible food that replaces meat on our tables up there," Mick countered. "On Earth, eating meat seems natural, because you're living under the curse in this fallen land. In God's holy presence in Heaven, you'd no more want to eat a hamburger made of cow meat, than you'd want to eat Baby—your dog."

"I'm actually glad to hear that," Wyatt said, chuckling. He had always been a little squeamish about eating different kinds of meat. Wyatt just couldn't stand the thought of killing animals for food, but he always supposed it was an ultimate result of living under the curse, and had become accustomed to it. He also knew that animals didn't first die until the fall of mankind, as taught in *Genesis 3.*

Wyatt was always tickled when he thought about something his friend's son, Bryan, said when he was very young. Bryan said that he didn't want to "eat his friends" when referring to eating meat. *Good point, kid,* Wyatt thought. *Leave it to a child to see with that kind of clarity.* Although Wyatt knew there was nothing biblically wrong with the eating of meat, he felt like Bryan's feelings were looked at through the prism of a child's innocence, and desire for nothing to have to die. That really touched his heart.

Mick continued, "Let's not forget that in *Genesis 2:19-20,* God brought to Adam all of the animals to name. To me, that would indicate the Lord obviously has a special love for His animals; one that many people—*especially Christians*—clearly underestimate."

"So tell me, Mick, how can you tolerate eating meat or fish on your jaunts to Earth?"

"That's actually a very good question—*when in Rome,* dude. Although this food isn't nearly as good as it is in Heaven, when I'm here on Earth, I have to eat—just like you. So curiously enough, while I'm down here, it doesn't repulse me to eat meat. When I'm at home in Heaven, it's seems pretty disgusting."

"Why is that?"

"Like I said partner, it's all part of the territory. I'm behind enemy lines right now, and I have to live by the local rules. You see, visiting this fallen land for an angel requires us to live within the current human living conditions."

"I take it then, that not all angels have the ability to come down here and eat our food, even if they wanted to?"

"Only certain angels—like me for instance—have the ability to handle it down here, in a human-like body."

"Why is that?" Wyatt asked.

"It's because, just like all of God's creation, we were each created for a specific purpose. It breaks down like this—God has given only certain angels the ability to have our heavenly presence pass through the flaming sword, temporarily adapting into human-like bodies. Now then, this process only lasts as long as we are on the sinful Earth."

"Really?"

"Yes. When we go back to Heaven, we revert to our heavenly appearance."

"Why do you think that is?" Wyatt asked.

"It's because the Lord won't tolerate the sight of sinful flesh in His Holy presence in Heaven."

"I see. I'm tracking with you, and I can't think of anything to contradict your claim," Wyatt said.

"On the other hand, my counterparts have a *whole* different set of rules."

"Counterparts? Do you mean other angels?"

"Well, sort of. They're not angels anymore—try again."

"Demons?"

"Unfortunately yes," Mick said. "I don't dig those guys."

"Can you tell me more about them?"

"Of course. But first, I want to finish up about angels."

"Okay, but—"

"So, what I will tell you is this—there's an invisible but real world outside of Heaven. It's just beyond what you can see and hear, but it's definitely real. In addition, demons and angels are in constant warfare in this *world of the air*. Please read *Colossians 1:16* for me . . . if you don't mind."

"No problem." Wyatt flipped to the correct passage . . ."*For by Him all things were created; things in heaven and on earth, visible and invisible, whether thrones or powers or rulers or authorities; all things were created by Him and for Him."*

"Essentially, the Earth turned into a battle ground after the fall of mankind; after original sin. And like I said, certain angels like me are designed to be able to assume a human-like body and launch missions into your world, as if we are human. However, demons can't do this."

"Why is that?"

"Because their bodies can't actually become true, physical bodies. In their natural state, they can only exist in the dimension of the air, because it's part of their banishment. Sometimes they can make themselves *appear* to take shape, but the only way they can have a real, physical presence is to take over an existing person." He hesitated for a moment. "Yeah, the whole demon possession thing is real. *But,* only an unsaved human can be possessed. In other words, Satan and his vile demons are not permitted to inhabit a person who's truly given their life to Christ. So, once you're saved, you belong to God."

"So, exorcisms and the like—?"

"Real stuff, dude. I see demons on my missions to Earth all the time. The truth is, I can always recognize them for who they are; though most demons give me a pretty wide berth. Remember, we all used to be in Heaven, serving God together."

"So . . . members of the dozen and certain other angel groups can have their bodies temporarily transform into human-like bodies on Earth?"

"Yep."

"Hmmm," Wyatt mumbled. "However, demons must possess unsaved people before they can take on human bodily form?"

"Bingo."

"That's interesting. Well, do you have anything else to say about demons, angels, and their bodies?" Wyatt asked.

"Yep. Just to clarify, I can spot demons in both dimensions—angels too. We've all known each other for a very long time."

"Okay. So, tell me more about the other 'angel rules.'" Wyatt made the quotations symbols with his fingers.

"Well, angels also possess free will. Although we live in Heaven, no one—including us—knows the time that Christ will return. But like I said before, if we fall or get banished, there's no hope for our redemption, since we're not made in God's image, like humans are."

"No news, there."

"We're God's servants and we don't marry. See *Matthew 22:30.*"

"You'd look pretty funny in a tux, anyway," Wyatt quipped. He quickly turned to the passage and read it silently. *This guy Mick sure knows his Scripture—can he really be an angel?* he wondered.

"I suppose you're right," Mick agreed. "I'm not real big on formalities. Anyways, here's the most important thing about angels; other than the body stuff I just told you about. Now then, I need you to listen to me *very closely,* and make sure you hear this right."

"I'm listening, Mick."

"See *Revelation 19:10* and *22:9.* Please read them to yourself and tell me what you think."

Wyatt read both passages and said, "I see what you're saying; that angels are *created* beings, and therefore aren't worthy of worship."

"Indeed!"

"Actually, based on these Scriptures, it appears that angels fully understand God, because they don't want to be worshipped."

"How right, you are. That may be the single, most significant difference between angels and humans. Of course, the obvious exception is the fallen angel Lucifer. He was so prideful that he wanted to be worshipped just like the Lord—that's why God shipped his sorry rear-end out of Heaven." Wyatt could sense the disgust in Mick's voice. Not anger, just disgust. "We also suspect that Lucifer was offended at having to serve humans," the angel added.

Wyatt thought about Mick's point for a few moments, then asked, "Is this the reason why you're such a seemingly regular guy, Mick? I mean, you look like an average guy in his fifties who likes to ride his Harley on the weekends . . . not to mention the fact you use the word *dude* so much."

"Wyatt my man, you shoulda been a rocket scientist," Mick quipped. "Yes, it's very true that I have to be able to blend in with the society which I'm visiting. I couldn't very well deliver holy missions and fix demonic messes if I didn't look like one of you, could I? Think about it! If I looked and spoke all ethereal and holy—like some of the other angels—how could I effectively deliver the offer of a mission from the Lord? Yes, that *powerful angel appearance* has happened in several angelic visits throughout biblical history. However, that wouldn't work in my case."

"I'm not following you."

"Listen, if I didn't approach my missions the way that I do, you people would be dropping to your knees to worship me. Trust me on this—I'm not worthy of your worship. Only *God* is worthy of worship."

"Good point," Wyatt agreed. By this time, they had finished their breakfast and were ready to resume their walk. Wyatt waved Ruth over, got the check, then gave her his credit card. When she returned, he signed the check, leaving her a nice gratuity. After re-depositing his credit card and receipt into his wallet, he asked, "Are you ready to roll, Mick?"

"Let's bounce, homey!"

"Are you kidding me—*a hip hop angel?*" Wyatt asked, smiling. They both stood up and stretched their legs.

"Not really. But let me say this—there's nothing wrong with hip hop music, dude. It's only when the lyrics are *filthy and disrespectful* that it goes bad. Hey, there are some rapping Christians nowadays, you know."

"Yeah, I suppose there are," Wyatt said. "Anyway, where do you want to go to next . . . and what's our next topic?"

"Let's head out into the market, and see where the wind blows us," Mick said. "And for our next topic, let's talk about *vampires.*"

7

VAMPIRES!

A s it approached mid-morning, Mick and Wyatt exited the Athenian and turned right, winding their way south, towards Pike Place Fish Market. From Wyatt's perspective, what started out as an unexpected rendezvous at his favorite coffee café, surprisingly turned into a gripping dialogue; he now found himself fully immersed in their growing discussion. *The market's increased activity also seems to be a personification of our little chat,* he thought.

Mick and Wyatt strolled along at a carefree pace, ostensibly without a specific destination in mind. It occurred to Wyatt that thus far, their discussion had centered on some very basic, "big picture" fundamentals about good and evil. It seemed to him that they were actually concentrating on the basic tenets of spiritual warfare. Unbeknownst to Wyatt, however, was the fact that their discourse was steadily sailing towards deeper water in his sea of emotions.

It remained cool and overcast outside, and the open hallway of the Main Arcade had a pleasant ambiance and comfortably cool temperature. The bustling sounds of business began to surround them as they walked, and it almost seemed as though the market's growing activity had also become very much like a bloodstream flowing vibrantly throughout a large body. In the near distance, they could hear a musician playing his acoustic guitar at the market's entrance, adding a festive tone to sensory array. To

Wyatt, a diverse stimulation of your senses always accompanies a trip to Pike Place Market. They slowly moved towards the fish mongers of Pike Place Fish Market, the heart of activity.

"Vampires huh?" Wyatt asked, launching them back on track. "I can't *wait* to hear this."

"Yep, vampires. It's an interesting subject, dontcha think?"

"Based on what I know of you so far Mick, I'd be surprised if you didn't already know that I've always enjoyed scary movies; particularly, the vampire ones."

"Then I guess you won't be surprised," Mick said grinning. "My reconnaissance reports are really good."

"Alrighty then," Wyatt said. "Well, let me first say that although I've always liked vampire stories, I'm far from fascinated—and *certainly* not obsessed with them. In fact, for most of my life, I felt like a *bad Christian* because I liked vampire movies and books. Actually, it was only about a decade ago that I realized if you look at the horror genre in the proper light, it can be quite interesting. Not only that, but having a strong hold of your faith can help you deal with just about anything."

"Hold on partner, I think I'm with you here. Observing the horror genre is not necessarily a bad thing—that falls under both the good versus evil, and art imitating life, categories. Falling under its allure, becoming obsessed by it, or by following an anti-Christian agenda because of it; well then, that's when it turns to sin. And, it's *really* bad when it negatively affects children. That should be avoided at all costs."

"That makes sense to me," Wyatt agreed.

"Truthfully however, if you want to win any war, you have to study the enemy and know everything about them. Let's face it. The enemy, Satan, often uses Hollywood and the entertainment industry to promote his own, anti-Christian agenda. However, that's a topic for a little later."

"I have to admit, I've always been fascinated with the battles between good and evil," Wyatt said. "But I can't stand the idea of unnecessary violence—it really sickens me. However, I'm always looking for good to triumph over evil. You and I both know that evil exists in this world, whether we like it or not—"

"And good versus evil will definitely be reflected in your art; that is, books and movies, etc. Watching a scary movie or reading a horror book doesn't automatically mean you worship it. In your case, it simply means you understand that evil exists—at least until Christ returns to ultimately wipe it all away. Remember, spooky movies aren't necessarily evil; they only tell a story *about* evil. And one more thing—just for clarity. We're *clearly* talking about adults, here. Since children are impressionable, parents should exercise all due prudence in monitoring their children's intake of the arts; that is, movies, TV programs, books, and the like."

"I agree with you—one-hundred percent."

"Actually," Mick continued, "teaching children about Jesus and His battles with Satan will allow them to identify the evil in society which they'll inevitably experience once they're adults. Sadly, most kids often see far too much evil before they even have a chance to grow up."

"Clearly, parents should be *parents*—not buddies to their kids. They can be buddies with their children when their kids are grown. In the meantime, I agree with you that children should be taught about this battle between good and evil—God versus Satan."

"Agreed," Mick said.

They stopped for a moment at the fish market, which was starting to come alive with the buzz of conversations, flying fish, and widespread picture taking. Personally, Wyatt couldn't stand looking at all of the dead fish carcasses, due to his dislike of seafood. However, he did enjoy the flying fish show, and he often pondered the irony of having moved to a seafood capital like Seattle. "If you don't mind, let's go over to Market Spice for a minute," Wyatt said. "I need to get another box of tea."

"You got it," Mick said. They wandered past the flying fish on their right, quickly covering the short distance into Market Spice. The store was quiet, and there were only two other people in the entire shop. Wyatt quickly located the box of tea he came for, then moved over to the register. In the meantime, Mick went over to the sample area and poured himself a tiny cup of complimentary tea.

After Wyatt paid for his purchase and put the box of tea in his backpack, he looked over at Mick a few feet away and chided "Don't you ever get filled up on hot beverages?"

"No, not really. Actually, I'm just about ready for another latte. But I suppose that I'll have to wait until we get near a good coffee shop for that."

"I guarantee we won't have to go very far to find one."

"Cool," the angel said. *"I know that's right."*

"Hey, I need to go into DeLaurenti next," Wyatt said. "I need to pick up a few things for dinner tonight with Miss Charlene."

"That'll work—lead on." It was completely lost on Wyatt that the mention of Charlene was no surprise at all to Mick.

They walked the short distance in the Economy Arcade and turned right—then left—into DeLaurenti Specialty Food and Wine. As they entered the store, the memories came flooding head-on at Wyatt. However, he was successful in fending off the pain brigade this time, because he had already prepared himself for their expected offensive.

Vanessa had dearly loved this store, and she could wander aimlessly around it for what seemed like hours. The fresh food counter was to the right, just past the registers. The shelves of exotic dry goods were on the left. Wyatt led Mick through the store and towards the back left, which also opened onto First Avenue.

The store's café was empty, but many beautiful pre-made sandwiches and desserts were already packed in the fresh food case, awaiting the hungry crowds that would soon arrive. Wyatt picked the corner of a bench table facing the window, which looked out onto First Avenue. He quickly sat down, followed by Mick. *It's always such a relaxing feeling to find a quiet spot in the market,* Wyatt thought. "This looks like a nice spot to continue our chat about vampires," he said.

"This suits me fine," Mick said. "But again, I want a latte after this—*your treat.*"

"Okay Mr. Angel. But please, don't start whining about it," Wyatt joked. "And trust me, I already knew that *I'd* be the one reaching for my wallet. It appears that you already have me trained pretty darned well."

"Here we go!" Mick said, ignoring Wyatt's quip. "Vampires . . . well, let me give you the answer first. The whole vampire lore which has fascinated so many people and that's become so popular in your culture today comes down to one thing—vampire mythology developed as a direct result of *demons.* You heard me right—demons. Demons are the source of the whole thing, and the archetype from whence all of the vampire stuff sprung. Let me stop there for a minute. I know I just solved another one of the great mysteries of life for you, and you might need to have your thoughts catch up with me."

Wyatt thought for a moment, and then said coolly, "I'm afraid you'll have to present your whole case before I can comment any further."

"Okay, fine. Let's start out with the most common vampire attributes—they only live in darkness, and die if they're exposed to sunlight; they live by taking the blood of life; they possess strength much greater than man; and they have super human healing powers. Also, you have to invite them into your home before they can enter."

"What about garlic, a stake through the heart, and all the rest?"

"Much of that stuff comes from the cultures where the legends originated. You see, vampire-like beings are deeply rooted in virtually every civilization throughout history. The point here is that these attributes are very *demon-like*. Do you remember what I said a little while ago about the only way a demon can take bodily form?"

"I sure do."

"You see, they're not like me. To be able to move from the invisible dimension into this one, a demon must inhabit a non-saved human's body. However, the important thing to remember is that Satan is absolutely *not* as powerful as God—not by a long shot! People often make that mistake."

Wyatt knew this was absolutely true. Satan and his demons don't possess godly powers, and Satan is not omnipresent like the Lord. Demons are actually fallen angels, and are therefore created beings, just like both the heavenly angels and humans. While demons appear to have powers more substantial than humans, the power of Jesus Christ and the Holy Spirit are much greater than the evil ones; God is actually unlimited in scope. Ultimately, after being tossed into the lake of fire in the future, demons will have no power over anything anymore, except maybe their own minions. "Okay then, how about some of the more popular vampire stories which involve the romanticizing of those bloodsuckers?" Wyatt asked. "What about that?"

"Oh yeah, that foolishness . . . I'm afraid that's also been around for a long time. Believe me; it's nothing new, my friend."

"What do you mean by that?"

"You see, there's a seductive element to the vampire lore, and it's similar to the attraction to Satan's evil ways and rebellion against God. You know about that nutty stuff in the mainstream books and movies regarding 'sexy vampires', don't you?"

"Yes. That's actually what I'm talking about."

"Yeah, well, all of that nonsense is similar to the seductive allure of sin, and Satan's wily overtures toward convincing Eve to disobey God in the Garden of Eden. Do you remember what's written in the first seven verses of *Genesis 3?*"

"Of course I do," Wyatt said. "Everything was copasetic in paradise until Eve was tempted by Satan in the Garden of Eden. After she and Adam sinned, all Hell broke loose—literally."

"That's right—it was *the* most pivotal event in all of human history; that is until Christ died on the cross to atone for it. Before original sin, Adam and Eve lived in a perfect world in total commune with the Lord.

After that, bad stuff indeed. Every iota of death and suffering throughout the entirety of human history can be traced back to that one, single tragic event—mankind's original sin."

"And it's all because Adam and Eve fell victim to the first *vampire,* Satan?"

"You catch on quickly, grasshopper."

"Are you kidding me—a *Kung Fu* reference? There's a bunch of young folks who don't even know who he is."

"You got it. The dude in that old TV show was *awesome.* The stories were always the same—he went around enjoying his peaceful walkabout until some jackasses would give him a hard time. It seems that the baddies were always surprised when he put his foot in their faces and beat the snot out of them."

Wyatt chuckled, "Well now; that's an interesting synopsis."

"Yep. It's all because the main character represented *good* and the bad guys represented—"

"Okay, okay," Wyatt interrupted. "Good versus evil—I get it. Let's get back to your theory about vampires and Satan."

"I'm afraid this isn't some random theory—it's the truth. Falling victim to Satan is very similar to what happens to humans in the vampire lore. When they're seduced by the dark one and become like him, they're forever trapped with their own evil powers. However, their immortality is not the happy kind that's promised by the Lord."

Wyatt thought for a moment, then replied, "You're not going to say that Jesus Christ is like Van Helsing, are you?"

"C'mon dude—are you *crazy?* There's *no one* like the Lord. Besides, Van Helsing is part of the Dracula legend. Dracula was a vampire, but not all vampires are like Dracula."

"Hmmm . . . you know, they say that Dracula's name was inspired by Vlad Tepes from the fifteenth century."

"Indeed it was. By the way, Vlad Tepes was a straight up, evil demon possessed maniac. That particular demon possessed a man, and later did the whole impaling thing under the guise of Prince Vlad III of Wallachia . . . by the way, I used to know that guy."

"You knew Vlad Tepes?"

"Of course I did. Well, I know the demon who possessed him. It breaks down like this—Vlad was possessed by a demon, and all demons are fallen angels. All angels were once together with God in Heaven, until Lucifer was cast out with the angels who aligned with him. *RYB dude!* Check out *Revelation 12:9 . . .* badda-bing."

"Did you slip a mickey into my coffee at breakfast? I'm must be getting loopy, because you're starting to make more-and-more sense."

"What can I say? The truth is the truth."

"So why are you here, Mick?" Wyatt asked, suddenly changing back to serious.

"Listen, we'll talk about that later on, my friend," Mick said, rolling with the probing question. "We first need to get to know each other a little more. *Listen up sonny—you just may learn something!"* he continued, simulating an old man's voice. This was an obvious attempt at distraction.

"I suppose I can't do anything about you being in charge," Wyatt said.

"Cheer up, my friend. You're actually going to be really glad I showed up here today."

"Okay, but I do need to get a few things in here," Wyatt said. They got up from their seats and began to roam around the bountiful aisles of imported and domestic food. Wyatt looked eagerly at the cheeses in the refrigerated case, but picked up a mini-loaf of freshly baked Italian bread wrapped in a paper bag, instead.

As they continued their browsing in the store, Mick only seemed to take interest in what Wyatt was interested in. They looked at small bottles of balsamic vinegar, exotic olive oils, oddly expensive salts, imported cans of red peppers, and many other bistro-like products. The two new pals then ventured upstairs and began looking at some of the wines. Wyatt picked up an inexpensive Italian Chianti, and the two went back downstairs. After picking out a nice bag of imported pasta, they went to the register and checked out. Wyatt paid with his credit card, signed the slip, and then placed the items into his backpack. Mick and Wyatt then ventured back out into the market.

"How's about that latte now?" Wyatt asked cheerfully.

"Geez—I thought you'd never ask."

"I suggest we hit the original Starbucks on Pike Place."

"Spoken like a true coffee connoisseur . . . lead the way, Jeeves."

Mick and Wyatt strolled back towards Pike Place, passing the fish market and the Rachel the Pig statue as they went. The main road through the market was fully open to traffic, though not many vehicles were passing through on it. They continued walking on the right hand side of the street on the sidewalk, heading north.

The two of them took their time chatting about the various shops and restaurants as they meandered along. Occasionally, they stopped to chat up one of the food vendors. Between them both, they engaged in a thorough evaluation of the items which were being offered at each shop. After a while, they took back to the street to speed up their arrival at Starbucks; it was high time for a latte. They stayed on the right hand side of the uneven brick road as they chatted.

As they walked, Wyatt asked, "Mick, tell me more about Satan. I mean, evil—the vampire lore—wars—famine—slavery . . . geez, I could go on and on listing bad things. However, none of this would've ever happened if Lucifer hadn't fallen, and then subsequently tempted Adam and Eve, right?"

"Right you are, Wyatt."

"So tell me this—why in the world does Satan try so hard to corrupt mankind?"

"Well, let me first tell you that Lucifer was the most highly favored and beautiful of all of us angels. However, his sin of pride pushed him to want to compete with the Lord. If you really think about it, that's completely ridiculous, because Lucifer was a created being—just like you and me."

"Meaning?"

"What I mean is this—Satan is not eternal like God."

"I understand that part, but I'm still not getting it."

"Essentially, I'm saying the Lord has always existed, and that's a pretty heavy concept for anyone to comprehend—even angels. In order for your head to not explode, you just simply have to accept this fact, because finite minds cannot comprehend infinite concepts—like God's eternal nature. It would be like asking an amoeba to do advanced calculus—it's simply far beyond what limited minds can possibly comprehend . . . and like I said, this is true even for us angels, who know God personally."

Wyatt shook his head, "Wow. You actually know the King of kings. That kind of blows my mind."

"Fringe benefits of the job, dude," Mick grinned.

They leisurely strolled for a couple more blocks before landing at the original Starbucks. There were already some musicians outside the store, who were really getting cranked up. The market's street performers, also known as "buskers," had to be licensed to be able to perform in the market. Mick and Wyatt were both drawn to the current group of singers, who were really good. They moved in closer with five or six other market patrons as they listened to four older African-American men singing a Motown style song. Wyatt noticed that the singers had some CD's for sale, and he felt sure that they had sold quite a few. Mick and Wyatt enjoyed the singing for a minute or so, before entering the ancient Taj Mahal of coffee.

The venerable ambiance in the store was in stark contrast to the countless new Starbucks stores, which seemed to be popping up in every town, both large and small. Wyatt was pleasantly surprised when they even opened a Starbucks at the Kroger in his hometown of Jefferson, Georgia.

The two thirsty men ordered their drinks from the young man at the register, then waited at the end of the counter for their barista to do her magic. As they waited for their coffees, Wyatt continued his questions about Satan. "Sooo . . . Lucifer got kicked out of Heaven and has been causing trouble ever since, huh?"

"Yep. Do you still have your Bible handy?"

Wyatt pulled it out of his pocket. "Got it," he said. "What're we looking up?"

"*1 Peter 5:8.*"

Wyatt quickly flipped to the passage and read aloud . . ."*Be self-controlled and alert. Your enemy the devil prowls around like a roaring lion looking for someone to devour.*"

"You know, that's one of the most concise and direct passages in the entire Bible . . . and there's really not a whole lot I can add to it."

"Yeah, it's pretty straightforward," Wyatt agreed.

"Satan is very much like a predator. The Evil One is only interested in feeding his own vanity by trying to take from the Lord what is His. Listen to me now, God will put up with this for a little while—*but not forever.* Unfortunately, none of us knows for how long. In the end, though, when the Lord decides the time is right, He'll slam the door shut on all evil . . . and do you know what else?"

"What's that?"

"For the life of me, I just can't understand why Satan and his demons would even *think* about such an absurd thing as to challenge the Lord."

"I've actually been wondering about that too," Wyatt agreed.

"However, you need to always remember that no matter how strong you think you are, Satan has been at this for a *very long* time. He's very, very dangerous—as are his legion of demons. Remember, these guys all used to be my buds, back in the day."

Wyatt nodded, "I suppose they were."

"I will tell you this one little tidbit . . . and I suggest you *never* forget it . . . demons are very powerful—they should *not* be underestimated."

"That makes sense. So, why don't people realize this, and resist these obviously bad guys?" Wyatt asked.

"That, my friend, is part of Satan's Trifecta of Tricks."

"Trifecta of Tricks—what are they?"

"Well, that's what we in the trade call them. Anyways, the first trick is this—that Satan and his demons simply don't exist. The evil ones do their level best to make people believe they're only metaphorical or legendary, not real. Believe me, they're *real.*"

"I'm tracking with you so far."

"Good deal. Second, demons *can* and *do* possess people, and have them do evil things in the name of righteousness. In the past century, Hitler, Stalin, and Hussein are only a few examples of this. The truth is, there have been a *huge* number of bloodthirsty tyrants throughout the ages—the list actually goes on and on."

"That also stands to reason."

"Geez, I'm glad you're able to keep up with me," Mick quipped. "Third, demons can convince all people—*even saved Christians*—to do sinful things by whispering temptations into their ears, and by trying to get humans to take the evil road to vanity and narcissism. By the way, that's the road to perdition which Lucifer so tragically took."

"The Bible does make it clear that Satan's way is the proverbial *highway to hell,*" Wyatt agreed.

"True enough. Anyways, demons like to stay in the background, causing trouble and wreaking havoc and mayhem on both humanity and God's beautiful creation. They do this silently and anonymously, so as to not attract too much attention to themselves."

"You know, hearing all of this makes me both angry and sad," Wyatt said.

"Me too, dude . . . go ahead and read *2 Corinthians 11:14-15* for me, please."

Just then, the barista named Britney called out their order, *"I have a double tall, soy, three Splenda latte for Wyatt; and a quad venti, breve, five sugar latte for Mick."*

"Right here darlin'!" Mick said, holding his hand up.

Britney handed them their drinks and they thanked her. Mick and Wyatt then moved over to the front window of the store, where no one else was standing.

Wyatt had a smirk sweep across his face as he asked, "How many calories are in that thing, Mick?"

"I ain't worried about it, dude. It won't make me look fat in my jeans, if that's what you mean."

"Oh, c'mon—there must be a gazillion calories in that one cup of coffee. It's got a ton of sugar, and do you know how many calories there are in half and half?"

"That's another fringe benefit of the job, my friend—I can't get fat. Remember, when I go back through the flaming sword into Heaven, my body is reverted back to a perfect, heavenly appearance. In fact, you'll have a perfect, *physical* body when you get to Heaven, so that applies to you as well."

"Does that mean I can eat as many french fries as I want in Heaven and not gain weight?"

"Yep. The only difference is, while you'll enjoy feasting in Heaven, you won't consider overindulging. Don't forget—food on Earth can be used as an unhealthy crutch, just like booze, drugs, sex, gambling, etc. In Heaven, there's no temptation to overindulge, or to be a glutton."

"I'm more interested in the fries thing, Mick."

"Okay, okay! Don't have a hissy fit," Mick said, grinning. "In Heaven, you can eat all the fries you want—all day—smothered in whatever formerly fattening toppings you want . . . happy now?"

"Actually, I am."

"Well, like I said before, the food up there is *much* better than you can possibly comprehend . . . just remember, no bacon bits."

"Bummer . . . I think."

"Listen Wyatt, we have food in Heaven that's a hundred times better than bacon, and nothing has to die to enjoy it. Please don't forget this— one day, Christ will wipe away all weeping and crying. That's in Isa—"

"Isaiah 65!" Wyatt interrupted. "Right?"

"Right-O, dude. *Isaiah 65:19,* to be precise."

"Gotcha, Mick. Okay, here's the passage you ordered up," Wyatt said, getting back on track. "Let's see, *2 Corinthians 11:14-15 . . . And no wonder, for Satan himself masquerades as an angel of light. It is not surprising then, if his servants masquerade as servants of righteousness. Their end will be what their actions deserve."*

"See what I mean?" Mick asked. "That's another one of Satan's tricks. And trust me when I tell you this—Satan has pulled off this terrible deception many, many times in the past. It's actually one of the most-used plays in the Evil One's play book."

"I see. So you're saying that Satan has tricked people throughout history by appearing as an emissary from the Lord?"

"Yep—exactly. His demons have done the same, exact thing."

"Okay, I see what you mean," Wyatt said. "It seems to be a fair statement that one should never underestimate Satan. And if anyone is selling something as *good,* it must be able to stand up to scriptural scrutiny. Do you agree?"

"Of course I agree."

"Good deal. So, where do you want to go to next, old timer?"

"Hang on," Mick said. "Before we go, I have one more thing about vampires." The number of customers in line at Starbucks was beginning to grow, but they both stood near the front window of the shop, relatively alone. "Oh, and I think I'll ignore that *old timer* reference."

"I thought we already covered that subject . . . vampires, I mean."

"We did, but we actually only scratched the surface," Mick said. "I have another important point to make; one which you need to keep in mind as it relates to demons. Now listen to me, because this is *very* important."

"Don't worry—I'm with you."

"Okay, we've touched on this subject a little bit so far, but we really need to go over it again. I want you to *never, never, never,* forget this . . . ." He hesitated for a moment before saying, "Again, let's bounce over to the vampire lore so that we can get a good frame of reference."

"Shoot."

"What is a vampire's primary weakness in most all of the vampire mythologies?"

Wyatt thought for a moment, "They can't go out during the day?"

"Well . . . yes. More precisely, they can't go into the *light* of day. The light will destroy vampires, because they're truly the princes of darkness. In the light, they'll burn up or explode, or whatever. They can't survive in the light; or rather, the *Truth* of the light. They can only survive in the darkness of their own miserable immortality. You know, it's not a small coincidence that Jesus said in *John 8:12* that He is the *light of the world.* Does that sound familiar at all?"

The angel's argument hit Wyatt like a ton of bricks. *Wow!* he thought. *Mick is right on the money with this.* He began thinking through the various vampire books, movies, and television programs he had watched throughout his life, and his head began to spin. "Mick, I need a minute to think about all of this. Your points make sense, but I need to wrap my head around the whole thing."

"While you're doing that, go ahead and look up *Jude 1:6* for me. After that, we'll get out of here and go do some more wandering."

"Gotcha," Wyatt said in a distant voice. His thoughts meandered through many different vampire stories, from Stephen King, Anne Rice, the old "Dark Shadows" soap opera, Darren McGavin in the "Night Stalker," and many others. His mind raced. All of the sudden, a thought hit him, "Hey, I think you forgot to mention *the* major vampire weakness in most vampire mythologies."

Mick grinned, "I was hoping you would figure out that the *Cross* is a major weapon against vampires, just like the demons and Satan. That's exactly the point I want you to *never* forget—the power of Christ is much greater than all evil. *Grasshopper,* you're almost ready to take the pebble from my hand."

"The Cross *is* a major weapon against vampires in most vampire stories," Wyatt agreed. "They can't *stand* to see it, and back away from its power."

"Amen!"

"Mick, I'm sorry—I almost forgot. Here's *Jude 1:6*." Wyatt paged over to the book of Jude and read . . ."*And the angels who did not keep their positions of authority but abandoned their own home – these He has kept in darkness, bound with everlasting chains for judgment on the great Day.*"

"Yep, you got it dude. You see, even a knucklehead like you can *RYB* and learn something," Mick teased, unable to hold back a laugh.

"Ha-ha . . . so in summary, the vampire legends are really indicative of our battle with demons on the fallen Earth. Essentially, it's *art imitating life.* The demons are wreaking havoc on God's creation until the Day of Judgment, but they're only limited in their powers. They can't beat God, although they're trying their level best to do so. They also use tricks and deception in the invisible-but-real world to battle humanity. Now then, all of this happened because the vain, fallen angel and first *vampire* named Satan, tempted Eve in the Garden of Eden. It seems that she was drawn to Satan's allure to rebel against God . . . am I on target, here?"

"You sure are! Oh, and one *more* last thing." Mick gently took the Bible from Wyatt's hands and flipped through a few pages. When he found his place, he read aloud "This is from *James 2:19 . . . You believe that there is one God. Good! Even the demons believe that – and shudder . . .* Now *that,* my friend, is a strong statement about who has the upper hand in this battle we're engaged in, doesn't it?"

"It surely does . . . so in conclusion, you don't think watching a vampire movie is necessarily a bad thing, huh?"

"Nope. *Not unless you are rooting for the vampires to win!*"

"Hmmm," Wyatt mumbled. "By the way, didn't you say that you had the Bible memorized?"

"Of course I have it memorized."

"I'm just checking . . . ." By this time, the Starbucks had become officially crowded with many of the market's visitors; they obviously came to order up their favorite coffee drink from the original flagship of the Starbucks fleet. That meant it was time for Mick and Wyatt to make their exit, to find a quieter place. "I know a less crowded spot nearby, Mick. Do you wanna get out of here?" Wyatt asked.

"10-4-let's skedaddle," Mick said, and they exited Starbucks in search of their next destination. Wyatt was blissfully unaware that their next discussion was going to venture deep into his jungle of emotional anguish.

8

TWO SONS

In a quest to find a quieter spot for the continuance of their chat, the thoroughly caffeinated pilgrims made their way back onto Pike Place. Outside of Starbucks, they were greeted with a Jerry Garcia looking banjo player who had replaced the singing group; he was really giving it his all. Pockets of sunshine began to peek through the late morning clouds and mist, the latter of which were beginning to peel away, giving way to a beautiful day.

Mick and Wyatt turned right on Pike Place, walking north at their now normal, relaxed pace. In what seemed like no time at all, Wyatt ushered them into a mini-mall looking area—their next discussion locale. There were several nice shops in this enclosed area, including Sabra Mediterranean, Emmett Watson's Oyster Bar, Pike Place Parcels, and The Soap Box, among others. Since The Soap Box was a favorite store of Vanessa's, the pain brigade gathered together another assault, launching itself at his heart. As panicky feelings of loss came rushing at him, a simultaneous wave of gloom passed through his soul.

Continuing to shake off the doldrums, Wyatt dropped off Miss Charlene's letters at a nearby U.S. mail drop box. Luckily and perhaps not coincidentally, Mick quickly spoke up, "Hey dude, can we get some oysters at Emmett Watson's today?"

Wyatt felt like Mick sounded very much like a child asking his parents for something. *The dichotomy of Mick's personality is a pleasant curiosity,* he thought. *One minute, he is confident in his faith and knowledge of the LORD; the other, he is very childlike and exuberant over the simplest things.* "Perhaps, but I don't wanna eat lunch there," Wyatt said. "I don't dig seafood you know."

"I know. Well, where else do you have in mind for our mid-day meal?"

"Seriously—are you getting hungry again *already?*"

"A little," Mick said. "But mostly, I'm just planning ahead. That's kind of my thing, you know."

"That's fine with me; but first, how does this bench look for the continuation of our chat?" There was a bench in the center of the shopping area, near a stairway, which led to another group of shops upstairs. Wyatt looked over at the wooden picture frame which had two holes cut out for sticking your face through, intended for taking pictures. He and his son Danny had posed in that frame themselves, on many vacation trips to Seattle in the past. His mind naturally began to drift towards his estranged son . . . .

"The bench is fine for now," Mick said, and they both sat down. Just then, three ladies made their way out of the soap store, all carrying large bags and chattering among themselves. As the ladies walked out towards Pike Place, their voices began to fade, like echoes in a large cave. The bench area then fell into an almost dead silence.

"Hey Mick—"

"Okay, Wyatt," Mick interrupted. "We need to take our discussion up to the next level."

Wyatt shrugged in surrender, "That's fine with me. What's next?"

"I need to talk to you about two different sons."

"Two 'suns', as in stars in the galaxy?"

"No, two sons; s-o-n-s," Mick said, letting it sink in for a moment.

Wyatt sighed, feeling crestfallen; disappointment swept over him once again. "I suppose you already know about my son Danny, huh?"

"Yep, I know all about Danny."

Wyatt unwittingly shook his head. Up until then, there was a very solid ongoing discussion between the two, with a lot of give and take. Changing their conversational dynamic to a discussion about his estranged son Danny, might change their course from a healthy Bible talk, into a heart breaking one. Wyatt found himself mentally retreating. "Look, I'm still not sure about this whole thing with you today, Mick. Anyone can Google these days."

Mick gazed seriously into Wyatt's eyes and said, "You really need to listen to me now. It's high-time for you to give up that skeptical nonsense," he said, firmly. "I like our joking around and all, but I also know that you have good instincts. You also have the Holy Spirit, Who lives within you."

"Yeah, and—?"

"I'm quite sure that you now realize this isn't some kind of hoax, and that I am indeed, a legitimate messenger from Heaven."

"I wasn't saying that you weren't—"

"Now listen," Mick interrupted. "I'm gonna insist you that give me some indulgence here, and you'll see what I am telling you is the truth. But before we go any further, I really want to know where you're buying me lunch in a little while. What's the deal?"

Wyatt laughed at the unexpected question. This burst his bubble of tension. "Mick, you sure have an unorthodox way of doing things."

The angel nodded, "That's from many years of practice, my friend." After a moment, he continued, "Well, help a brother out and tell me where we're gonna go." Mick purposely used this off-balance technique to keep people from guarding them self. He had many centuries of practice under his belt in dealing with humans, and he knew the first thing to do was to break down their pride barriers through unexpected directions in their conversations. Mick knew that it was only after he got inside these barriers that he could really communicate with someone. He understood that it was nearly impossible to get anywhere with a human, unless he could crack their outer shell, which unwittingly develops as a defense mechanism in an often cruel, fallen world.

"Okay, I was thinking about taking you to Pike Brewing," Wyatt said. "The food is fantastic, and if you want a cold beer, they make their own."

"I think I'll stick with coffee . . . so how's their seafood?"

"Good I suppose—if you like stinkin' seafood."

"Okay, Pike Brewing it is!"

Wyatt shook his head. "I see you working there, Mick," he said, and the angel smiled. "Now then; let's get back to business. I'm over the initial shock of you talking about Danny."

"Good deal—my strategy worked. You can trust me Wyatt. It goes against my charter to do anything that'll hurt my clients."

"Clients? Geez, that sounds pretty *official.*"

"Trust me—it is. Now then, when we're having lunch in a little while, we'll delve into all that stuff that happened with Vanessa last year. But for right now, let's start with your son, Danny. The other son who we'll discuss is Jesus Christ, the Son of God."

"I suppose that makes sense," Wyatt said.

"First off, we both know that Danny is an extremely gifted young man. However, he's gifted in ways which you may not fully realize."

"What do you mean by that?" Wyatt asked.

"True enough, he graduated from the University of Georgia in only two and a half years. However, his gifts of learning and knowledge, *pale* in comparison to his gift of discernment in the Holy Spirit."

"Geez, you could've fooled me," Wyatt bemoaned.

"Look dude, as bright as Danny is, he's still only in his twenties. We both know that the car accident which took Vanessa's life was *not* your fault. The fact that he didn't know how to deal with his grief shows his lack of spiritual *maturity,* not ignorance."

Wyatt sighed, "I suppose you're right."

"Listen—God has a plan for everyone, and when your duties have been completed, He brings you home to the place that He's prepared specifically for each of you."

"*John 14:1-3*-right?" Wyatt asked.

"Bingo. Dying down here and going to Heaven is a *reward*, not a punishment. Like I said, we'll talk about Vanessa and all of the turmoil from last year over lunch. But for right now, let's stay on track with Danny."

"Mick, you've gotta know that Danny and I have barely spoken since the funeral."

The angel nodded, "I understand. But all of that's about to change."

"What makes you say that?"

"Well, this is where you'll *really* need to begin your leap of faith with me today. Remember, angels are essentially messengers."

"Is there any truth to the myth about guardian angels?" Wyatt asked, digressing.

"Sure there is. All of us angels have specialties. In your lifetime, you've probably had three or four dozen angels helping you from the invisible dimension."

"Really?"

"Yep. Guardian angels do exist, but each person doesn't have just one angel assigned to them. Like I said before, we all have specialties. Angels in the guardian group actually work in unison with each other, and they generally work within families and groups of people who know each other."

"Hmmm," Wyatt mumbled. "Do you have any specific examples?"

"Of course," Mick said. "When you got out of high school, you did all of that drinking and woman-chasing at college—remember that?"

Embarrassed, Wyatt admitted, "Yeah, I suppose I do, but—"

"Listen—you don't need to make excuses with me. It happens to a *lot* of people. All human beings sin—I well understand that. But, the good news is that the Lord has a way of taking former party animals and using them for His purposes."

"I sure am glad to hear that."

"Anyways, there are some angels who specialize in protecting people when they do dumb things—like getting liquored-up. Actually, some of these angels were looking after you during that rebellious time of your life."

"Well, I suppose that makes sense. It seems to me that some very passionate born-again Christians are former hellions. It also seems like I've had an invisible helping hand at various times in my life."

"Yep. God is always at work in His kingdom . . . and speaking of former *hellions,* how about Paul, the artist formerly known as Saul of Tarsus?"

"Good point. He persecuted Christians—"

"And was converted into a believer by Christ, Himself, on the road to Damascus. Paul ended up turning into arguably *the* greatest evangelist of all time. By the way, he's a pretty cool dude, you know."

"So where is all of this going?" Wyatt asked.

"You asked about guardian angels."

"Oh yeah. So you're saying that myriad of angels help us through our life on the current Earth, directed by the Lord, right?"

"That's it. You actually got stuck with me today because the bosses decided that they wanted you for a slightly bigger purpose. Yep, you've stepped up in the world, and graduated up to *the Mick-ster!*"

"How lucky for me," Wyatt chided. "So what exactly *is* that purpose?"

"Once again, we'll discuss that topic later today."

"Fine," Wyatt relented. "Then can you tell me more about your specific duties, instead?"

"All you really need to know about me and my homeys—that is, other angels—is that we kick demon butts and fight their evil ways."

"Oh, I forgot. You're not a 'girly man', are you?"

"No, I'm *certainly not!*" Mick said, grinning. "Staying close to that analogy, I guess that you could say that I'm a demon *terminator!*"

"Great, a self-aggrandizing angel," Wyatt quipped. "So tell me there, Mick . . . what exactly do you have to say about Danny?"

Mick paused and looked down for a few moments, "Well, how can I say this—?"

"How can you say, *what?*"

"Well, it seems that Danny and I have already had a little chat."

A perplexed look swept across Wyatt's face, "What? When? Where?"

"Chill, dude—don't have a hissy fit. Danny and I had a little chat yesterday, and he's onboard with me now. He also knows that I'm meeting with you here, today."

Wyatt shook his head, "This better not be some kind of sick joke."

"Trust me, it's not. So the good news is this—later on, when we get to back to your place, Danny is expecting a call from us."

Still stunned, Wyatt quickly rebounded, "Okay then, if you can hook me up with Danny, then I suppose you're worth *every penny* I'm shelling out on you for food and coffee today."

"Thank you?!?!?"

Wyatt chuckled nervously. He then asked, "By the way, where is Danny?"

"Oh, he lives in Minneapolis."

"I thought so," Wyatt said. "By the way, what's he doing way up there? Does he have a job?"

"Yep. He's actually doing quite well. He has a small apartment in downtown Minneapolis, and works for a fairly large investment bank."

"Why Minneapolis? Did he move there for the job—or a girlfriend?"

"Neither. He moved there first, and then found a job in his field. The truth is, he was largely inspired to move to the Twin Cities because of the trips the three of you took there when he was a kid. I suppose he wanted to get away from Georgia after his mama passed away . . . just like you."

It's true, Wyatt thought. Over the years, Minneapolis had been the destination of three different winter break trips for himself, Danny, and Vanessa. Whenever it was possible, his family loved going to the Mall of

America for a winter boondoggle of shopping and recreation. The Twin Cities had indeed become a special place for the Hunter family.

"Yeah, he studied that finance stuff at UGA," Wyatt said, changing directions. "I'm afraid the apple fell far from the tree on that one—I hate big business and finance."

"True enough. But, you're still pretty good with handling money. Hey, you put him through college without Danny having to pay back any student loans, didn't you?"

Wyatt nodded, "Yeah, I suppose you're right. But, he also got a lot of scholarship money."

"I understand that. But the King smiled on Danny by blessing him with both a bright mind, and a fiscally responsible set of parents."

"Gee thanks," Wyatt said. He felt excited at the prospect of speaking with his son.

"Anyways, Danny is very anxious to speak with you later today, after supper."

"Won't that be too late?"

"Nope, Minneapolis is only a couple of hours ahead of us, so we'll call him right after dinner. Besides, I don't think it matters to him. Danny is really looking forward to hearing from us. He greatly misses you."

Wyatt's heart melted and his eyes became misty. It had been very difficult for him to deal with moving forward in his new life without having any contact with his only son. As a result, he simply buried the pain. Thus far, his discussion with Mick was pulling the pain out of the darkness, and his emotions were trying to keep pace with its progress. "Okay, let's move on . . . ."

"I gotcha, good buddy. Listen, I wanted to first speak with you about your own son as a prelude to talking about God's Son."

Wyatt shook his head, "Mick, you should've been a lawyer," he said.

"What, become a lawyer and then have to spend an eternity in *Hell* because of it?"

"A lawyer joke? Well . . . I suppose I asked for that one . . . anyway, please continue."

"Well, I'm not gonna beat any dead horses here. From my reconnaissance reports, I know that you've studied all of the Lee Strobel, 'The Case For—' series, right?"

Wyatt bristled, "Yes I have—all of them . . . Faith, The Real Jesus, Christ, Creator, Christmas, Easter . . . ."

"Yep, all excellent books. Essentially, those books prepared you for a bigger role in evangelism and the spreading of the Gospel of Christ by teaching you some basics about Christian Apologetics."

"How so . . . or rather, *why* are you claiming that I'll have a *bigger role?*"

Mick ignored his question. "You know, even though God sent His only Son to die for humanity's sins, the Christian faith has been under a heated attack for some time now. Well, I'd like for you to just think about that for a minute. How would you feel if you sent Danny to die for billions and billions of people; yet many of them still rejected his sacrifice?"

Wyatt considered this for a moment, "I suppose I'd be well beyond mad, and incredibly frustrated. What father wouldn't be?"

"That's my point—exactly."

"And further, *who* can ignore the kind of sacrifice that Christ made for mankind?"

"Who? I suppose it's lost people who only know the way of being preoccupied with them self. *That's who.* By the way, that's also the way of the world, not the way of the Lord."

"So what's your point? I get the part about God's incredible sacrifice. You know, when *The Passion of the Christ* came out a few years ago, it really seemed to fire up the entire Christian community . . . it graphically pointed out the depth of what Jesus did for us."

"It did. But, that was only part of the beginning." After a few moments, Mick continued, "It's hard to watch that movie without a waterfall of tears, isn't it?"

"It certainly is. It really drove home for me, and millions of others, exactly what the Lord did for us; undeserving though we are."

"True enough. But here's my point," Mick said. "The Christian faith needs to continue to advance and teach a more biblically correct approach to helping others towards the Cross. Bible prophesies seem to be hitting a crescendo, and the United States is at the forefront of the cultural battle versus Satan. Moving forward, a person's need to really understand the Bible is only going to get more-and-more important."

"Why? Isn't that kinda arrogant to say? The United States is not the only country in the world, you know."

"No, it's not arrogant at all."

"Why, then?"

"It's because the U.S. is the wealthiest large country on Earth. It's also a predominantly Judeo-Christian nation. And no matter what the secularists in your country say, the U.S. was founded by men and women of great faith in God."

"That's true."

"Listen to me, now. Satan is really coming after the U.S., so what we really need is more Bible based teaching to fight against him. But, we need to do it in a way which regular folks can understand."

"What makes you say that?"

"It's simple—there are literally millions of people in your country alone, who profess to have a 'belief in God', but are turned off by some of the mistakes that church leaders have made in the past. Losing just one person who would ordinarily be open to a relationship with Christ is a terrible loss, so I'm afraid the stakes in this game are immense."

"I'm tracking with you, Mick. God made a tremendous sacrifice for us, yet millions are still headed the wrong way when they die. If they don't surrender to Christ, they'll end up spending all of eternity without Him."

"You're darn tootin' they're heading the wrong way, and we all have a responsibility to do what God asks us to."

"I see. So what's next? I'm all ears."

"Where's your Bible?" Mick asked.

"In your jacket pocket. I gave it to you in Starbucks."

"Oh yeah." Mick reached into his leather jacket and pulled out the Bible and handed it to Wyatt. "Here dude, why don't you read for us? *Beauty before age.*"

"Okay—whatever that means," Wyatt said. "What're we looking at?"

"*Luke 10:27.*"

Wyatt read aloud . . ."*He answered: Love the Lord your God with all your heart and with all your soul and with all your strength and with all your mind; and, Love your neighbor as yourself.*"

"Yepper, those are the two new commandments of the new covenant. *It ain't rocket science, is it?*"

"No, I suppose it's not," Wyatt agreed.

"The point here is that you have to love God—and—also love your neighbor. However, there's a whole lot more to understanding the *love your neighbor* part then you might think."

"What are you driving at?"

"Simply this—how can you truly love your neighbor if you aren't willing to at least share the most important thing in the universe with them? How can you really say you care if you aren't willing to guide them towards the greatest gift of all, which is Christ?"

Wyatt nodded, "I suppose that makes sense. Do you have any examples of this?"

"I do," Mick said. "If you were safely at the edge of a volcano and someone you knew was hanging on a ledge twenty feet below, would you rebuke them for getting too close to the edge, or would you tie a rope securely to a tree and throw it down to them?"

"I'd throw the rope down to them, of course."

"Okay. The next question is this—would you use a rope too thin to hold their weight, or one that was strong enough?"

"I'd use a rope that was strong enough. Where are you going with this?"

"The point here is that although some well-intentioned people have mistakenly tried to share the Gospel too forcefully, it still has to be shared. In other words, you can't just watch from the edge of the volcano as people drop into the fire. Caring Christians must realize that without salvation, everyone drops into the eternal fires of Hell."

"Geez," Wyatt said. "This is starting to sound like a hellfire and brimstone sermon."

"That's not *hellfire and brimstone* you throw at the unsaved. It's merely what the Bible says about your eternal fate if you reject Jesus Christ. What the unsaved need is the *rope,* which of course, is the Bible. Basically, God has chosen His children to reach out to the lost. I believe that He really wants you to have the same passion for His lost sheep as He does."

"I understand your analogy, but I've always felt that it wasn't our job to save people. It's God's job to—"

"It *is* God's job—through the Holy Spirit—to convict each person. The problem is that some churches get too wrapped up into judging others, instead of trying to toss them a rope. Human nature is one where people tend to feel good about themselves by judging others; that's why Jesus warned against it so strongly. Sometimes it's like hearing a bratty kid saying 'nya nya, look what *I* have and *you* don't'."

Wyatt chuckled, "I agree, Mick. I was distrustful of churches for many years because of that sanctimonious attitude. However, I finally moved past it, into a strong relationship with both Christ and His church."

"Yes, there are many inappropriate ways to witness. On the positive side, we've already talked about some of the contemporary theologians who are doing a mighty good work for God. However, we need more feet-on-the-street in this cultural battle for the hearts and minds of your fellow humans. Let's face it; if the U.S. is strong, your ability to help other nations is strong. A weak U.S. is a major win for Satan; who by the way is doing a good job of watering down Christianity today. Especially in your country."

"I agree with that," Wyatt said. "I can't stand it when I hear cop-out phrases, like referring to the Lord as 'the big man upstairs', or 'the deity'. All of that, just because having a belief in God may offend some people."

"Hmmm . . . go on," the angel said.

"I think we need to call Him God, or the King, or Yahweh, or the Lord, or whatever else the Bible says. Believing in the Lord doesn't automatically make you judgmental of others; it only means you believe in the Gospel of Christ and its Truth."

By this time, the shopping area where they were sitting was seeing increased activity. Several people were passing Mick and Wyatt, heading into Emmett Watson's and Sabra for lunch. However, because of how engrossed they were with their discussion, the guys barely noticed.

"I agree," Mick said, "and your relationship with the Savior should make you more like Him, not less. Anyways, let's take a look at another passage."

"Okay, whaddaya got?" Wyatt asked.

"*2 Timothy 2:24-25.*"

"Okay . . . *And the Lord's servant must not quarrel; instead, he must be kind to everyone, able to teach, not resentful. Those who oppose him he must gently instruct, in the hope that God will grant them repentance leading them to a knowledge of the truth.*"

"What does that mean to you?" Mick asked.

"To me, it means you can't force someone to accept the gift of Jesus. It also means the job of evangelism is to speak the truth, not force the truth. In other words, it's *not* our job to save people. Only God can do that."

"Amen!"

"*Hey, that's the point I was making a minute ago.*"

"Your point was *correctamundo.* I'm afraid that passage of Scripture has not been adhered to by some churches for centuries . . . but that's also changing."

"Gee thanks, Fonz."

"*Ehhhhhhhhhh!*" Mick said, doing his best Fonzie impression. They both chuckled.

"Actually," Wyatt began, "I've observed much of the Christian faith move in a very positive direction in just the past ten to fifteen years."

"I agree. Not to try to one-up you dude, but think about what I've seen, myself. I've witnessed the Inquisition, the Salem witch trials, and countless cults spring up and do unspeakable things, *in the name of Jesus.* It sickened me to see these things happen; yet God allowed them to happen."

"Why?"

"It's because all people are given the ability to make their own choices in life. Do you know what else makes me sick?"

"Missing an old episode of 'Happy Days'?" Wyatt quipped.

"Good one dude, but no. What I really can't stand is all of that *soul mate* baloney that sprang up a few years ago."

Wyatt shook his head, grinning. As usual, Mick took an unexpected direction in their conversation. "Yeah, I agree. To me, all of that stuff is a bunch of malarkey. But, why don't you give me your take on it—you seem to be pretty convicted in your statement."

"Okay then," Mick said. "Do you remember what I said about all good gifts coming from the Father?"

"I do."

"Well, that certainly includes relationships. You see, people still try to keep themselves at the center of the universe by claiming that just one person is their soul's complement—barf—gag! That overly sentimental garbage is for people who watch too many of Hollywood's chick flicks."

"Yeah, but chick flicks are only movies, not reality," Wyatt said.

"Bingo! You just touched on my point, exactly. The reality is that some people are guided towards a very symbiotic relationship, then end up getting and staying married. The problem with some of those folks is they often don't realize that a good marriage is a *blessing;* it's not because they're any better than anyone else. Christ loves all of His children equally."

"I think some people who've been married for a long time can easily forget that."

"You're right. I understand that in order to have a good marriage, it does take a huge commitment from both a husband and a wife. Indeed, both partners have to work at it. However, they would be well advised to not take credit for the success of their marriage. But rather, they should be thankful to the Lord, instead."

"Point taken, Mick. A good marriage is not necessarily about each one being a *good person*—which is impossible. It's more about them being blessed by the One who is perfect."

Mick nodded. "On the other hand, some people aren't willing to wait for God to bless them, and they become impatient and jump into relationships which they really aren't suited for."

"That's also true."

"They want that perfect relationship when *they* want it, not when He wants it. Too often, they don't put God at the center of those relationships, and many of them result in disaster."

"I can't argue with that," Wyatt agreed.

"The same thing is true for all blessings in your lives; that's the primary reason why there's so much divorce. People become impatient and jump into relationships which they know deep-down aren't right. In other words, they try to force God's hand. Essentially, they favor their own will, instead of His."

"Why do you think people choose their own will over God's?"

"A lot of times, it happens due to societal and cultural expectations. Other times, it's because people put their own wishes ahead of all else. You have to remember, God is most definitely in charge of your life, even down to the minutest details. Sometimes when you pray for something or someone, the answer is simply a 'no'. Again, people are so self-centered, they aren't willing to yield to *His* will. But rather, they prefer their own."

"So . . . are you saying that you don't like chick flicks?" Wyatt chided.

"Oh, I suppose they're okay. Actually, I'm quite fascinated with most of your media; that is your books, movies, television programs, and the internet—the whole shootin' match. Of course, there's both good and bad in all of it, just like your lives. Well, just like your lives until you get home to Heaven to be with the Father."

"So, you *do* like chick flicks, huh?" Wyatt persisted.

"Fine dude—*yes*. I like chick flicks. Are you gonna revoke my man-club membership now?"

Wyatt shook his head, "I'm afraid the ole *man-club* likely has a restriction on angels."

"And I suppose you *don't* like chick flicks, huh?" Mick said.

"Yeah, I like some of them . . . hey, what's the most 'chicky' of the chick flicks?"

"I'd have to say, *The Notebook,*" Mick said. "How about you?"

"Well, how about the one that we talked about earlier, *Sleepless in Seattle?* Or, just about any Hugh Grant movie."

"Good choices. And by the way, if you ever get a chance to see me mix it up with a demon, you won't be so quick to revoke my man-club membership," Mick said coolly.

"You get into physical altercations with demons?"

"Sometimes. However, I try to go easy on them, because it's actually an unsaved person's body who a demon inhabits. But yes, I sometimes have to kick some demon-booty. Remember, my group is like a Special Forces unit."

"Geez, I thought that was only metaphorical," Wyatt said.

Mick's facial expression quickly turned serious, "Listen dude, we're embroiled in a war with the dark forces, and the fates of all humans are at stake. I'll do whatever I have to do to help win souls for God, and to carry out His holy orders. It's as simple as that."

Wyatt was humbled and quickly changed the subject, "Speaking about souls, do you have anything else to say about the whole soul mate thing? I think I'm about ready to start making our way towards the restaurant."

"Yep. It's pretty simple. Your true soul mate is the Lord, Jesus Christ. He's the only one who won't abandon you; He doesn't care if you are having a bad hair day; He doesn't have any kind of agenda; and most importantly, He made you with His own hands, and knows you better than any human or angel ever can."

"Good points. But, it's pretty hard sometimes. We're humans after all, and since *Genesis 3*, we've been restricted from eating from the tree of life; the tree that can sustain us into immortality with God. It's hard Mick, without having any direct contact with the Lord."

"I won't argue with any of that. I can only point out that God provides for all of your needs. However, the most important part of appreciating His bounty is that you lose yourself and yield to Him—that's what *faith* is all about. He'll grant you your ticket to Heaven by having faith in Jesus Christ, and by accepting His sacrifice on the Cross. Works certainly do matter, but they won't get you into Heaven—*Jesus is the only way.*"

Wyatt nodded, "I understand. Anyway, let's get up and start walking. My legs are getting stiff."

"Cool. Let's roll."

Mick and Wyatt exited the Soames-Dunn Building and turned left. As they headed south on Pike Place, they could smell the various foods being prepared for the lunchtime crowd. Even though the market had far fewer tourists that day than it typically had in the summer, it was definitely at full tilt. Interestingly, the important discussion between the two new friends was at full churn, as well. Mick and Wyatt walked slowly, as they moved back towards the heart of the market.

"Do you smell that?" Wyatt asked.

"Smell what?"

"That buttery aroma." They walked past Piroshky Piroshky, the market's incredible Russian bakery. As they did so, the pleasant aroma of both sweet and savory pastries was a wonderful assault on your sense of smell. They stopped and stood outside the shop for a moment, but Mick remained quiet and a little solemn.

"Dude, that smells like some of the feasts that we have back home," the angel said.

"You're bragging again, Mick."

"Sorry . . . you know; you're really gonna like it in Heaven. Vanessa loves how much she gets to cook and prepare feasts for all of her family and friends up there." Mick's words were spoken so matter-of-factly, it surprised Wyatt.

By now, Wyatt knew in his heart and mind that he was having an extraordinary day; one which he wouldn't expect for anyone to ever experience. However, he remained confused over why the Lord had chosen him to receive a visit from an angel. "Mick, please tell me about Vanessa."

"I will. But first, I need to finish up about God's Son."

"Okay my friend. But please—tell me if she's alright."

"Wyatt, she's *more* than alright . . . are we good for now?"

"I suppose so."

"Good. Let's cross over." Mick and Wyatt had arrived at the corner of Stewart Street and Pike Place. They crossed the street and turned left, with Mick leading the way. Slowly walking up the inclined street, the angel said, "Please pull out your Bible and turn to *Colossians 4:5.*"

Wyatt had his backpack on, but he had kept the Bible in his pocket. He pulled it out and read aloud . . ."*Be wise in the way you act toward outsiders; make the most of every opportunity.*"

"That's what the key to sharing the Gospel is all about. Prepare yourselves by taking several daily doses of the Bible; in other words, *RYB dude.* Pray constantly for the Holy Spirit to reveal God's plan to you, and stay vigilant for opportunities to share the good news about Christ with others. Although you can't force feed this to people, you must remain prepared to help others when the opportunity arises. Ultimately, each person must make their own, personal decision regarding whether they accept or reject the Lord."

"I understand," Wyatt said.

"Well, that's about all that I wanted to cover regarding 'two sons' for now. Any questions?" Mick asked. They stood at the corner of Stewart Street and Post Alley.

Wyatt thought for a moment, and then asked, "Is the fact that you're helping me reunite with my son, one of the gifts that you mentioned when we first spoke, earlier today?"

"Indeed it is, Wyatt. But I do need to tell you that talking to Danny tonight is only the appetizer. I can't *wait* to serve you the main course."

9

THE TURMOIL

Mick and Wyatt continued their walk along Post Alley between Stewart and Pine Streets. As usual, Wyatt had no idea where they would end up next. Despite that, he did know they were moving in the general direction of their lunch destination at Pike Brewing; he was actually hoping to get in ahead of the lunch-time crowd.

Wyatt's mind drifted towards why he had been chosen to meet an angel, when Mick suddenly asked, "Dude, tell me about the lottery thing. What was that like for you?"

Wyatt snapped back to reality, "Well Mick, what can I say? After losing my dog, my mother, *and* my wife, all within a period of a few months . . . oh, and don't forget that my only son stopped speaking to me after my wife's funeral—"

"Whoa there Wyatt—hang on partner," Mick said, raising his hands in a halting motion. "We don't need to drag all of that out right now. I was just asking—"

"Oh c'mon, Mick! After losing Vanessa and my mom, one of the hardest things I had to do, was to put Scout to sleep! On top of that, my son decided that it was *me* who was at fault for my wife's death."

Mick simply put his hand on Wyatt's shoulder in an effort to soothe him. After a few moments, Wyatt said, "I'm sorry. I didn't mean to go off on a tangent."

Mick nodded, then gently guided Wyatt back on track, "The lottery thing—?"

"Yeah, the lottery thing was a very unexpected blessing."

"Please tell me what happened."

"Well, it was late on a Thursday afternoon in September of last year, and I was coming home from a two day business trip to the Carolinas. Vanessa's funeral had been about five weeks earlier, and I wasn't feeling particularly well that day. Anyway, I made my usual stop at a gas station at I-85 and exit 137 to fuel up, and after doing so, I went into the store and bought a couple of lottery tickets . . . ." Wyatt paused for a moment.

"Please—go on," the angel encouraged.

"Well, even though I really don't like gambling, I used to buy a couple of tickets a week, because I always figured that just in case God wanted to bless me, I should give Him the chance."

"I'm not sure I agree with that," Mick said. "But please—go on."

"Anyway, I bought one of those, *win a thousand dollars a week for life* tickets, and guess what? That next Sunday morning when I checked the numbers, all six matched my ticket. The following day on Monday, I went down to the main lottery office in Atlanta and claimed my prize, but not without a very nervous Sunday of anticipation."

"So, you're loaded now, huh?" Mick chided.

"No, it wasn't enough to retire on; what with inflation and all. But, it was enough to sell my house in Georgia, then buy an awesome two bedroom, two bath condo in Seattle on Alaskan Way. That's something I never dreamed I'd *ever* be able to afford."

"That sounds pretty cool to me," Mick said.

"It is. But do you wanna know something? I've always wondered why it happened *after* Vanessa passed. She would've definitely wanted to move out here."

"You know the answer to that one, Wyatt. God's plan for Vanessa was merely different than yours. I can assure you of this—she's enjoying her fellowship with Christ right now, in her heavenly mansion. Believe me; Vanessa's permanent home in Heaven is *much* better than any earthly condo—by a long stretch."

"I suppose you're right," Wyatt agreed.

"Listen, that's also the reason why Jesus is your soul mate, not any human being. Don't forget—people's lives on Earth are finite. Only God is eternal."

By this time, they arrived on Pine Street and turned right. When Wyatt looked up, he knew exactly why they had come that way. Right before them stood Vanessa's favorite kitchen store, Sur La Table. They actually passed the other side of the store before entering Post Alley, but Wyatt was looking at his Bible, and hadn't paid much attention. To their left was the beautiful Inn At The Market hotel, a place that Wyatt had always wanted to patronize before he moved to Seattle.

"I'm not sure why I didn't notice where we were going after turning left on Stewart," Wyatt said. "I guess I was looking up the last passage."

"I was actually distracting you," Mick admitted.

"This was her favorite place—"

"I know Wyatt," Mick interrupted, gently. "Listen, we have much to talk about regarding your bride, and I felt like this store would be the best place to start." Directly across the street was the Seattle's Best café where their conversation had started that very morning. "Dude, how's about I show off a little of my *angel knowledge* and tell you all about your story with Vanessa?"

Wyatt shrugged, "Sure. I don't see why not."

"Let's see . . . you and Vanessa have known each other since grade school. You were actually best buddies up until the summer before your senior year in high school; she was two years behind you. Anyways, you started dating, and continued to do so until March of your senior year. That's when you got the bright idea to dump her so you could date other women when you went to college at the University of Georgia that fall. How's that so far?"

"So far so good, but you make me sound like a philanderer when you say that I dumped her to date other women. Hey, I was only seventeen at the time." They continued to stand on the sidewalk outside of Sur La Table.

"The truth is the truth . . . anyways, after some experience at college, you changed your mind about dating Vanessa, who was then a junior in high school. But oops, you messed up! She had another boyfriend by then, and she wasn't interested. Vanessa ended up dating that same boy until they graduated from high school. Then she dumped him and came back to you."

"Yes. By then, I had dropped out of UGA and started working as a junior salesman in the trucking business for a mentor and good friend of mine. I actually stayed in that line of work for around two decades, until

I moved out here. You know, I spent a lot of time on the road, probably ninety or so nights a year."

"Right," Mick said. "Well, as it turned out, you and Vanessa didn't take long to get married after you two got back together. She went to nursing school while you worked, and bingo! A year later, Danny was born. Vanessa was able to finish nursing school later on, and worked part time in the health care business for a while. In the meantime, you made a nice living as your experience progressed; all was good in your little world."

"We were so proud of Danny and what he did in school, and later, in college. It seemed to come easy to him, and we were always amazed at how quickly he understood and picked up on things."

"Yep, he was truly blessed. The King brought you and Vanessa together to bring Danny into the world and to raise him. Plus, you folks have a good marriage."

"Don't you mean *had* a good marriage, Mick?"

"Well . . . sort of."

"What about that passage in *Matthew 22* about—?"

"You mean about marriage after death?" Mick interrupted. "Yes, *Matthew 22:30* is where the Lord said . . . *For when the dead rise, they will neither marry nor be given in marriage. In this respect they will be like the angels in heaven* . . . Christ was speaking to the Sadducees who were trying to trap Him. Of course, He quickly exposed them as being ignorant, compared to Himself."

"That's interesting."

"Let me ask you a question," Mick continued, "does it make any sense at all that the significant relationships you have on Earth won't be significant in Heaven?"

"I guess not."

"Ask yourself this—would an all-powerful God who is *very* involved in your lives; One who gives you a significant opportunity to choose where you want to spend eternity, completely of your own volition; do you think He would actually fail to restore your family connections in Heaven? *Does that make any sense at all?!?!?*" Mick was very emphatic, and Wyatt was taken aback because of it.

"No, I suppose it doesn't."

"Well then, while it's true your eternal marriage is with Christ, He absolutely restores your Christian relationships in Heaven. Of course, this only includes your family and friends who surrender to Him."

"I suppose that makes sense," Wyatt said.

"The people who you meet and love on this Earth are in your life for a good reason—God's reason! Don't forget this—Jesus is in the redemption business. It's an absolutely absurd notion that He would bring you to an eternal life which is completely unfamiliar to you."

"That's good to hear," Wyatt said.

"Your redemption will ultimately bring you physically into the presence of God. However, the stain of sin will be completely removed by Jesus. In the same way, all of your loved ones who are in Christ will be with you physically—just as they are now. But again, the relationships will be perfect, without the stain of sin. God will also restore a perfect Eden for you, including animals. Remember now, from the beginning of creation, these are things that God intended for mankind. Basically, God isn't creating a completely new world; He's redeeming the old one, and restoring it to His original plan."

"I see."

"C'mon Wyatt. You know full-well that what I'm saying is true," Mick said.

The angel's semi-tirade had Wyatt back on his heels, "Hang on, Mick. I was just commenting on what many Christians say about marriage in Heaven . . . or the lack thereof."

RYB dude! Don't listen to what others say about God's Holy Word. Check it out for yourself. If you read the whole passage, you'll see the whole *context.* Jesus was under a verbal attack by some naysayers, who were trying to discredit Him. Listen, the relationships with your wife, family, and friends will be different in Heaven than they are down here, but they'll be infinitely *better!* You'll just have to hunker down and trust God on that. Don't forget what I said a little while ago about the whole soul mate thing."

"I understand, but it just seems like—"

"It just seems like Satan has tried to make people *not* want to go to Heaven by twisting what the Bible says about marriage in Heaven?"

Wyatt shrugged, "I suppose that makes sense, Mick. Anyway, can we go inside for a minute? I enjoy looking at all the cooking stuff."

Then, in an amazingly calm voice Mick said, "You should see all of the cool cooking stuff that Vanessa has these days."

"Are you for real???" Wyatt asked.

"Of course I am. Please don't forget how awesome the Lord is, and don't put Him into that little box which Satan and company have convinced some people to do."

"Are you talking about how unbelievers think of Jesus?"

"Yep. But, this list also includes Christians who believe in things about God and His Holy Word, without ever cracking open a Bible. God made *everything* that you see. He's not a small God—He's a great big, humongous God."

"10-4, my fired-up angelic buddy," Wyatt said. With that, they walked up the few stairs to Sur La Table's front door, and entered over the threshold into a kitchen version of paradise.

Once inside, they weaved their way around aisles of pots and pans, observing every kitchen gadget one can imagine. When they came to a utensil knick-knack section, Wyatt picked out a pair of plastic salad mixing forks. They were only ten bucks and he thought they would come in handy when preparing that night's salad with Miss Charlene.

"What're those?" Mick asked.

"Salad thingies . . . and if you say one thing about my man-club membership—"

"Whoa dude! I'm just asking," Mick said, grinning.

"Me and Miss Charlene like to have a fresh salad with our dinners."

"I actually like salads myself."

"By the way, you talk about Vanessa like you actually know her."

"That's because *I do* know her."

Wyatt stopped in his tracks. He once again started to get a queasy feeling in his stomach, wondering, *what if this guy is perpetrating the most incredible hoax of all time?* Deep inside he knew better, but since their conversation had begun so suddenly and unexpectedly, he still felt somewhat hesitant. As they walked towards the register, he asked, "Mick, when was the last time that you saw Vanessa?"

"Actually, not long ago."

"You're continuing to give me cryptic answers about her."

"Okay then—fine. I saw her last week."

Wyatt sighed, "Geez Mick, I don't know about all of this . . . ."

"Listen, I'm really trying to ease you into this part of our discussion," Mick said gently. "This is the most delicate part of our chat today, and I don't want to scare you off, or make you feel paranoid."

"Okay, but I'm not finished with my questions yet," Wyatt said. He checked out and put the salad implements into his growing backpack. After exiting the store, they made their way across Pine Street, making a bee line back onto Post Alley.

As they walked past the Seattle's Best Coffee shop, the now open windows provided the familiar aroma of freshly brewed coffee and espresso. When Mick glanced into the café, his walking thudded to a complete stop. He then proceeded to stare intently at someone standing in line at the counter. Wyatt's "spider senses" began tingling, and he sensed a sweeping emotional change in Mick. After standing there for only a moment, Mick began walking again, but he didn't say a word. The angel stared straight ahead and was completely quiet.

"What's wrong, Mick?"

"I'll tell you when we get to the restaurant. I really need to sit down, so I can regain my cool."

Walking in silence, they finished the short distance on the diagonal Post Alley, quickly landing on Pike Place. The produce and seafood vendors were very busy by then, and the market was much louder than earlier. However, Mick remained curiously quiet. Wyatt led the way towards the restaurant, passing by Rachel the Pig and the fish market once again. After a couple of turns, they passed by their previous shopping stop at DeLaurenti. After another a short distance, they reached the entrance to "The Pike." Continuing down the stairs, they made their way into the restaurant.

"Ma'am, can you kindly direct us towards the *used coffee* department?" Mick asked the hostess.

"Excuse me?" she asked.

"Sorry—I mean, where's your restroom?"

"Oh," she giggled. "It's down the hall on your left."

Both Mick and Wyatt headed down the hallway to the restroom. When they returned to the hostess area, the young lady was waiting for them. "Okay then, two for lunch?" she asked.

"Absolutely," the angel said.

There was a good sized crowd in the restaurant that day, and the volume of conversations was fairly loud. Mick and Wyatt were promptly seated in a booth near the kitchen, where the hostess advised them that their server would be with them in a moment. She then went about her business.

Wyatt quickly asked, "Okay Mick—*what's going on?* You completely spazzed out back there. Something's not right."

Mick sighed, "Well Wyatt, it looks like my mission with you just kicked into hyper-space."

"Please knock off that cryptic baloney, Mick. What's going on?"

"Okay, okay! Once again, I'll give you the answer first. Do you remember all that stuff about my group—*the dozen*—that we talked about at breakfast?"

"Of course I do."

"Well, we've actually been together for a long time now, embroiled in our battles against the enemy. But for most of our history together, we've actually only had eleven members."

"Really—why is that?"

"You see, one of our original members was kicked out of Heaven by the Lord to join his fellow flunk-outs in Demonville. Yep, he was once one of us; now he's one of them. Get it?"

"Do you mean that one of your former members—?"

"Yes. One of our original members in the dozen is now a demon—a former angel."

"When did this happen?"

"DP—Divine Privilege. The Bible doesn't actually tell you when Lucifer and his angels were booted out, and I'm afraid I can't divulge that information to you."

"Do you have any idea why?"

"I'm not sure. But, it's probably because this topic is an important part of Heaven's orientation program for all new citizens."

"Did you say, *orientation?*"

"I did. All new entrants into Heaven get a thorough review of their life—as well as an overview of the history of the world—at their heavenly orientation. By the way, I hear it's a very good program."

"Hmmm," Wyatt mumbled. "Will all of God's mysteries be revealed then?"

"No dummy, not *all* of them. The King's knowledge and power are eternal, and therefore clearly outside of all understanding. That means none of us—angel or human—will ever know *all* of God's mysteries."

"I see."

"The point here is this . . . in Heaven, you'll learn a heckuva lot more than you currently know—particularly about the first two of the three eras of human history."

"Help me out on this one, please," Wyatt said sheepishly. "I'm afraid I'm at a loss."

"*RYB dude!* The first era was creation and life in paradise. That's covered under *Genesis 1* and *2*. Now then, *Genesis 3* started the second or current era, which started with the fall of mankind—initiated by Satan in the form of a serpent. The final era starts in *Revelation 21*, which is in the future. Some folks actually believe it's in the very near future. Anyways, as you're probably aware, most of human history—as you now know it—is contained between *Genesis 3* and *Revelation 20.*"

"So, when will this third era begin?"

"DP, dude. Not even an angel like me knows the answer to that question."

"Yeah, I suppose that makes sense."

"Therefore," Mick continued, "because I'm a soldier, I'll just keep fighting ahead, until this battle is over. That's what soldiers do, you know."

"I can't argue with that," Wyatt said.

"Let me also say that very soon, you might become a soldier for Jesus Christ, as well."

"Me—a soldier?"

"Yep. Not an angelic soldier, like *yours truly*. But a human soldier, of course."

"That's very interesting . . . anyway, when are you gonna tell me about whatever or whoever you saw in the Seattle's Best that got you so spooked?"

"Oh yeah. It was actually angel number four from our group. His name is Damon. And by the way, I'm not spooked—I'm angry!"

"Why?"

"I'm getting to that. You see, demons in both dimensions—both the invisible and in this one—can't hide from me. As we were walking, I sensed Damon's repugnant presence. So, when I looked into the café, I saw the human body who he inhabits, standing in line for a coffee."

"Did he see you?"

"It doesn't matter. He's only here because he knows that I'm on a new mission to see you."

"Hmmm," Wyatt mumbled. "Why—?"

"Yeah," Mick interrupted. "I'm afraid those demonic scavengers sometimes track we-angels in an effort to sabotage whatever our missions are. It seems that they really like to jump in the middle of something good and foul it up; but, they really hate it when we step in and fix their bad deeds. Well, I should rather say, fix the aftermath of their destruction—*like now.*"

"What does Damon look like this time?"

"Good question. He was that good looking, sandy haired dude who was dressed in an expensive business suit."

"For real?"

"Unfortunately, yes. You know something . . . *that Damon is a real jackass!*" Mick fumed.

"You seem pretty fired up, Mick. Is there anything I can do to help?"

"Just follow my lead and listen to what I'm telling you. I'll never lead you astray, and will always do everything I can to protect you."

"I realize that Mick. So what's our plan now?"

Seemingly on cue, their server named Mimi came up and asked, "What's up guys? What can I get you started with?"

"Mimi, I believe I'll just have a cup of coffee," Mick said.

"And I'll have a hot tea and a glass of water," Wyatt blurted.

Mick smiled, "We'll be ready to order when you get back, darlin'."

"I'll be back in a flash," Mimi said, proceeding towards the beverage station.

They both sat quietly for a minute, reviewing the menu. There was a lot going on in their discussion, and this unexpected development with Damon seemed to really throw fuel into the fire. Mick broke their silence, "So, what're you getting to eat there, dude?"

"I'm not real sure yet. Hey Mick, how well do you know Damon?"

"Unfortunately, I know him real well."

"Why is that?"

"Because he was actually under my command in the dozen. You see, he wanted to be in charge of our group, so he was booted out of Heaven, partially because of his jealousy of me. Anyways, since his ouster, I've literally been all over this globe battling him. He's very devious, and I'm very leery of him."

Just then, Mimi brought their drinks and asked, "What are we having today, guys?" Mimi was an attractive twenty-two year old young lady with a raspy voice.

"Honey, I'll have the salmon sandwich," Mick said.

"And I'll take the Son of Reuben sandwich," Wyatt said slowly, still looking at the menu.

"I'll get y'alls order right in," she said. Mick and Wyatt prepared their beverages as the lunchtime crowd continued to grow. The higher noise level in the restaurant was in stark contrast to their earlier talking venues.

"It sounds like Mimi's from your old neck of the woods," Mick said.

"Nice work, Sherlock," Wyatt retorted. "Actually, I'm glad to see you lighten up a little," he added.

This caused Mick to grin, "My good man, I'll have you know that I have a great fondness for the folks in the south. *Y'all* tend to be very expressive about your faith in the Lord, and it always makes me happy when I have missions down there."

"Have you spent much time in Georgia?"

"I'm afraid I've probably spent more time in Georgia than *you,* my friend," Mick exaggerated. "Have you ever heard of the Civil War?"

"Right," Wyatt said. "But before we get off track again, let's get back to Damon. Once again, what's the plan?"

"Well," Mick sighed, "I think I'll just let ole pretty boy make the first move, while we continue our discussion. If Damon interferes, I'll just have to put a serious *smack down* on that evil little schmuck."

Wyatt chuckled, "It sounds to me like you're watching *way* too many of our movies, Mick."

"In this case, don't you mean rasslin'?"

"Now I *know* that you've spent some time down south if you're talking about professional wrestling."

"That's *rasslin* dude, not *wrestling.* What kind of southerner are you anyways?"

"Apparently, not as good as you are," Wyatt laughed.

"Seriously though, I'll deal with Damon later. Don't worry, you're in good hands with me."

"Gee, thanks for the Allstate commercial . . . so, what do you want to talk about next?"

"Dying," Mick said, suddenly solemn. "Well, at least that's what you folks think it is. To me, it's actually more like *living* for the very first time."

"That's an odd perspective."

"Not really. Think of it like this—for Christians, it's really like shedding an old, temporary shell for a permanent one."

Wyatt was quiet for a moment, "I suppose it's finally time to talk about Vanessa, huh?"

"Indeed it is. Like I mentioned earlier, the car accident that took Vanessa's life wasn't your fault. Also, Jesus wouldn't have let it happen, if it didn't ultimately serve His purposes. Now then, do you understand what I just said, or is this just the kind of concept that many Christians agree with, but don't really believe in their hearts?"

"Yes, I understand it. I suppose I really didn't fault myself for the accident that took Vanessa, until Danny blamed me. It was then that I started second guessing everything which happened that night."

"I understand. However, that's precisely when your reliance on Christ should kick in. Remember, no matter how much people may love and care about you, they'll never love you like the Lord does." Mick pointed upwards. "All people are fallible and usually look first and foremost at their own interests and feelings; not to mention the fact that you're all mortal, and will ultimately die in this life. However, Christ is always there for you. He gives each of you the hope which is necessary to get you through this ordeal down here."

"Yeah, I guess that it's hard to look at my only son and see his shortcomings. I know in the bottom of my heart that he was wrong to abandon me during the most difficult time of my life."

"Actually, he and I spoke at length about that yesterday. And believe me, he's ready to make amends. You see, that issue had to be dealt with first—before I could come here to see you today."

Pleasantly surprised, Wyatt said, "This is really good news . . . I really don't know what to say. Thank you so much."

"Thank Him!" Mick said, looking upwards.

After a few moments, Wyatt asked, "Weren't we talking about dying?"

Just then, the food runner brought out their food and asked them if they needed anything further. They didn't, so they prayed and began to eat.

"Dying. Yep. Well my boy, I have a good movie analogy for you on this subject."

"Surprise, surprise!" Wyatt said, using his best Gomer Pyle impression. Mick ignored him.

"I assume you've seen *Indiana Jones and the Last Crusade?*"

"Only about a million times, Mick."

"Okay. Do you know the part towards the end where Indy has to walk across that big chasm to get over to where the knight and holy grails are?"

"I know it well. It's one of my favorite parts of the movie."

"Cool. So, if you'll remember, Indy had a choice to make. He could stay on the path, which he knew was correct, and take the uncomfortable but necessary *leap of faith* . . . or . . . he could have turned back and gotten killed. Well, have you ever thought about—?"

"I get it!" Wyatt interrupted. "Dying is like that chasm he was afraid to fall into."

Mick nodded emphatically, "It sure is."

"No matter how strong your faith is, it's still a terrifying thing for a human to face death. And no matter how much you may know your eternal destination when you die, you can't help but to have some measure of trepidation within yourself. You can't totally eliminate that feeling of, LORD—*you'd better be there!* I believe you can have the strongest faith in the world, but many people still have that nagging doubt—"

"Exactly dude!" Mick agreed. "Just like in the movie, Jesus is the unseen bridge across the chasm. You absolutely *must* take that *leap of faith,* and let him carry you across the chasm of death, because Christ is the only One who can do so. Again, that's art imitating life."

"Indeed. Anyway, whenever I have any kind of doubts, instead of just letting them fester, I take them to the Lord in prayer. I apologize for not totally trusting in Him, and I constantly ask God to continue to correct, instruct, and guide me."

"That's exactly how each of you should handle any issue with the Lord. Take it to Him in prayer, RYB, and consult other Christians and your local church. By the way, pastors love to help with that kind of thing . . . I call that the Church of One concept, but I don't want to go into that until a little bit later."

"That's fine. So, you're saying that dying for a human is a terrifying thing to deal with, regardless of someone's level of faith? It seems that facing that chasm of death can scare just about anyone, huh?"

"Absolutely," Mick agreed. "But the Lord will be there for you—if you simply ask Him to be."

"You know, that reminds me of an old expression," Wyatt said. "It goes something like this—*everyone wants to get to Heaven, but nobody wants to die!* I think that sentiment is what best sums up what we're talking about."

"It sure does," Mick agreed. "And it really does a good job of describing the human experience." They continued to eat their lunches. "So, how's that Reuben working out for you?"

"It's really good. But don't hold your breath waiting for me to ask you about your smelly salmon sandwich."

"And to think that I was really beginning to like you, Wyatt."

After chomping down a large french fry, Wyatt asked, "Hey Mick, tell me more about all of the former angel banishments. Can you tell me the story of when Lucifer and his angels were kicked to the curb?"

"Hmmm, let's see . . . what can I tell you?" Mick thought out loud. "Well, I mentioned earlier that the age of us angels falls under DP. So, it's a *no-can-do,* on that. However, I believe you can glean some information from the Bible on this subject. Let's see if you can figure it out . . . ."

"Alright, then." Wyatt gave it some thought for a few moments, "After Day 6 of creation in *Genesis 1,* God said His creation was *very good.* Angels getting booted out of Heaven and creation being *very good* are at odds, so the banishment must have happened after the end of *Genesis 1.*"

"Go on," Mick encouraged. "I like your methodology."

"*Genesis 2* basically goes back and gives some details about creation, and why God created Eve for Adam. So let's see, *Genesis 3:1* speaks of Satan in the form of a serpent showing up—"

"You're getting there."

"So, it seems like the banishment might have happened in-between *Genesis 1:31* and *Genesis 3:1.* Does that make any sense?"

"It does make sense, but what about *Job 38:4-7?*" Mick asked.

Wyatt quickly read the passage. "I'm confused. It sounds like the angels were around before creation in this passage, but it doesn't say anything about when the bad angels were banished. Are you going to cop out and fall back into DP?"

"DP is *not* a cop out—God has His reasons for not telling you certain things. I really think it's a good idea to totally trust in Him, and He'll ultimately reveal His ways to you . . . in His time."

"I suppose that makes sense."

"Anyways, from the human perspective, there are good arguments on all of the theories on this issue. However, what you need to remember is that it really doesn't matter for your current lives. The important point here is that leading others towards Christ is what *really* matters. When we-angels were created, and when the bad angels were banished, is not really important for you to know right now—*or God would have told you in the Bible!* I'm afraid you're going to have to wait for your orientation program in Heaven before you get your answers to questions like this. By the way, I have no more comments about this. DP kicks in here—sorry."

"Have additional angels been banished since the original fall?"

"Kindly see my last statement," Mick said firmly.

"So . . . you can't tell me when Damon fell, huh?"

"Nope."

"Geez . . . well, I suppose I'll find out one day."

"You will—don't worry."

They sat quietly for a few minutes enjoying their sandwiches until Wyatt spoke up and said, "I can't wait until Vanessa and I can talk about all this stuff."

"Actually, she can't wait, either."

"Didn't you say that you saw her last week?"

"Are you sure that you're ready to talk about this?"

Wyatt sighed, "I think so."

"Okay, here we go . . . I suppose that what I'm about to tell you is a 'coming attraction' to the overall gifts I mentioned earlier, so dummy up. You need to listen closely to me—got it?"

"Yes boss," Wyatt said.

"Now then . . . here it is . . . Vanessa prepared a great feast last week before I got deployed on this mission. That's her job up there, and of course she loves it. It seems that her love of food and her propensity to nurture people through her cooking has carried forth into Heaven. The King made her for that purpose, and now it serve's His purposes."

"Wow . . . really?"

"Absolutely. That's the way it is for all saved Christians when you get to Heaven. But sadly, so many of Christ's followers don't actually think about how *real* Heaven truly is . . . and by the way, Vanessa makes an awesome mac and cheese."

"So you're telling me you actually had a feast in Heaven last week . . . *and Vanessa prepared it?*"

"Well, she and the others in her group. But yes. Lots of her saved family members and friends were there as well, along with a few of us in the dozen. There were also some other angels, and of course, Jesus Christ, Himself."

Wyatt shook his head slowly, "Mick, that really sounds far-fetched," he said. "That's the kind of thing which sounds too good to be true."

"I understand. But it's true, nonetheless."

"I mean, I just can't picture the Lord being with people at a feast."

"RYB dude! Look up *John 21:1-14.*"

Wyatt looked up the passage and took a minute or so to read through it. "Okay Mick, what's your point?"

"Just this—Christ appeared several times to His disciples after His resurrection. This time, they hauled in a major catch of fish and He dined with them. Remember, this was *after His death and resurrection*. Well, if He feasted with His disciples then, why would he *not* feast with his children in Heaven?"

"I have no answer for that. I mean . . . I know that we earlier discussed the fact that there is absolutely feasting in Heaven. But somehow, it seems so unreal."

"I have an answer for you, and it's actually pretty simple," Mick said. "The sad fact is, many Christians short-sell their King, and often think of Him as being boring and aloof. That type of thinking has been promoted by the enemy—*and we know who that is!* Anyone who has any real sense of our Father, *and* who'll read their Bible, knows that Jesus Christ is all about eternal joy. Well, feasting is a very important part of fellowship on the current Earth—and in Heaven. Ultimately, it'll become a major socializing event on the new Earth."

"That makes sense. It's actually pretty awesome when you think about it . . . so, is Vanessa happy?"

"She's *very* happy, and she's living without any worries or pain like she had on Earth. Vanessa is also performing the duties which make both her and the Lord happy. That's the cool thing about living in total commune with the Father. So relax dude, she's in good shape up there."

"Did she mention me at all?" Wyatt asked.

"I'll get back to you later on that one," Mick said.

Mimi dropped by to check on them as they were almost finished eating. Wyatt asked for the check, got out his credit card, and gave it to her. He then continued, "Mick, all of this stuff makes sense to me. But like I said, it sometimes seems a little far-fetched. I mean . . . I understand and embrace the truth of Christ and all . . . but it's so hard to imagine actually seeing Him."

"Take heart my friend—that's a fairly common thought. In other words, I don't think you should feel like the Lone Ranger on that one."

"What do you mean?" Wyatt asked.

"It's simple. God designed it that way so that when you make the leap of faith and trust in Christ, you're actually doing something that's difficult—not easy. Unfortunately, many folks take the easy road and just push God into the background for dealing with later on. The problem is, sometimes that 'later on' never comes before it's too late. Due to the fact that some people can't imagine God's greatness in your cynical and fallen world, they cop out and procrastinate. In other words, they put the Lord on the back burner."

"That seems pretty foolish to me. I mean, any of us can die at any moment."

"Yep, it sure seems short-sighted to me, as well."

"So . . . do you feel like talking about atheists?" Wyatt asked.

"Nope, not yet. I wanna talk about sharing the Gospel of Christ."

"Isn't that what we've been talking about all day?"

"Yes, but let me explain. What I want to tell you is this—let's say that you need to share the Gospel with a non-believer one hundred times before they open their heart to God—"

"Didn't we talk about the appropriateness of how you witness to others earlier?"

"We did, but that's not what I'm talking about. We spoke about the fact that it's not up to any one person to save another—that's God's job; to save people that is."

"What's your point?" Wyatt asked. Although he understood the importance of sowing the seeds of Christ and letting God do His part, the method by which some people try to share the Word by pushing an unsaved person into a corner, then belligerently showering them with Scripture, was something he truly detested.

"Again, if it takes someone a hundred times to hear about the Lord before opening their heart to Him, you can't possibly know if you're number one, or number ninety nine—and it shouldn't matter to you. Remember, your job is to be a disciple and spread the word. The Lord will do the rest. Trying to do anything more than speaking the truth is equivalent to trying to play God. Am I making any sense, here?"

"Yes, but I still don't understand—?"

"Listen," Mick interrupted. "Much damage has been done in God's kingdom by people who think they 'save' people by forcing a decision prematurely. In those cases, a decision for Christ didn't actually happen, and the damage must be undone before these people will ever listen to the Gospel Truth again."

"So a decision for Christ needs to be made sincerely and from the bottom of someone's heart? Is that what you're saying?"

"Exactly!"

"Okay, you'll get no argument from me on that," Wyatt agreed.

"Alright. I suppose we can move along for now."

Mimi brought the little credit card tray with both copies of their bill, then thanked them for stopping in. Wyatt left her a nice gratuity before preparing to leave.

"Mick, do you want to go confront Damon? I'm pretty sure we can still find him."

"We don't have to go find him—he's sitting right over there." Mick motioned over towards the east end of the restaurant.

A chill ran up Wyatt's spine. *If this angel-thing is correct, then the demon-thing also has to be,* he thought. *Is that handsome guy sitting a few tables over actually a demon?* he wondered. It was hard for him to tell. "What should we do?" he asked.

"Like I said, nothing yet. I don't think he'll mess with us too much today. But, I could be wrong. I'm guessing that he's just nosing around and doing a little flaunting. Demons do that a lot, you know."

"I thought you said that you're leery of demons."

"I said that I was leery of *Damon*; and yes, I'm also leery of all demons. However, I'm not scared of them, because I have the power of God behind me."

"That must be nice."

"Listen . . . you have His power too, and I'm here to teach you how to use it. God's Holy Word is your best weapon against the princes of darkness. Please trust me on this."

Wyatt looked at Mick quizzically, but decided to not press him. "Okay then, where do you want to go next, and what shall we talk about?"

"I'm glad you asked. Let's go over near that movie store on one of the Down Under levels of the Main Arcade. Oh, and I need to stop and get a haircut also."

"After all this food and coffee—now I have to buy you a haircut?"

Mick raised an eyebrow and leveled, "Yes, *Mr. Lottery*, you have to buy me a haircut." Wyatt smiled at this. "Let's get going."

As they left the restaurant, Mick stared down Damon, who only shot back a cheesy smile. In an effort to try to glean as much insight as he could about their relationship, Wyatt watched both of them back and forth—angel and demon. This ancient battle between the good angels and the evil ones has raged on for ages. And now, very unexpectedly, Wyatt Hunter found himself caught squarely in the middle of their war.

10
HOLLYWOOD

With their appetites temporarily satisfied, Mick and Wyatt walked mostly in silence, making their way back towards the Main Arcade. Along the way, they occasionally stopped to enjoy some of the diverse wonders of the market. Several of the interesting shops in the Economy Market and LaSalle Buildings caught Mick's attention; in particular, the Daily Dozen Donuts shop.

Right in front of the small shop was a donut frying machine, which allows the market's patrons to get a close look at the preparation of those delectable mini donuts. Mick beamed like a kid as he watched the donut making process, and soon found himself in the company of three children. After a few moments, both the angel and the youngsters clapped heartily as they watched the donuts flip in the fryer. This prompted Wyatt to chuckle, remembering that Mick was actually wearing a Krispy Kreme tee shirt—something he would never have expected from an angel before that day.

For a fleeting moment, Wyatt thought he must be going insane. A donut loving, coffee drinking, Bible knowing, anti-demon guy, who excessively uses the word *dude,* entered his life just a few hours ago, claiming to be a member of the heavenly host. This angel not only claimed to be in contact with God Himself; but also, that he ate some of his late wife's mac and cheese in Heaven just last week. Thus far, this whole experience seemed so surreal . . . yet also, very real.

Although their unfolding discussion felt right in his heart, the logical, *Mr. Spock* part of his mind just couldn't eliminate the nagging, bastion of doubt regarding Mick's authenticity. However, since he really believed something unique and very special was indeed happening that day, he decided to proceed, based on his heartfelt feelings. Guided by his unorthodox messenger, Wyatt decided to completely relax during this very interesting walk through the market.

They made their way back past the fish market once again. This time, they had to squeeze around the throng of tourists, most of whom had their cameras and cell phones out, taking pictures. The people were smiling; the children were laughing; the sound of clapping was heard in all directions; and most of all, the salmon flew through the air. This place was truly the beating heart of Pike Place Market.

Continuing past the fish market crowd, they made their way down the steps, which led into the lower levels and the Down Under shops. This was also the south-bound entry point for the Pike Place Hill Climb, which Wyatt had taken north-bound just a few hours ago, to start this unexpected adventure. At the bottom of the stairs, Mick had to excuse himself to use the restroom again, so Wyatt waited over by the railing and breathed out a deep sigh.

When Mick re-emerged, Wyatt said, "Well, I can safely say that I've learned at least *something* from you today, Mick . . ."

"What's that, my friend?"

"I haven't once asked you why an angel has to use the restroom."

Mick chuckled, "Yeah, well I'm glad you're listening. While I'm on this side of the flaming sword, my body acts very similar to yours—only it's much more handsome."

"In that case, it would be pretty much the shocker-of-all-shockers if you didn't have to relieve yourself—what with all the coffee you drink and all . . . however, I'm not so sure about that *handsome* part."

"Look here, dudemeister. I'm sorry to break this to you, but I'm still not done with my coffee pilgrimage, yet."

"Are you kidding me?"

"Nope—not one single bit. Later on, we still need to stop at the Tully's on Western Avenue."

"Why is that?"

"Because Tully's has good coffee, a cozy fireplace, and extra comfy chairs—all just *waiting* for us to arrive. What more could you want?"

Wyatt shook his head, "No offense Mick, but sometimes you sound like a little kid."

"I'll take that as a compliment. Are you familiar with *Matthew 18:3?*"

"Isn't that where Jesus instructs us to become more like children?"

"Yep, it sure is. The humility of a child and their dependence on our heavenly Father is what it's all about."

"Hmmm. I can't argue with that, can I?"

"Nope. I'm afraid not"

Mick and Wyatt made their way down some more stairs and began wandering around the venerable Down Under shops. It was always much quieter in these lower levels of the market, as the environs assumed a much quieter solitude. The ancient wooden floors underfoot had a certain old-fashioned creak, which only added to the ambiance of a bygone era. The relaxed pace in the Down Under areas clashed greatly with the pleasant noise and frenzy just above their heads on the main level of the market.

Their first official stop Down Under was at a barber shop for Mick's haircut. They walked into the shop, which was empty of patrons, and Mick sat down in one of the chairs. Wyatt sat down and watched with amusement as the barber put a smock over Mick and asked him how he wanted his hair cut.

"How come she didn't ask me if I wanted *my* hair cut?" Wyatt joked.

"She's not dumb, dude," Mick said. A little chuckle slipped out.

Wyatt grinned, "You might want to avoid that kind of terminology while someone has a sharp instrument in their hand."

"Sage advice," Mick agreed. He then said to the barber, "Hey darlin', please just take about an inch off the bottom." The barber began her work in preparing the angel's hair by unraveling his pony tail. While she did that, the guys continued their discussion.

"Mick, I know you're leading this parade and all, but I'd like to talk to you about people being superficial. Is that okay with you?"

"That suits me fine—lead on."

"Well, I used to know a lady who once said to me that she thought that the kind of car someone drives is a clear indication about how they really feel about them self . . . she actually thought the car you drive has a direct correlation with your self-esteem."

"That's interesting."

"Well, I have to admit, it always stuck with me because I was shocked at how incredibly shallow it was."

"Word, dude!"

Shaking his head, Wyatt continued, "I often wonder what it is in our society that would make someone be influenced to say such a ridiculous thing . . . or, was that just a whacky, isolated statement?"

"No Wyatt, it's definitely embedded in your society—only Christ can bring you up from the depths of that kind of superficiality. Actually, this fits in well with our next lesson, so I'm really glad you brought that up."

"No charge, Mick," Wyatt quipped.

The barber continued to comb and trim Mick's half-gray, half-blondish, long locks. "Anyways," the angel said. "I'm not surprised to hear a ridiculous statement like that. You also don't have to look very far in the entertainment world to see that kind of superficial sentiment. Music too—or should I say *especially*—is included in the promotion of that flawed thought process. Let's face it . . . the evil ones have a penchant for utilizing the various media outlets to promote their anti-Christian agenda. One of their all-time smartest marketing campaigns was to make it cool to be self-centered, and to *look out for number one."*

"I've heard that a lot."

"What a crock! That goes directly against Christ's second great commandment, which is to love your neighbor as you love yourself."

"Didn't you say that you liked our various sources of entertainment?"

"I *do* like them. They're an interesting way to observe life on this fallen Earth, and they're often quite entertaining. But, there's a huge difference—I have Christ *first* in my life. As a result, I view the evil that's woven into the many entertainment choices from the correct perspective. It's sort of like when you mature in Christ; you're then able to put on a kind of eyeglasses that allow you to see the world from God's perspective, not the world's."

"So what are you saying?"

"I'm saying that if you strongly have Christ in every fiber of your being, then everything you look at, read, listen-to, or whatever, can be viewed from the correct perspective. Therefore, once you put on your *God glasses,* so to speak, you can look at anything in the world, and it won't adversely affect you. If you don't know Jesus, then you end up saying shallow things like, *the car you drive is an indication of how you feel about yourself*—an obviously outrageous statement."

"You know, Mick, I've always felt like the opposite was true in that car scenario. Doesn't it make sense that people who feel poorly about themselves sometimes compensate by trying to impress others with the flash of an overpriced car?"

"Grasshopper, you have just snatched the pebble from my hand. I'm proud of you."

"Thank you—*thank you very much,*" Wyatt said, doing a very poor Elvis imitation.

"Listen, having a nice car isn't necessarily a bad thing. However, it doesn't have anything to do with who you really are . . . I'm with you on this one, dude."

"Good deal," Wyatt said.

"And one more thing. Always remember who Jesus Christ was when He lived on Earth, and always remember what He did while He was here. Think about how He spent His time, and with whom He spent it."

"What do you mean?"

"You see, the Lord spent His time in the trenches, dealing directly with the sinners. While he was disgusted with sin, He always loved the sinner."

"Oh, I see. Yeah, I'm down with the whole *hate the sin, love the sinner,* thing."

"Good—that's very important. You have to understand, the battles are won on the battle field. However, you can't take it too far—that would be a *serious* mistake."

"Meaning??? Do you have an example for me?"

"I do. If you said that you needed to watch porno movies for five hours a week to 'study' the phenomenon, you'd be lying. Remember, you can't fool the Lord. He knows the intention of every thought you have."

"I believe that's in the Old Testament, somewhere."

"The porno thing, no. The intention thing, yes," Mick said with a grin. "It's in *1 Chronicles 28:9.* Would you kindly do me the honor?"

"Sure thing." Wyatt pulled out his Bible and looked for the passage. "Okay, here goes . . . *And you, my son Solomon, acknowledge the God of your father, and serve him with wholehearted devotion and with a willing mind, for the LORD searches every heart and understands every motive behind the thoughts. If you seek him, he will be found by you; but if you forsake him, he will reject you forever* . . . that makes your point pretty well, Mick."

After a couple of minutes, Mick said to the barber, "Hey darlin', will you kindly get me a mirror so I can have a look at your progress?" He then checked out his hair and declared, "That'll about do it on the hair, dear . . . now Wyatt, do you have anything to add concerning that last passage?"

Wyatt was looking at an old National Geographic magazine, and kept his attention on it as he replied, "Not really. It's pretty much an in-your-facer. How can you misconstrue that?"

"You can't, but people try. Essentially, that's the 'big picture' reason why people reject a relationship with God—they simply don't want to have any accountability to anyone, other than themselves."

"Yeah, and they also want to make themselves the center of the universe, not God."

"Yeparoo dude, you're correct." Mick turned towards the barber, "So, how much for the cut, young lady?" Wyatt already had his wallet out and paid the barber as they both stood up. The twosome then ventured back into the Down Under shops area.

Mick and Wyatt meandered and browsed for a while, until arriving at the Golden Age Collectibles shop, which had many different items from the world of entertainment. The brightly lit store had several life-size, stand-up pictures of entertainers, just outside of its entrance. After a brief search, they found some chairs not too far away to continue their discussion.

"Wyatt, are you aware that movies and entertainment can be a double-edged sword?"

"I think so . . . but just to be safe, what exactly do you mean by, *double-edged sword?*"

"A double-edged sword is anything that can be very good if used properly, but very bad if used improperly. Well, if you use your *God glasses* to view the world, and you're actively engaged in spreading the Gospel of the Lord, the various types of entertainment can be a really fun escape from the seriousness of spiritual battles."

"I'm with you so far."

"On the other hand, if all you do is while away your time reading comics and surfing the internet, the entertainment world can be quite destructive . . . particularly for kids."

"Go on," Wyatt said.

"Quite frankly, I really like a lot of your movies, TV shows, books, and music. But, I can't stand to see people living their lives for fiction. To be properly balanced, you'd be well advised to put Jesus first, then all other things after Him. Is this making any sense?"

"Certainly, but what're you driving at, here?"

"Well, let me ask you a blunt question . . . does it seem to you that a lot of the entertainment industry is against God?"

"Yeah, I suppose it does seem that way, sometimes," Wyatt agreed. "You've been around this game a whole lot longer than me. So what's your take on the whole *Hollywood liberals* thing?"

"Hollywood isn't innately evil, and neither is entertainment. What *is* evil, are the sneaky intentions of demons who influence the Hollywood entertainment mouthpiece to espouse their anti-Jesus sentiments."

"Okay—?"

"Listen, it's easy for demons to whisper in the ears of people who have lots of money thrown at them. After a while, it's hard for a human to stay humble after all of that adulation from the general public. In other words, how can a person not grounded in Jesus stay humble like Christ, when they constantly deal with throngs of people who practically worship them? Remember, we've already talked about how angels aren't worthy of worship—and neither are any people—*especially celebrities!* Only God is worthy of our worship."

"I agree, Mick. But of course, we're not just talking about movie stars, here. The same is true in several of the other types of entertainment, as well."

"Such as—?"

"Like you just said, the music business comes to mind."

"Go on."

"Well, basically, I believe the music business is equally as bad about the inappropriate hero worship of people, just like the other entertainment types are."

"You'll get no argument from me," Mick agreed.

"Believe me, I absolutely understand that only God is worthy of our worship."

"Right you are, dude. Do you have any specific examples from the world of music?"

"How about Elvis, for one?"

"I *love* Elvis!" Mick snapped back.

"I like Elvis too. However, I don't think he should he be semi-worshipped just because he was a good singer—should he?"

"Of course not. But it's easy for me, because I always have my *God glasses* on as a way to view your world. Plus, I'm an angel—and a pretty darned tough one at that. Anyways, we only worship the Lord. No one else is even close."

"Yes Mick, you're definitely a tough-but-humble hombre. And I'd like to stress the word *humble*."

"Just to let you know, this *humble hombre* is still thinking about his next latte . . . just in case you forgot."

"Noted," Wyatt said. "Now, let's get back to Elvis."

"Okay, let's see . . . Elvis's songs are good, worshipping him is bad. Agreed. Now, let's move on to a more recent example—Michael Jackson."

Wyatt sighed with resignation, "I just knew the subject of him would come up when we started talking about this," he bemoaned. "I really liked his music and abilities just fine. And he certainly had a huge impact on his generation. However, his abilities were God given, and he absolutely didn't deserve to be glorified like a semi-deity—*no human being should be!* Did you watch his funeral?"

"No, not really."

"Me neither."

"You know," Mick began, "there's a good reason why so many people act more distraught about a celebrity's passing than an average Joe, and we just touched on it a little while ago."

"And that is—?"

"Somewhere in everyone's heart is the need to worship. The problem is that all too often, people choose poorly who they actually *do* worship. Unfortunately, that technique is part of the oldest deception in the book for Satan and company."

"What deception is that?"

"The evil ones don't have to influence a person to worship demons or any other god; they only need to get a person to *not* worship Jesus Christ."

"That makes sense," Wyatt agreed. "I never thought of it like that before."

"These celebrities and singers are actually easy targets to get people all worked up about," Mick said.

"What do you mean?"

"For example, if I hear the intro to 'Jailhouse Rock', I get excited about how much I like that song. The difference is that I enjoy the work that the Lord allowed in bringing the song together, through all of the folks who were involved in its recording. The people who worship celebrities, get excited about the actual celebrity *them self*. The difference between the two is immense . . . are you hearing what I'm saying?"

"Yes, I'm hearing you. People often forget the fact that the celebrities who they adore so much were created by God, and were given their abilities *by Him*. He also saw to it that they rose to a level where they could affect others with their gifts. So in the end, it's really all about the Lord's greatness—not any celebrity's accomplishments."

"You're right on track with that, my friend," Mick agreed.

"You know, I often sympathize with the many people who live in relative obscurity, who possess equal or better talent than famous celebrities. It makes me wonder what would've happened if God had chosen them over the people who became famous, instead."

"I'm not quite following you," Mick said.

"Essentially, no one rises to prominence without God's consent. That's really what I'm trying to say."

"Oh, okay. I see what you're saying, and I agree. That same thing goes for the Hollywood crowd, singers, politicians—the whole lot. It's a shame that often times, these folks don't remember who gave them their natural talents, which got them to where they are. I suppose they feel like they achieved their success due to their own hard work."

"What exactly do you mean by *natural talents?*" Wyatt asked.

"Natural talents are ones that both saved and non-saved people have. Gifts of the Holy Spirit only come from the Lord . . . and only someone who loves Him can have those."

"I see," Wyatt said. "Switching gears now, do you think it's okay for entertainers to be so vocal about political things which they may not fully understand?"

"Well, if you are talking about the United States, of course they have the *legal* right to speak-out on politics."

"Oh c'mon—you can give me more than that."

"Chill out dude—I'm getting there. What I will say is this; being famous doesn't give you the right to act like an expert on something which you're probably not qualified to speak about. Unfortunately, being a celebrity emboldens people to speak out—but often about the wrong things."

"Okay then, what should they speak out about?"

"Now you're asking the right question! We're engaged in a war with Satan and his minions," Mick said. "They should speak up for Christ, who gave them all that they have. What I'm also saying is that being a rich celebrity doesn't allow anyone to graduate past having an abiding faith in the Lord. You know, the current mortality rate among humans is one-hundred percent, dontcha?"

"I suppose that's right," Wyatt agreed.

"Well, do famous people actually think they can take their riches with them when they die? Is *leaving their mark* really all that important when they're dead?!?!?!"

Wyatt shrugged, "I suppose not. But why do we keep talking about the entertainment industry, Mick?"

"Because of its immense influence on your society—especially the young folks."

"Yeah, that makes sense. So, how about cutting to the chase?"

"Fine dude, here it is . . . most people who accept Christ as their Savior do so by their early teens. Many more make this critical decision by the age of twenty. Well, the enemy well-understands this, and uses the fame and stardom of some celebrities to promote their anti-God message, via the world of entertainment. Of course, this is the weapon of choice for Satan and his crew. Too much love of money, power, and the lust for fame, are vices which have been around for most of human history. I'm afraid they're also easy devices for the evil ones to utilize; all in an effort to influence non-faith minded people to carry out their evil agenda."

"I see."

"And unfortunately, their primary targets are young folks. Young people are greatly influenced by these celebrities, and many Christ believing parents only try to shield their children from the whole thing. While that's certainly a good idea, it simply doesn't go far enough. Teaching children about Christ and this very significant battle that you're all born into—in other words, *spiritual warfare*—is a vastly under-utilized way to protect children . . . at least, in my opinion it is."

"Are you saying that parents should—what?"

"I'm saying parents should prepare their children for the battles which they'll inevitably encounter in life. Trying to keep them shielded from evil in the media will only go so far, because sooner-or-later, the enemy will ultimately find a way to get through to them."

"I agree—the evil ones are very persistent," Wyatt said.

"Essentially, what I'm saying is that by providing an external shield, parents are only going *half-way* in protecting their children. They should also help to immunize their children from evil by arming them with the knowledge of the enemy, and just how *real* this enemy is. This is basically an internal protection for each child. I believe that children need both external and internal protection to have a strong walk with the Lord, and to stay on His path during their formative years. Don't forget this—the Word of God is the greatest weapon which anyone can use against Satan and his cohorts."

"Geez, that sure seems to be a regular theme with you."

"Indeed it is. Later on, we'll talk about the weapons to use against the enemy, which are listed in *Ephesians 6*. But for now, just realize that on this fallen Earth, you can't hide from Satan. Everyone is best advised to protect their children—*and themselves*—by being armed with the power of Christ and His Holy Word. Am I making any sense, here?"

"Yes, you're making perfect sense, Mick. By the way, why are you emphasizing this with me? My kid is in his twenties."

"We'll get into the specifics of your mission later today. Do you remember what I said in the beginning? I'm simply a messenger, and I'm here for the purpose offering you a mission."

"Yes, I remember that. But I'm still confused by it. Anyway, I just wish that my *messenger* had been a little better looking than you—no offense."

Mick chuckled, "Actually we do have some prettier angels than me in the dozen. But I suppose you could say that you lucked-out and got me today."

"Lovely. So . . . what else do you want to talk about regarding Hollywood and the entertainment industry?"

"Just a few more things. Let's start with *Proverbs 16:18.*"

"And I suppose you want *me* to read?" Wyatt asked.

"Geez, I thought I already had you trained better than that."

"Better than what?" Wyatt played dumb.

"I'm the teacher and you're the student—got it???"

"Fine," Wyatt sighed, cracking a smile. "Give me a second . . . what was that reference again?"

"Proverbs 16:18."

"Okay, here we go . . . *Pride goes before destruction, a haughty spirit before a fall.*"

"See what I mean?" the angel asked.

"No, not exactly."

"Well, let's start out with the seven deadly sins. Although they aren't listed as such in the Bible, they're still very dangerous . . . and *pride* is arguably the foundation for all of them."

"Really, why?" Wyatt asked.

"Because pride was the sin that got my former compadres kicked out of Heaven. Although that was a terrible day in history, you can rest assured, it didn't happen without God's complete knowledge and acquiescence. Anyways, it's hard for celebrities to avoid falling into the pride trap, and it's easy for the enemy to use them when they do. Bad things end up happening after that."

"Yeah, I hear ya," Wyatt agreed.

A comfortable silence settled in between the new friends as they watched patrons come and go from the various shops. Wyatt lapsed into deep thought for a moment as a subtle wave of relaxation draped over his soul. This pleasant affliction often accompanied him when he visited Pike Place Market—especially the Down Under area.

Angel and human continued to soak in the tranquility as they watched shoppers of all ages move throughout the majestic hallways. The quieter hum of activity was accentuated by the ancient feel to the Down Under shops. Since the entire market had an incredibly diverse array of different shopping venues throughout several buildings and levels, the whole campus left Wyatt almost believing that each section of the market was akin to different parts of one large body.

Logically, Wyatt knew that something which was inanimate like the market, couldn't possibly be alive. However, there was a *certain something* about this special place; it made him feel like Pike Place Market was an old friend, who he needed to visit from time-to-time. This always gave him a wonderful sense of peace.

Mick's previous words regarding the danger of pride actually sent Wyatt into deeper reflection regarding the entertainment industry. While he thoroughly enjoyed many movies and television programs in the secular world, he still felt it was unnecessary for the Lord's message to be ignored—and even corrupted—by many filmmakers and television show producers. He remained deep in thought as his mind raced through several of the movies he had recently watched. A light bulb suddenly turned on in his head, and he declared, "Mick, I just watched a movie called, *The Reader* recently, and I was just thinking about what you said earlier regarding the use of the Bible as a survival manual."

"Okay dude-ly, what's on you mind?"

"Well, it's an excellent film, and I think it won some awards. Anyway, the story is about a teenage boy who had his first sexual experience with an older woman, and it had a profoundly negative effect on the rest of his life. After they see each other for a while, the woman takes off and disappears.

The man later marries another woman and becomes a successful lawyer. However, he's never quite the same. As it turns out later on, the first woman is arrested, tried, and sent to prison for something she did during World War II."

"So what happens next?"

"Well, prison isn't good to this woman. Anyway, after about twenty years, the man ends up helping the woman get ready for her release. But before her emancipation, she kills herself."

"Geez, that sounds pretty melancholy. It also sounds like it may be a cleverly disguised chick flick," Mick chided.

"Perhaps you're right . . . the point here is that the main guy in the film is never the same after falling into sin with this woman. Well, I was just considering the fact that God tells us that we shouldn't have premarital sex. However, many people ignore that instruction. In the case of the story in this film, it ruined this man for much of his life. As a result, he later had trouble with true *emotional* intimacy with both his wife and his daughter."

Mick unwittingly raised an eyebrow, "I'm still waiting for the punch line, here."

"Well, I suppose I'm saying that the actual sin of fornication will not make you burn in Hell. Christ atoned for all of our sins—only rejecting the Lord will send you to Hell."

"So, are you saying it's okay to be one of those 'eleventh hour Christians' who think they can do whatever they want, commit any and all sins, then apologize to the Lord before they die, and everything is okay?"

"No—absolutely not. That's insincere, and no one can fool the creator of all things. God gives us a set of instructions in the Bible, and if we follow them, we greatly increase our probability of happiness and success. If we follow our own ways instead of His, we must face the consequences."

"How true," the angel agreed.

"I'm also saying that God knows what He's doing, and if we use His Holy Word as a *survival manual* like you said, it can only stand to help us get through this often difficult life down here."

"Amen to that."

"Basically, I've learned that living a life full of faithfulness to the Lord is really important, Mick, and it's the only way you can experience a truly enjoyable walk with Him."

"I hear you. So, if someone sins all of their life, but accepts Christ at the end, are they going to Hell?"

"No. Christ knows the intentions of our hearts. We just talked about God knowing our intentions in *1 Chronicles* a little while ago. You can't fool our Creator, because He knows if someone comes to Him in sincerity for forgiveness."

"Spoken like a true prodigy who has his *God glasses* on," Mick said. "The Lord absolutely knows you better than you know yourself. Following the Bible's instructions will not guarantee you'll avoid tribulations. However, it does increase the probability you'll have fewer of them. *Matthew 24:9 says . . . Then you will be handed over to be persecuted and put to death, and you will be hated by all nations because of me.*"

"Don't worry, Mick. I understand that life won't be easy. Anyway, the main guy in the movie paid the price for his sin. And as we discussed earlier, sin is essentially disobedience of God's commands. At the end of the movie, the man took his daughter to a place where he and his older lady friend had gone, way back when they were involved. All-in-all, the man was emotionally opening up to his daughter, and thereby recovering from his sin from many years before. I have to say, it really was a good movie, and it had some good lessons . . . if you're paying attention."

"I'm not sure that your take on the movie is the same as what others think," Mick said, "but I must say . . . I do like your thought process."

"You're probably right. Hey, do you want to get up and start walking again?"

"Sure thing. But let's cover one more topic while we're talking about superficiality, Hollywood, celebrities and the like. Are you familiar with *2 Corinthians 5:1-10?*"

"Is that the one about our earthly 'tents' and how we eagerly await our heavenly bodies?"

"It sure is, but there's more. Verse six says that as long as you're in your earthly bodies, you're away from the Lord. It also says that you'll ultimately answer for your actions during the time you're in your earthly bodies. In other words, even for Christians, works do matter."

"I've often heard that . . . but it can sometimes seem a little confusing. Can you explain that further?"

"Sure thing," Mick said. "Works won't *save* a person. But, if you're a Christian and don't do the works God wants you to, then you won't receive His rewards."

"I see."

"However, the *real* question out of all of a person's options is this—what are you going to do about Christ's offer of salvation? Do you want to spend seventy five or eighty years serving yourself, only to spend eternity regretting it? Or, would you rather surrender to Christ and help serve others, thereby serving God? Doing the latter can guarantee your rewards for eternity. And believe me, that's a *long time!* Don't forget this—good looks ultimately fade in your current bodies . . . ."

Wyatt thought about this for a few moments, then said, "I think a good example of your last statement is Farrah Fawcett."

"Do tell."

"Well, back in the seventies, she was a pin up girl and an international phenomenon. Three and a half decades later, she had a terrible cancer take her life."

"And—?"

"No matter how beautiful any person is during their prime," Wyatt began, "looks most definitely fade, and our current bodies age and wear down. It was definitely a shame about Ms. Fawcett, but it's a shame when anyone dies."

"It's only a shame when anyone dies *without Christ*, dude. Being a celebrity doesn't matter to God. Only knowing His Son matters."

Wyatt pondered that for a moment, then asked, "What're your final thoughts here, Mick? Do you have any additional words of wisdom on this subject?"

"I do. Study everything in society and *RYB, dude.* Do your best to relate to the unsaved, and try to show them the joy in the Gospel of Christ. As a result of this, you'll ultimately stick out like a sore thumb in a superficial society."

"I'm sure you're right about that."

"Also, don't try to attract attention to yourself, just because you follow the Lord. I suggest that you simply follow His example, and study how He lived His life in the Bible. Being Christ-like means emulating Him, but it doesn't include the judging of others—that's God's job, not yours. In fact, if you judge others, you'll essentially be deciding who to tell about Christ based on that judgment, rather than on the basis of God's leading."

"That all sounds reasonable to me."

"Wyatt, we need more people out there injecting the good news about Jesus—and the message of His sacrifice—into the mainstream media. The problem is, a big part of the Hollywood culture seems to center on human pleasures to the exclusion of the Lord. I'm afraid the vast majority of the whole establishment seems to take pride in spreading anti-God rhetoric. We simply need to fight back."

"Is it time to step up our battle with Satan and his nasty influence?"

"It's time to *get it on,* dude! Are you ready?"

"You bet."

And with that, Mick and Wyatt continued their very interesting day.

11
CHURCH OF ONE

The two new friends—angel and human—continued walking north along the Down Under hallway. Between the magic shop; the health store; the bags & backpacks store; and myriad of others, there was much for them to peruse and enjoy. They took their time as they wandered. After a while, they approached the north ramp, back up into the Main Arcade. As they did so, the noise level took on a commensurate increase.

"Okay my good man, I wanna talk to you about a very important concept concerning your overall faith and relationship with God," Mick said. "In observing you for the last several years, I believe that you understand this concept very well. That's actually one of the many reasons why you've been chosen for a mission."

"Okay, so when do I actually *get* my mission—or whatever this thing is that you're talking about?" Wyatt asked.

"I already told you—we'll talk about that later on. Can I finish?"

"My bad. I didn't know that you were back on a roll."

The angel sighed, "I'm sorry, dude—I'm just feeling a little tense."

"Why?"

Mick shook his head, "It seems as though that dirt bag Damon has decided to follow us." Wyatt turned around and spotted Damon, who was about thirty feet back. However, he was well out of earshot. The demon was meandering around the front of several different stores, trying to appear as if he was shopping. "Don't worry," Mick said. "He can't hear us—let's continue."

Mick and Wyatt proceeded up the ramp and back into the Main Arcade. They turned left and stopped at the Mick's Peppourri shop, where the pepper jellies were out of this world. After tasting a couple of samples, they proceeded through the nearby doors and out onto the covered skybridge over Western Avenue. The skybridge led over to an elevator, which connected the market with several floors of a parking garage.

Mick chose the center of the skybridge as the place to continue their chat. He knew it was an excellent vantage point to observe the comings and goings of the market and the parking garage, as well as any potential demonic provocateurs, like Damon. This new vantage point also had excellent views of downtown, the waterfront, and the port of Seattle, across the bay.

It was still crisp outside, and the sun occasionally peeked through the clouds. The temperature was in the high fifties, and both Mick and Wyatt stood with their hands on the chilly metal railing, leaning over as they looked south over Western Avenue, a few floors below. Wyatt's instincts now told him that it was time to dig back into the serious stuff.

"Like I was saying a few minutes ago," Mick said. "I believe you understand this next concept very well. However, I still need to go through it with you in-depth. It will actually be an important part of the message in your mission."

"That's fine with me—shoot."

"Here goes . . . to achieve your highest level of fellowship with Christ here on Earth, and to increase your ability to evangelize and share the Gospel, you have to develop a strong Church of One."

"Church of One?"

"Yep. Now, what this means is that every Christian must solidify the foundation of their own personal *church* with the Father, before they can be an effective disciple of Christ to others. In other words, it's absolutely essential that the first church which you support and nurture is your *own* church with God—just you and Him. Because in the end, it's just between you and Him anyways."

"That's interesting—go on."

"It's just like a soldier in the army," Mick said. "A soldier isn't sent out to fight any battles until they're trained and equipped to do so."

"And—?"

"Basically, if you're not communing with God on a daily basis—in studying the Bible, prayer, and fellowship—you won't be equipped to do God's work . . . or bring Him glory. Is this making any sense so far?"

"Oh, I see. Sure thing—I'm tracking with you," Wyatt said. "You're saying that each person has to start with their own church with the Father before they can be effective in serving others—right?"

"Right. However, the benefits aren't just for the serving of others. It'll also help protect you from the enemy's attacks."

"How so?"

"It's because an effective Church of One is both an offensive and a defensive strategy. If your own personal relationship with God is strong, then you're strong. If it's weak, then you're likely going to be spiritually weak. Believe me when I tell you this—the Lord needs strong soldiers to fight in this battle against the evil ones. To be a strong soldier, you'll absolutely need a solid Church of One."

"For *once,* I think I'm going to agree with you on this," Wyatt chided. "But, I'm going to need a *whole* lot more information to completely understand what you're saying."

"I can handle that. Now listen, there are four basic tenets or elements to the Church of One, and each one is very important. The problem lies with the fact that many Christians don't have all of these fundamentals in their repertoire. Truthfully, when you don't execute on all four elements, you end up leaving yourself spiritually vulnerable."

"So what are these four elements?"

"Okie-dokie, here they are—Direct Line, The Word, Inside the Walls, and Outside the Fortress. That's it—cha-ching! Give this man a latte."

Wyatt grinned, "I'm sure glad to see you relaxing a little, Mick."

"Listen up, dude. There are some very good reasons why I'm emphasizing these things with you today. You'll come to understand this later on at your place, but not before you buy me dinner at Ivar's on the Waterfront."

Surprised, Wyatt grumbled, "Oh no—*are you talking about dinner already?*"

"Of course. After a little while, we'll head down the hill climb so you can treat me to some of that awesome Ivar's clam chowder . . . if that's okay with you."

Wyatt shrugged, "What's up with you and all of this comfort food, Mick?"

"It's but a small price to pay, bud-dro."

"Fine," Wyatt relented. "I'll order some french fries and feed the sea gulls . . . can we get back to the four elements now?"

"Sure thing. At first, the term *Church of One* may sound a little self-centered, but it really isn't. The basic concept is that in order for you to have a healthy and productive *witness* for the Lord, you must first have a healthy and productive *relationship* with Him. To achieve that, you need to strengthen the four elements, so the foundation of your personal relationship with Jesus is strong and impermeable."

"Go on."

"Well dude, think of it like this. You know how when you get on an airplane—?"

"I thought you angels flew around through the air and didn't need airplanes."

"Oh c'mon—don't be such a *knucklehead*. Besides, that's a different kind of angel."

"Oh."

"Anyways, when I'm down here on Earth, I generally have to move around like the locals do. The only other option is to go back through the flaming sword and into Heaven once again . . . actually, it's kinda cool the way that I can instantly disappear into the invisible dimension."

"I was just joking, Mick."

"I wasn't. By the way, if we ever end up taking a flight together, I like to fly first class. The seats are bigger and the food is better."

"Geez, I'll have to write that down somewhere," Wyatt joked.

"Anyways, are you familiar with that silly safety demonstration which the air carriers are required by law to give you?"

"What, the *how-to-use the seatbelt* demo?"

"That's the one. Also, there's that hokey air mask dropping if they lose cabin pressure. Do you have a good mental picture of that?"

"Unfortunately, yes."

"Well then, tell me this . . . what exactly do they teach you when they talk about the air mask dropping?"

"Let's see," Wyatt said. "I've only seen it about a gazillion times over the years . . . oh yeah—they tell you to put on your own mask before you attempt to help others."

"Bingo, dude. Why do you think they tell you that?"

"To avoid lawsuits?"

Mick grinned and nodded, "Yeah, and what else?"

"Well, I suppose it's because you can't effectively help others if you're unable to breathe yourself . . . ." Wyatt trailed off. It suddenly hit him what Mick was driving at.

"*Exactly!* You can't help others if you can't breathe yourself. *That,* my friend, is why you have to develop your own Church of One. This absolutely must happen—*before* you can begin to help others towards Jesus."

Wyatt was impressed with Mick's analogy. "I see what you're saying, Mick. If your own, personal church is weak, then how can you be expected to evangelize and help others by spreading the Gospel . . . is that it?"

"It sure is. Hey . . . just in case you're wondering . . . later on, I think I'll have a mocha instead of a latte . . . just to let you know."

Wyatt sighed, "You sure are single-minded of purpose."

"I suppose I am," the angel admitted.

"Fine—we'll go get your mocha after we make our way out of here. Satisfied now?"

"I am. Anyways, it seems that you understand the analogy of the air mask. You simply can't be a fully effective disciple of Christ if you can't breathe on your own . . . or in this case, if you don't have a good relationship with the Lord."

"I gotcha. So, are you going to explain to me the different elements that make up the Church of One—or am I gonna have to beg you?"

Mick chuckled, "No, you won't have to beg. Let's start with the first one, Direct Line. What this one is all about is your prayer life. Now, I'm not talking about doing all of that chanting and repetition stuff. I'm talking about *real* prayer, here. You know the kind—where you take your thoughts, problems, concerns, worries, joy, jubilation . . . ." Mick trailed off for a moment. "Basically, God wants for you to take the good, the bad, and the ugly to the Cross in prayer. He wants for you to personally involve Him in every aspect of your life, because *He is* involved in every aspect of your life. If you have something that you're worried about, *take it to Him.* If you have something good happening in your life that makes you happy, *take it to Him.* Let's face it—God is already there, and He wants you to tell Him what's in your heart and on your mind."

"That makes sense to me."

"And one more thing," Mick said. "It's absolutely okay to discuss your life's issues with family and friends, because that's one of the reasons why He put those people in your life. However, please don't forget to include your heavenly Father in your everyday life."

"All of that rings true with me, Mick. I pray to the Lord wherever I am, and whenever I think of something I want to tell Him about. He's my father and my friend."

"Good deal. Oh, and one of my *extra secret* angel reconnaissance reports advised me that your favorite place to pray to the Lord is when you're in the shower."

"Are you for real about the reports? That sounds ridiculous."

"It's certainly *not* ridiculous. Do you think we don't keep an eye on people's progress down here?"

Wyatt's thoughts quickly retreated. "I suppose y'all do . . . but it'll creep me out if I think about it too much. Anyway, you're right about my praying in the shower. I keep a line of communication open with the Lord at all times, and I pray to Him whenever something comes to mind. Actually, the shower is a great place to talk to the Father, as well as driving in the car, sitting on the couch, or *walking through the market or a mall.*"

"In other words, you keep open a *direct line* with Him?"

"I suppose I do," Wyatt agreed.

"My friend, I can't emphasize strongly enough how important it is to communicate with the Father. Since God knows everything anyways, you might as well embrace His involvement in your lives. *Philippians 4:6* says . . . *Do not be anxious about anything, but in everything, by prayer and petition, with thanksgiving, present your requests to God* . . . Basically, I'll give you an 'A-minus' in this category for yourself, which is pretty darned good."

"Okay then, item number one is the Direct Line of prayer with God. I'd give myself an 'A-plus', but we'll let age over beauty decide this. 'A-minus' it is. So what's next?"

"The next item is—The Word."

"Let me guess, Mick. *The Word* is connected with *RYB*, right?"

"You got it dude—that's exactly right. Reading the Word of God with the right frame of mind and an open heart is absolutely critical in the building of each Christian's personal Church of One. In fact, you simply can't move forward in your Christian walk if you don't ever read the Bible. However, there are several different ways to approach this critical function."

"There sure are, Mick. I like to—"

"I'm going to give you a regular 'A' on this one," Mick interrupted. "We've been keenly watching how you subscribe to daily and periodic emails from several sources, then use Biblegateway.com to research the

Scriptures based on what you receive. Nice work! Unfortunately, many Christians attend church on Sunday, then don't crack open their Bibles—online or otherwise—the rest of the week."

"Thanks. As I see it, the trick to success with Bible study is that you not only need to find the right translation, but also the right time to read and study God's Holy Word. Honestly, I used to think the Bible was an old book, written thousands of years ago by ancient people, and—"

"And has no bearing on today's society? Yep, that's one of the more impressive lies pulled off by the enemy. The evil ones know the Word of God is both empowering and life changing, so they desperately try to keep people away from it. Speaking of that, it's time to pull out the Bible again, and look up *2 Timothy 3:16*."

Once again, Wyatt opened his Bible and quickly located the passage. "Okay Mick, here we go . . . *All Scripture is God-breathed and is useful for teaching, rebuking, correcting and training in righteousness.*"

"There ya go—that's like music to my ears. Did you pay attention to the part about Scripture being *God-breathed?* There's not too much confusion about that part, is there?"

"No, I guess there's not. Do you know something else, Mick? I remember an interesting tidbit from way back in my early career in the trucking business which applies to the Bible."

"Do tell."

"Well, all prices for freight had to be published in tariffs that were filed with a now defunct government agency. These tariffs were the prevailing authority on what was charged, and the filing of these tariffs was done by pricing managers. Basically, these guys were the resident experts on tariffs and their rules. Anyway, when I had the occasional need to ask one of the pricing managers a question about the price on a load of freight, they would inevitably ask me, *what does it say in the tariff?* Admittedly, it used to infuriate me, because I was being lazy and I wanted the quick answer. Well, maybe those guys had the right idea, but as it relates to Bible study also."

"That's interesting—please continue," Mick said.

"Well, all too often, people want answers to complex faith based questions, but they aren't willing to actually do any biblical research—or as you say, *RYB dude.* Nowadays, there's absolutely no excuse why either Christians or spiritual seekers can't find out the readily attainable answers to their questions . . . the amount of quality Christian literature is huge, and it continues to grow."

"El Dude-O, I have to agree with you one hundred percent on this. The whole face of Christianity has been evolving, and the Christian entertainment world is emerging as a force to be reckoned with. But with all of that said, the Word of God really doesn't make any sense unless you've taken some steps towards knowing the Lord."

"Now that you mention it, I suppose I didn't really start to understand the Bible until I got saved and baptized. It was at that point, I began my earnest journey towards the Lord, and He's been teaching me ever since. It seems the closer I move towards Him, the more the Holy Spirit reveals Himself to me."

"My friend, the Holy Spirit can't even *begin* to do His work in you, until you surrender to Christ and get baptized in the Holy Spirit. Those are some pretty important fundamentals in growing with the Lord."

"No doubt. When Vanessa and I got baptized several years ago, it was very emotional for both of us."

"Well I don't mean to freak you out here dude, but she told me over dinner the other night about how much she'll always remember the Sunday the both of you got baptized."

"Freak me out—*are you kidding me?* Listen, this whole chat with you today is still a little strange for me . . . and hearing you say over-and-over again that you saw Vanessa last week . . . and actually spoke with her over dinner in Heaven . . . well, that's *really* weird!"

"Oh; why is that?"

Wyatt shrugged, "Well, I suppose I'm still getting accustomed to this whole, *visit from an angel,* thing."

"Whoa dude—take it easy and RYB. The Lord promised you an eternal body in several passages of Scripture; many of which we've already discussed here today. What did you think happened in Heaven? Do you think it's not a *real* place up there?"

"I know it is—"

"Listen, hearing all of this from me today is a gift. I'm actually trying to ease your heart and mind so that you can carry out the mission the Lord has in mind for you. Remember, I'm only the messenger, here. Everything we're talking about comes from the Lord."

Wyatt was quiet for a few moments before asking, "Can I speak with Vanessa?"

"Absolutely, positively, *not.* I'd probably get banished if I tried something like that."

"Why?"

"Because each person has their own individual journey with the Lord, and everyone must make their own decisions. Now then, what I'm about to tell you is one of those *super critical* items for you to remember, so please listen up."

"This sounds serious."

"It is . . . God made all of you in His image, and each one of you since the banishment of Adam and Eve has had the ability to make your own decision regarding Him. During your lifetime on Earth, no one on their own—*and I mean no one*—will ever be able to definitively prove or disprove God's existence and sovereignty."

"Why do you think that is?"

"It's because this life of yours is a walk of *faith,* which from the world's perspective, is far from easy. Since *Hebrews 12:2* says that Jesus is the author and perfecter of your faith, it's clearly *impossible* to have enough faith on your own. In fact, it's understandably hard for people to keep their faith in a God who you can't see, but who you can certainly feel. Do you understand so far?"

"I do."

"Do you also remember when we earlier spoke about *Romans 1:20,* regarding God's invisible qualities?"

"I sure do."

"Well, what it's saying is that the evidence of God's mighty hand is behind everything you see in this world—it's all there. Again, if you can't see the Lord, then you're just not looking."

"So, you admit that a human's walk of faith isn't easy, huh?"

"Like I just said, it's not easy—*from the world's perspective.* That should lead you to seek God out. Then, when you open your heart to Jesus, it actually *is* easy."

"Hmmm," Wyatt mumbled.

"Listen to me now . . . you believe in God. However, it's not because you've proven God's existence; it's because the Lord has given you the faith to believe in Him."

"That's interesting," Wyatt said, and thought about it for a moment. "Mick, how do you explain your appearance to me today? Isn't that some kind of *proof* or something?"

"Not really. You already believed in God; I've merely convinced you that I was sent by Him. Even though you say I just freaked you out about Vanessa, I'm glad you fully embrace the significance of what's happening today."

"So what'll happen if I blow all this off later on?"

"Don't be ridiculous. If the time wasn't right for your mission, God wouldn't have bothered to send me to see you."

"If the time wasn't right for *what* mission?" Wyatt asked, frustrated. Mick gave him an incredulous look with a raised eyebrow. "Okay, *after* dinner," Wyatt said. "Let's move on."

Mick took a moment to look in all directions to ensure that Damon wasn't eavesdropping. Wyatt sensed what was going on and asked, "Hey Mick, can demons see or hear us from the invisible dimension right now?"

"Good question, my boy—no, the evil ones can't hear us right now. But, many up *there* can." Mick nodded towards Heaven.

"So what's blocking the demons from hearing us?"

"It's because only God is omnipresent, and we're under His mighty protection right now. Damon—or any other demon for that matter— would have to physically spy on us to hear what we're saying. Normally, they're able to use the invisible dimension to carry out their surveillance and their attacks. But for today, I suppose we can say that you're a privileged character. So don't worry. I'm good at this and I've got your back—so does the Lord."

Wyatt nodded, "Okay, so what's the next item up for bids in the Church of One?"

"Cute, dude. But don't be picking on one of my favorite all-time shows?"

"You actually like, *The Price is Right?*"

"You betcha—I'm *awesome* at that game. I really should try to get on that show one day—"

"Moving along," Wyatt interrupted. "I think *Inside the Walls* is next."

"It is," Mick agreed.

"So, are we talking about church attendance, here?"

"We are. Okay, I'm gonna have to give you a grade of 'C' in this area, dude. Inside the Walls is all about your home church."

"You're giving me a 'C'? C'mon Mick, I'm not that bad."

"I didn't say that you were *bad,* you're only just average."

"But—"

"Let me finish! Although church attendance and fellowship is a critical part of your Church of One, the truth is, too many Christians rely much too heavily on it. I understand that you, personally, don't have this problem,

and that's cool. The Lord designs each of you in different ways and for different purposes. It's apparent to me that you're more of a road warrior in your fellowship efforts."

"I am. Don't get me wrong, Mick. I like my church and the fellowship within the four walls of it, but it's not the only part of my walk with God."

"Understood. What you've actually improved on the most, is with your giving to the church . . . especially since the financial blessings you enjoyed before you moved out here."

Wyatt nodded, "Mick, I've always felt that giving to the church is a personal issue between each person and God; I can't help but to believe that He only wants for us to give joyfully."

"You're correct—that's actually in *2 Corinthians 9:6-7*. Anyways, the reason why people generally don't give abundantly to their church is because they're focused more on themselves, than on God. Many others simply don't trust churches."

"Can you blame people for not fully trusting churches? There's been an awful lot of abuse—"

"Yeah, and for every example of abuse, there've been substantially *more* cases of good things being done with the money which people do give to their church."

Wyatt shrugged, "Well, perhaps you're right. It took me awhile to get there, but now I write my check to the church before all others each month. I do wish that it hadn't taken me so long to get to that point, though."

"Right. But, you're also older and more mature as a Christian," Mick said. "It's only natural that the older you get, the more interested you become in kingdom affairs and Heaven."

"Maybe you're right. Anyway, even as my relationship with God has grown, going to church has only been one part of my walk of faith."

"Amen," Mick said.

"Hey Mick, do you think some people use church attendance as their only sustenance of faith?"

"Actually I do—that's why I mentioned it a minute ago."

"Well, I believe you're right. I once had a pastor back in Georgia tell me that he felt like the true work of God is done in the *community*, not inside the four walls of the church."

"That's true. However, let's not forget that the people who adore their church, usually get a sense of fellowship that's very important to them. Remember, church is still a good thing, even if you don't do anything outside of it for the Lord. All that means is you're not clicking on all four cylinders available to you . . . so to speak."

Wyatt nodded, "I like that old expression that says, *you're no more a Christian because you're sitting in a church, than you're a car because you're standing in the garage.*"

"True dat," Mick said, much to Wyatt's chagrin. "Church isn't everything, but it's definitely important."

They continued to stand on the skybridge, but by this time Mick had turned his back to the railing and was leaning up against it. He curiously turned his gaze to the right and concentrated on the entrance to the market. Wyatt noticed that Mick was staring at the doorway in total silence, so he turned around to see what had his attention. Suddenly, the doors opened, and they found themselves staring at the imposing specter of Damon. However, this time, unlike before, the demon was angrily glaring at them.

Wyatt was surprised, because instead of looking away and trying to be stealthy like before, Damon seemed much more direct in his approach. Nothing was said between Mick and Wyatt as the demon walked towards the elevator on their left. Just as he came up aside them, Damon said, *"You need to know – there's another side to the story!"* It gave Wyatt chills, because Damon was looking directly into his eyes when he said it. The demon then sauntered over to the elevator, which had just opened. Four people began to pile out of it as the door clanked open. Damon then entered the elevator and disappeared without looking back.

The four new market patrons chatted as they passed by Mick and Wyatt, into the market. After a few moments of silence, Mick said, "Listen to me, dude. Don't ever fear that guy or any of his kind. Although they're quite dangerous, you have the Creator of the universe behind you, so you're covered."

"Okay Mick, *to Hell with him*—literally. Let's get back on track . . . I think we were finishing up about the Inside the Walls part of our discussion."

"Right you are . . . by the way, I like you're fighting attitude. Anyways, as it relates to churches; they're generally either inwardly or outwardly focused. Inwardly focused churches generally spend their time serving the church members—kind of like a private club. Conversely, outwardly focused churches tend to spend their time serving the community. Now then, the most important attribute to consider before attending any church—inwardly focused or outwardly focused—is simply the knowing and praising of God."

"That makes sense."

"After that, each person must endeavor to find a place of worship which best suits their needs, and where they're the most comfortable. How much time each congregation spends on their own church, or community affairs and missions, is clearly up to pastor and its members. Essentially, church isn't the only thing there is to knowing the Lord, but it's definitely important and shouldn't be ignored."

"So what're you saying here?"

"I'm saying that praising God is of paramount importance. Period. And remember, every person is wired differently. I suggest that people concentrate on going to church, praising God with fellow Christians, praying, doing a daily RYB, and financially supporting your home church and Christian charities. Those are the important things."

"Okay, that seems pretty straightforward. So what's left?"

"Outside the Fortress is last, but certainly not least."

"Does this have to do with being an outwardly focused church?"

"Wrongamundo, dude. Outside the Fortress has to do with the fellowship of all churches, because the entirety of all churches makes up the one body of Christ. Denominations don't matter. Knowing Christ does . . . well, that's it. Are you about ready to head to Tully's?"

"Whoa there—slow down Mick. I'm going to need a little more meat on that bone," Wyatt demanded.

"I'm just kidding, dude. Let's turn to *Romans 12:4-5,* and by *let's,* I mean *you* . . . .

"Yes, Sarge," Wyatt said, flipping to the passage . . ."*Just as each of us has one body with many members, and these members do not all have the same function, so in Christ we who are many form one body, and each member belongs to all the others* . . ." He kept reading silently for a few moments. "Mick, the passages that follow confirm that God makes all of us with different gifts to use for His purposes."

Mick locked both of his hands behind his head and leaned back with a big smirk on his face. "Who's your daddy?"

Wyatt shook his head in disbelief at his unorthodox messenger, "Only you would say something like that, Mick."

The angel shrugged, "Anyways, Outside the Fortress is about the fellowship of all Christians, not just the folks who you attend church with on Sunday. Wyatt, this is where I'll give you a top-of-the-line 'A plus.' It's clearly your strongest category of the four. So, what do you think about that?"

"That'll work for me . . . anyway, my old traveling job lent itself to this type of fellowship. I used to spend ninety or so nights a year on the road, and I met lots of people along the way. Actually, I'd have to say, I've enjoyed fellowship with people from every corner of this country."

"True enough, but you did a good job of maximizing your opportunities. You always had your *faith radar* on when you met strangers, and you were always ready to talk with someone about their belief in God . . . that is, if they were open to it."

"So that's a good thing, huh?"

"Of course. You didn't hide from your faith, and neither did you push it on anyone, either. That's absolutely the way that it should be done. Essentially, you have to wait for your opportunities to share the Gospel. If you go too far, you inevitably turn people off, because they'll think that you're a religious zealot. But if you don't do it at all, then you're either brain dead, or you just don't care about others. I'm actually quite proud of what you've done in this area."

"Well, since I'm not traveling very much on business anymore, it's hard to do that as much as I used to. Back then, my opportunities were plentiful. But now, that's all changed . . . ."

"It's changed because *the* LORD wanted it changed. You're now doing a little freelance magazine writing, because *the* LORD wanted it to happen. You see, Jesus has been molding you for His purpose all along, not your own. Are you with me on this?"

"Yeah, I suppose I am," Wyatt agreed. "Can I assume we'll talk more in-depth about the Lord's purpose for me later on at my place after dinner?"

"If you mean dinner at Ivar's, then yes. Now seriously, if I were to counsel a typical Christian about how they can improve on their game . . . kind of like if I was a head coach on the sideline, calling in plays . . . ."

"This ought to be good," Wyatt mused.

Ignoring him, Mick continued, "Well, since it's often the weakest area for many people, as a coach, I would work the hardest on this last element—Outside the Fortress."

"What do you mean by that?"

"Basically, neglecting this area can interfere with optimizing someone's discipleship performance. Sometimes it almost seems as if some Christians feel like they're cheating on their home church if they attend a church service—or even enjoy fellowship—with one of their friends or family members, who attend another church. Of course, *that's ridiculous.* The passage you just read clearly says that all of you are indeed, one body of Christ."

"Geez Mick, thanks for noticing my efforts towards outreach. For a long time now, it's been my goal to help guide God's children towards Him, and to otherwise help the people who He's put in my path. You know, if people would only stop worrying about appearing religious and just open their hearts and minds, they just might find something special in a relationship with the Lord."

"Well-said, my friend."

"However, having said that, I also feel like we-Christians are now paying the price for the overzealous attitudes of some churches in the past. You know, even when Christ talked with the rich young ruler in *Luke 18:18-27,* He didn't force the man to surrender."

"Good point—maybe you're not such a bonehead after all," Mick chortled.

"Very funny."

"Anyways, I'm afraid you're correct," Mick said. "Based on where the whole face of faith is right now, I think that all Christians uniting and serving one basic purpose is more important than anything else. Of course, that purpose is to fight against the dark forces, and to share the Gospel of Christ. It's actually not very complicated, and it doesn't require a PhD to understand."

"I agree."

"So, why don't you bottom-line this whole thing for me," Mick said.

"Okay. So in review, executing on all four elements of the Church of One, which are a direct line of prayer with God, studying the Bible—His Holy Word, attending and fellowship in a local church, and lots of fellowship with all other Christians . . . that's what the Church of One is all about, right?"

"Spoken like a true prodigy, Wyatt. Are you ready to bounce outta here?"

"Sure thing. Hey—do you think we'll see Damon again?"

"Probably so. But now that I know what he's up to, I won't let him distract us."

"So tell me; how many demons have you battled with in the past?"

"Hundreds . . . thousands . . . maybe all of them at one time or another. Well, now that I'm thinking about my history, it seems that in the past several centuries, I mostly go up against Damon."

"That's odd."

"Perhaps you're right. Anyways, I suppose you could say that Damon and I are the Yankees and Red Sox of the angel-demon war."

Wyatt chuckled, "You're real big on analogies, aren't you?"

"Yep-a-roo—I sure am. I'm also real big on moving towards my next coffee. What do you say?"

With a big grin Wyatt declared, "Let's bounce, homey."

12

TWO MOTHERS

Weaving their way through the entry doors and into the market, a wave of sound from the bustling commerce came instantly rushing towards Mick and Wyatt. Once again, they passed the pepper jelly store on their left, and not far on their right, was the ramp to the Down Under shops where they had been just a little while before.

Angel and human took their time as they meandered both left and right upon entering the main hallway. Ultimately, they walked north through the market, which ran parallel to Pike Place. The whole area continued to be in full swing, and it was now impossible to move through the Main Arcade without dodging the many tourists and Seattleites. The afternoon weather was still cool, and the open doorways to the outside showed that clouds and overcast skies had eclipsed the partial sunshine.

The cornucopia of farm fresh produce, colorful flowers, jellies, and other interesting products, had the two of them making several stops as their stroll continued at a relaxed pace. Mick wanted to stop at the Chukar Cherries shop for a few samples, and in no time, he had the serving ladies practically eating out of his hand. *You just can't help but to be drawn to Mick,* Wyatt thought. *He has a humble charisma that's clearly infectious.*

"Hey dude, have you ever tried their chocolate covered cherries?" the angel asked.

"I've tried them before, Mick. They're very good."

"What do you mean by, *very good?* They're *awesome!*"

"Okay Mick, they're awesome."

"Do you think we should take some home to your place tonight?" Mick asked. "I'm sure that Miss Charlene might like some."

"Sure thing."

"Cool—"

"*Wait a minute!*" Wyatt interrupted. "I've only mentioned Miss Charlene in passing. How could you possibly know anything about her? And while you're at it, how do you have any idea that she might like chocolate covered cherries?"

"Oops," Mick replied sheepishly.

"What do you mean by, 'oops'?"

Mick shrugged, "Well, how can I say this?"

"How can you say *what???*"

"Now, don't be going all conspiracy-theory on me."

"*Conspiracy theory?* What on Earth are you talking about? Do you know Miss Charlene?"

"Well, yes . . . I suppose you could say that we've met."

"When?"

"The most recent time was last night," Mick said, and Wyatt raised an eyebrow. "We had a latte at the Starbucks on Alaskan Way; you know, the one south of your place."

Wyatt shook his head in disbelief. "So, I take it that wasn't the first time that y'all met, huh?"

Mick nodded, "That's correct. Listen, we'll get into all of that back at your place later. For right now, we need to move on to—"

"*Mick!?!*"

"What, dude?"

"*Never mind.*" Wyatt sighed, shaking his head.

"Listen, this is nothing to get sore over. Miss Charlene is simply a part of your mission's plan. To be even more honest, she's been involved for quite some time now."

"You've got some explaining to do, my friend. However, I know that I'll have to wait until later for that. I guess that I'm already used to that with you . . . and I'm not sore at you . . . I'm just surprised."

"Then you'll definitely dig what's in store after dinner," Mick said, grinning.

"Whatever," Wyatt said, still frustrated. "So what's next?"

"Headlining our next chat is a talk about two mothers."

"Two mothers? Well I suppose you're probably going to talk about my mother Abigail. She passed away last year during the dark times."

"Yeah, Miss Abbie . . . nice lady."

Although Mick was well aware of what transpired, Wyatt began a recap of events, "I'm afraid that mom died of lung cancer last year. Vanessa and I took care of her for a while, but we didn't have to do it for very long. Unfortunately, she died within a few months of being diagnosed."

"Wyatt, we were all proud of you for ministering-to, and reading Scripture to her during that whole ordeal."

"Thanks Mick, but it sure was hard on all of us—me, Vanessa, and Danny. Death is a really sad thing to deal with, but it hits you especially hard when it happens in your own home."

"Listen, I haven't been given permission to comment too much on Miss Abbie, today. However, you know all-to-well that you can use your knowledge of the Bible to determine which direction she went when she passed."

Wyatt sighed as he remembered the horror of watching his mother die. "She never abandoned her faith during the entire downfall, even when the cancer had gotten into her brain towards the end. She went crazy because of how fast the cancer spread, and she had to spend her last week at a hospice down in Athens."

"I understand my friend," Mick said gently. "But let's stay on track with the point I was trying to make. What was the most important part of that whole ordeal when Abbie was dying?"

"I suppose it was the fact that she had already accepted Christ, and she loved the Lord until the very end."

"You got it! So what does that mean now?"

"That she no longer has any physical maladies, and at this very moment, she's in God's holy presence—all without any pain or suffering."

"Good. That's exactly right."

"Yeah, but I miss her so much, Mick."

"Of course you miss her—what kind of son would you be if you didn't?"

"I hear you. Anyway, it was really hard in the end, because Vanessa and I had to care for mom as we watched her body deteriorate. Dad and mom actually split up a long time ago, so except for me and Vanessa, mom didn't really have anyone else to help her through that agonizing ordeal."

"Have you ever considered the possibility that perhaps the Lord allowed it to happen that way for some divine reason?"

"What do you mean?"

"Well, perhaps as her frail body gave out, God wanted for you and Vanessa to be the ones to escort her to Heaven's gate."

"Geez, I've never thought of it like that before."

"Listen, all things work together for the Lord's purposes, my friend. While I understand that you really miss your mom, isn't it more important that she's now in total happiness?"

Wyatt thought for a few moments before responding, "Well, I suppose if I were the Lord, I'd rather have her in Heaven with me, then down here in this mess."

Mick bristled, suddenly looking both pleased and surprised, "Wow—I can't begin to tell you how profound that statement was!"

"What are you talking about?"

"What I mean is this—many people, even the best Christians, have a hard time putting God's interests and desires before their own."

"If you say so."

"No dude, listen to me! You're absolutely right in what you just said. Ask yourself this—what's the more important issue, that both God and Miss Abbie are happy, or that *you* are happy for the few times a year that you got to see her?"

Wyatt was quiet for a few moments, "The former, I suppose."

"Okay then. If you truly have faith in the Lord and His promises, then you logically have to rejoice in the homecoming for all Christians." During their discussion, Mick and Wyatt continued walking north through the Main Arcade until they reached the North Arcade. They continued to walk slowly as Mick played the part of concert maestro. The angel had wisely chosen or directed most of the various conversation venues throughout the day, all in an effort to keep their discussions balanced and effective.

"I know, Mick," Wyatt said. "But it's really hard to watch your own mother die."

"Believe me—I realize that. But, let me ask you this . . . isn't it also hard to watch your only Son die on a cross due to the evil inherent in the hearts of a fallen mankind?"

Wyatt sighed loudly, but was quiet for a few moments. Like a good salesman, Mick said nothing, as well. "Mick, I can't argue with that. I know our Father made a huge sacrifice by sending His only Son to die for our sins . . . never mind."

"Don't 'never mind' me. I brought this up for a reason. Miss Abbie's passing last year was a transaction between her and the Father. If she truly surrendered to Jesus Christ as her Savior before she died—which she most certainly did—then you have nothing to worry about. *Your job* is to make sure that you direct as many rear-ends towards Heaven as you can, before you get to see her again—this time for eternity. After that, we can all have an awesome time together."

"Fine, Mick. I really do understand. But the loss of both my mother and my wife in the span of a couple of months was a little bit overwhelming, dontcha think?"

"Yes, dude. I can only imagine how tough that was for you, my friend. Although I'm different from you—and I can't directly relate to your kind of pain—I've seen some horrible atrocities for many, many years. I'm afraid that mankind living under the curse is no day at the park for any of us in God's creation."

Wyatt was quiet for a few moments, lapsing into deep thought. Mick followed suit and remained quiet, as well. After a minute or so of this, Wyatt mentally swam up from the depths of deep reflection and declared, "You know something, Mick? In thinking about the Church of One and mom, it seems to me that she probably wasn't clicking on all four cylinders."

"I'm all ears, dude."

"Well, in the end, we both know that Mom never turned her back on her Savior. However, when I look at the other parts of her faith, I see that she didn't follow the RYB practice very often; I don't believe that she attended church, except when she visited us from Jacksonville; and she only talked about the Lord if someone else brought Him up. While I'm not trying to be critical of her faith, I do think she would've enjoyed her walk with the Lord much more intensely if she had executed on some of the other fundamentals of the Church of One."

"Perhaps . . . but there may be some things about her faith that you simply aren't aware of right now."

"Maybe you're right," Wyatt agreed.

"Anyways, I understand that she did pray all of the time. Let's not underestimate the importance of prayer."

"She certainly did. That was definitely a strong area for her. But you know, as important as it is to constantly pray, if you don't read your Bible, you can easily fall into some of the secular traps that Satan lays for people."

"Can you give me an example of that?" Mick asked.

"Sure. I often hear people say that the Bible is *ancient, outdated, and not relevant for today's society.* It seems to me that Satan and his minions are trying to convince people that the Bible no long applies to our modern society. You know, I can't help but to see Satan's evil influence when I hear that kind of baloney . . . am I off base here?"

"Actually, no. We briefly touched on that earlier today, and you're absolutely right . . . I also think you should check out those awesome looking jars of honey over there." Mick pointed to a table where a vendor was selling raw honey and other honey products. Mick's radical subject changing continued, and Wyatt thought the angel had to be doing this for a reason. *This must be some kind of teaching technique or something,* he thought. He continued to ponder this interesting stranger, who was quickly becoming a good friend.

"And I suppose you figured out that I like to put honey in my coffee, huh?" Wyatt asked.

"Whatever gave you that idea?" Mick joked.

"Whatever . . . let's go check it out." They walked over to the vendor and asked a few questions. The ladies were very accommodating, and they knew their products well. Wyatt bought a jar of honey and a jar of bee pollen, then placed them into his burgeoning backpack. After that, Mick and Wyatt began their meandering once again.

By this time, they arrived at the horseshoe shaped area in the North Arcade, which had several day-vendor tables available. They turned left, moving towards the window area, which faced the waterfront and sported a good view of Western Avenue. There were a few consecutive unused tables that day, so Mick and Wyatt were able to get off the beaten path to continue their discussion in a relatively quiet spot.

Wyatt took off his backpack and laid it on one of the unused stools sitting nearby, then took a seat himself. Mick grabbed another stool and put it on the vendor's side of the table. The stools were a little beaten up, but they still worked pretty well. Although they were alone for the time being, they weren't far away from the fray.

"Okay then," Mick said. "To finish up about your mom, she lived her life just like all people do—she was born, lived, died, and either went to Heaven or Hell. That's the cycle for you folks, but that's not all there is to it. If you follow the Bible's teachings, you know that man was created in God's image, and that humans are God's crowning achievement. So, if nothing were to happen to someone at death, then logically, the Lord wouldn't be an all-powerful God."

"Why is that?"

"*Think about it.* It's because something in creation that God-Himself described as *very good* would be lost forever. If the Lord were to lose something like that, He would cease being all-powerful."

"That's a reasonable statement."

"Listen to me, now. You need to always remember this, because it's very important. God said at the end of *Genesis 1* that His creation was *very good.* So, that makes it impossible for Him to be both all-powerful, *and* to have his now fallen creation lost forever. Do you see what I mean?"

"I'm tracking with you," Wyatt said.

"Basically, whether anyone likes it or not, something happens to *everyone* at death. You either spend eternity with the Lord, or apart from Him. Period. End of story. The Bible actually indicates that all humans are born heading towards Hell because of your inherited sin-nature from Adam. Don't forget this—Hell essentially is eternal separation from God, which is obviously a very bad thing. After Christ's sacrifice on the Cross at Calvary, Jesus is now your life preserver. Do you have any further thoughts on that?"

"What, am I back in school now?"

"Yep, this is Eternal Fate 101."

Wyatt shook his head. "Okay, I think that yes—people must switch their direction away from Hell during their lifetime. Surrendering to Christ is a take-it or leave-it scenario."

"Good deal. Anyways, getting back to Miss Abbie, did your Mom *take it,* as you say?"

"Yes, she sure did."

"Good. Let's move along. You'll see her again."

Wyatt smiled, "Okay Mick, I understand what you're saying. By the way, you said a little while ago that she was a nice lady. Have you met her as well?"

"DP dude. I'm only authorized to speak about Vanessa."

"Why?"

"Later . . . ."

"Okay, fine." Wyatt was feeling a little antsy at this point and often liked to fidget with things. He pulled out his jar of honey, and began to roll it around in his hand, looking at the gooey liquid moving in circles around the jar. He then asked, "What's next, chief?"

Mick nodded, "Okay then, the second mother I want to talk about is the so-called *Mother Nature.*"

"This sounds interesting."

"As per our tradition, I'll start you out with the answer. Then, I'll explain why."

"How college professor of you."

"Listen up smarty, cause here it comes—*Mother Nature* isn't actually a *mother* at all. The correct expression should actually be *Father Nature,* because all of creation—and everything in it—comes from our heavenly Father."

Wyatt shrugged, "That's it?"

"Whaddaya mean *that's it?* Yeah, that's it."

"C'mon professor, give me some more info."

"Okay partner, it's like this. Satan and company not only know that God created everything, but they also know that He's omnipresent, and His mighty hand can be seen in all things. Now then, the whole Mother Nature thing was planted into several ancient pagan cultures many years ago by the evil ones. Why? Because from a demon's perspective, there's no better way to minimize their Creator's awesome handiwork, than to divert people's attention away from God's mighty hand behind everything that you see."

"This sounds like a little bit of a stretch so far. Can you give me some more info to consider?"

"Fine. Let's first look at the complexity of life issue. You've read several books that speak of the Intelligent Design movement, right?"

"I have. You know, I'm always surprised by the opponents of Intelligent Design, because they're so absolutely adamant, passionate, and even *angry* about the correctness of their pro-evolution positions. And to be perfectly honest, I find their overzealous passion to be quite disconcerting."

"Evolution of various species isn't the problem here, Wyatt. There's no argument that things absolutely do evolve. However, they only evolve within their own *kind.* Nothing in all of creation can evolve into another kind of life, so the common descent of all living things from an undirected single cell is the theory that's causing the problem. That position is clearly unbiblical, and it contradicts the Word of God in the book of Genesis."

"My impression from studying the Intelligent Design movement is that they're not actually endorsing any particular religion. Instead, they believe modern science has disproven Darwin's archaic theories."

"That's true," Mick agreed. "However, the chasm between scientists *of-faith* and scientists *against-faith* is growing at an alarming rate."

"It seems to me that the God-hating scientists seem to be out in force. I also believe they control of the majority of the science departments at colleges and universities. Unfortunately, they get sucked into the allure of mankind's intelligence, and all-to-often, they end up trying to do everything they can to disprove God's existence. Their impassioned efforts always make me wonder what their motives really are."

Mick nodded, "Indeed. Darwin's theory of evolution has actually become a huge rallying cry for unbelievers. Many of them act as if it's of paramount importance to try to prove their point, and the result of that would be to take people's faith away from them. The curious thing about the whole issue, is that if they were correct, your lives really have no meaning at all. Think about it—if there was no God, your life's only meaning would be to get what you can get before dying. After that, you would cease to exist."

"I hear you. Like I said, I just can't figure out why they're so impassioned—*they doth protest too much, methinks!*"

"Methinks you're correct."

They were quiet for a few moments as they pondered the sad reality of their current discussion. Wyatt finally broke their silence, "Seriously Mick, it's really a sad existence to be all caught up in the limits of both humanism and human intelligence. Without the Lord, I couldn't get up each day and face the possibility of death, and the subsequent non-existence of not only all that I have, but also all that I've ever done. How can *anyone* face that?"

"You've got me on that one. I've never understood Satan's lie. Not to sound mean or anything, but folks who can't see a loving Creator behind all of the wonder and beauty in nature, are really missing the boat. Do you remember the passage in *Romans 1:20* regarding God's invisible qualities being apparent, so that no one has an excuse?"

"Sure I do. We've already discussed it a bunch of times today."

"You need to always remember this—speak the truth about Jesus and don't let yourself get angry at the unbelievers of the world. If you get nasty about it, you're falling into one of Satan's traps."

"But unbelievers can be so arrogant at times, Mick. So many intelligent people in the world—who are also unbelievers—often carry around such an unpleasant bravado. They also seem to think that people of faith are really not all that bright, and that faith in God is for dumb, unenlightened people. How can you *not* get angry at that kind of attitude?"

"By being compassionate, just like Jesus. Let's not forget the sad fact that there are also a group of sanctimonious people of faith who seem to relish the judgment of others. Those folks are just as adamant about spewing unloving and judgmental attitudes towards unbelievers, as any unbeliever's condescending attitudes towards people of faith are. In my opinion, they're both wrong."

"I suppose you're right," Wyatt said.

"Again, you're correct that many unbelievers seem to think that people who believe in the Lord are just simply stupid. However, many people of faith act just like the Pharisees did, and they look down their noses at the spiritually needy."

"I understand. Anyway, *Romans 1:20* seems to be a real go-to passage of Scripture for you."

"That's because it's in my top five Scriptures," Mick said.

"You have a *top five* Scriptures?"

"Doesn't everybody?"

Wyatt shook his head, "I'll plead the fifth for now . . . but I'll also work on that and get back to you."

"10-4, dude."

"By the way, how can I ever contact you after today?"

Mick grinned, "Who says I'm leaving? Maybe I'm planning on moving in with you."

"Oh geez. Please don't freak me out again, Mick. If you moved in with me, you'd certainly drink all of my coffee; not to mention the fact that you'd probably wear out all of my favorite war DVD's."

"Maybe so—"

"You'd also drive me bananas with your incessant use of the word, *dude!*"

"Word, dude!" the angel chuckled.

"Anyway Mick, are you familiar with the *dissent from Darwin* website?"

"Actually, I am. My boss-man Michael and I discussed it just a short time ago."

"So what do you think about it?"

"First off, we've been very frustrated with the lies about God's creation for a long time now. We then wondered why it took so long for the scientific community to come to its senses and tell the truth about the holes in Darwin's theories."

"Hmmm," Wyatt mumbled.

Suddenly bristling, Mick said, "Hey, I just told you about some angel inner sanctum stuff."

"I thought you guys knew everything," Wyatt said.

"Only the Lord knows everything, dummy."

"Oh."

"Although I must admit, we are privy to a lot of inside information."

"Okay, *Mr. Inner Sanctum*. Can you explain to me why people are often so idealistic when they're young?"

"Of course I can—*RYB, dude!* Look up *Ecclesiastes 1:12-18* and you'll see about the futility of earthly wisdom. Essentially, if you don't learn at an early age the importance of humility before the throne of God, a young person can be sucked into the arrogant, pseudo-intellectual vacuum that Satan and his minions have created."

"What do you mean by that?" Wyatt asked.

"Okay, it's like this. When you're young, people typically get all caught up in trying to *save the world*. Well, if you live a normal life, it typically humbles you and teaches you important lessons. So, if you're really smart, you learn to stop trying to save the world, and instead, start trying to *save your neighbor*. The saving of the world is God's business; so it's best to leave that to Him. Mankind is not in the least bit capable of saving the world—only destroying it."

"Wow. That's kind of . . . geez, I don't know what say."

"Actually," Mick began, "only Jesus Christ is capable of saving the world—*and* saving your neighbor."

"Amen to that," Wyatt agreed.

"Anyways, that's straight from the angel inner sanctum, my good man. Don't worry though, there's no charge for that."

"Gee, thanks???" Wyatt joked.

"Okay then, let's make sure that we finish talking about Mother Nature . . . before I forget."

"I get it. Father Nature. What's next?"

"No, we're not quite done yet, so listen up, knucklehead. Yahweh is the only God throughout all of mankind's history who can bring together all of the things in the universe. You see, only His presence explains all things—no other religion does that."

"I don't get it," Wyatt said.

"Well, it's like this. Some people worship nature; some people worship various gods and goddesses; some people worship false idols; but they all only scratch the surface. Only *Yahweh*—the *real* God, can explain everything in nature *and* in science."

"I'm still lost."

"Use your noodle, Wyatt! The most difficult concept for the human mind to comprehend is the eternal nature of God. As you know from studying the Intelligent Design movement, everything in creation has to have a starting point, and life's complexity points towards an intelligent creator. Anyone who has an open mind and who doesn't have an agenda can easily see that."

"Go on—"

"Anyways, the point here is that human intelligence and the discoveries in the field of science only go so far. You need to remember that, *God is the master scientist.* He created all things and is omnipresent. Ergo, everything in science points towards His mighty hand. Are you familiar with Francis S. Collins?"

"Yeah—isn't he the scientist who headed up the mapping of the human genome project?"

"He sure is. Well, it seems that he found *God* the deeper he delved into the complexity of DNA. That's what I mean when I say the Lord is the *master scientist.* His mighty fingerprints are all over even the minutest complexity of life details."

"Actually, I read through Collins' book. Although I'm not sure what I think about his position on evolution, I respect his opinion. Okay Mick, I think I'm tracking with you."

"Good. Now, I only have a couple of more things before we head over for our afternoon coffee extravaganza."

"You mean *your* extravaganza."

"Fine dude, *my* extravaganza. Anyways, let's talk about those idealistic animal rights groups who use heavy handed techniques to get their point across."

"Okay, shoot."

"Later this afternoon we'll dig back into God's love for His animals. But first, let me just say, there's a huge difference between the folks who work with humane societies, and the arrogant and hateful people who try to judge others for the eating of meat or the use of animal products."

"Sure there is. Being humane to animals is expected by God. Let me see . . . ." Wyatt pulled out his Bible and found his own, hand written concordance on a piece of paper in the back of it. *"Proverbs 12:10* says . . .

A righteous man cares for the needs of his animal, but the kindest acts of the wicked are cruel."

"Right-O. While you're at it, look up *Romans 14:21."*

Wyatt read aloud . . ."*It is better not to eat meat or drink wine or to do anything else that will cause your brother to fall."*

"Got it. One more, before I make my point. Read to yourself *Hebrews 10:1-10."*

Wyatt took a minute or so and read the passage. He read of Christ being the new sacrifice, and that the old way of sacrifices and burnt offerings were not pleasing to God, because Christ changed everything. "Okay *mister coffee,* what's your point in all of this?"

"Put on your seatbelt, because *here we go!* The whole point here is that if you don't love and care for God's animals, then you're obviously not pleasing Him. You see, God originally made animals for mankind's enjoyment. Well, it seems to me that the heavy-handed animal rights people generally have a very narrow view of creation and redemption."

"What do you mean by that?"

"Basically, I believe if these folks would simply try a little *RYB,* they'll understand that God didn't originally create animals for food; that only happened after original sin and the fall of mankind. Let's face it—God is the one who gave mankind meat to eat, and people eating meat is now a normal part of life here on this fallen Earth. However, people who enjoy eating meat should respect those who don't—and people who don't enjoy eating meat should respect those who do."

"I'm with you," Wyatt said.

"One important note, here. Because the Lord has allowed meat to be used as food, there's nothing wrong with huntsmen who use hunting as a source for food. However, simply hunting for the shear thrill of killing—without any intention of eating the meat—is just cruelty to God's creation."

"I suppose you're right about that, also."

"So to summarize, looking down on others with arrogance because of their favorable position on animals being used for food is not pleasing to God. It's *His* creation, not theirs. The Bible clearly states in *Revelation 21:4* that there will be no more death. So at some point in the future, there'll be no more death for either people *or* animals."

"I sure can't wait until that happens," Wyatt said.

"Well, that's pretty much all I have to say on that subject. God isn't cruel because He wants humans to die, and for animals to be used for food.

These things only happened as aftershocks of Adam and Eve's earthquake of disobedience in the Garden of Eden."

"I'm with you on all of this, Mick. So, do you have any last, parting shots before we move on?"

"Yep, one last thing. Let's talk about your favorite band, Rush."

"Rush?" Wyatt's love for the music by the Canadian trio dated back to his high school days. He still enjoyed their music, even today.

"Yep. That song they wrote called *Xanadu*—do you know the one?"

"Of course I do."

"Well, why don't you give me your take on the story behind the song."

"With pleasure. If I remember correctly, the song is based on an unfinished poem," Wyatt said, and Mick nodded. "I believe the story represents mankind's desire to live in a beautiful, utopian place, in a state of immortality. Sadly though, the guy in the song finds out that being immortal isn't exactly all that it's cracked up to be."

"Good. Now, looking at the song through your *God glasses,* what else do you see?"

"Well, I suppose I see the futility of trying to be immortal on a fallen Earth. I also believe the desire for immortality is imbedded into each person's heart."

"Nice work—that's the point I'm trying to make here. It's essential for you to view all art forms through your *God glasses,* so you can separate the good from the bad. When you can do that, your witness for the Lord will be that much stronger."

"So, can I assume that you like Rush?"

"Sure—I like a lot of their stuff. Those guys are three virtuosos who really rock, and whose lyrics aren't mired in filth and perversion."

"Of course, I agree. I've actually seen them in concert about a dozen times."

Mick nodded, "Alright partner, you've delayed me for long enough," he said, changing directions. "It's time to head to Tully's."

Wyatt nodded in agreement. As they got up to leave, he asked, "Hey Mick, I know that God is all powerful and all, but why does He allow so much pain and death down here? You know, sometimes, it seems like we live in complete madness and utter chaos."

"It's actually quite simple, my friend. It's because God wants all of you to exercise your own freedom of choice regarding His Son, Jesus Christ."

"I see."

"Although He very much wants for you to make the right choices, it's strictly up to you to do so."

"Why do you think that is?"

Mick's eyes flashed conviction, "Ask yourself this—why would God want to spend an eternity with a bunch of drones? The people who choose Christ will be rewarded for exercising their own free will in choosing to follow Him. In other words, the Lord won't *force* you to love Him—that's not love at all. He wants you to *choose* to love Him—that's true love. Am I making any sense here?"

"You sure are."

"However, we have to be careful about how we toss around the term *free will,*" Mick cautioned.

Wyatt look confused for a moment. "Are you talking about the Calvinism versus Arminianism debate?"

"Indeed, I am."

"So, which one is correct?"

"I'm afraid both of those perspectives are from a flawed, man-centered point of view," Mick said. "The Lord is neither a Calvinist nor an Arminianist."

"Meaning?"

"Some things are just simply beyond mankind's ability to fully comprehend . . . and any human will indeed have a very small 'god' if they claim to fully have the mind of the Lord, which is well beyond all human understanding."

"So what are you saying, here?"

"It's God's way that He elects mankind unto salvation, because you can't do it yourselves. However, He lets each person choose Him."

"How does He do that?"

"Listen, let's not get into all of that right now," Mick said. "In the end, choosing Christ is the answer—it's just that simple. Everything else pales in comparison to this basic truth."

Wyatt nodded, "On a brighter note," he said. "The song, *Free Will* is another great Rush tune."

"It surely is my good man," Mick agreed. *"It surely is."*

13

DEVIL'S FOOD

Everything seemed to be suddenly in motion in the North Arcade, as Mick and Wyatt stood up and stretched, preparing for their re-entry into the fray. With his gaze slowly panning from left to right, Wyatt surveyed the adjacent area. He noticed a steady flow of shoppers from their recessed vantage point, and all vital signs in the market seemed to be normal. With that, they proceeded to saddle up and venture back out into the crowds.

As they made their way out of the horseshoe shaped area and into the North Arcade hallway, Mick took particular notice of the incredible array of fresh-cut flowers for sale. The sight and smell of the flowers was captivating, so the angel insisted that they stop at a few of the vendors, so he could chat-up the owners. Wyatt smiled to himself as Mick continued to interact with people in that special way which he seemed to have perfected over the years.

They made their way towards the north end of the market, enjoying several other shops along the way. When they eventually re-emerged onto Pike Place, they continued walking north. There, they discovered several day-vendor booths, which were set up outside, offering their wares.

When they came to the near-pointed corner where Pike Place almost intersected with Western Avenue at Virginia Street, they crossed over and continued north. To their left was Victor Steinbrueck Park, which was

153

filled with numerous people that afternoon. Wyatt made a mental note that they should stop in the park for a while once they were through having their coffee.

They continued to move north along Western Avenue, mostly in a comfortable silence. As they passed by the Cutters Bayhouse restaurant on their left, the pain brigade fired an offensive at Wyatt—he and Vanessa had eaten at Cutters several times in years past. The restaurant had excellent views of Elliot Bay, and the food was outstanding.

As they walked, Wyatt wondered why the pain brigade had neglected to launch anything at him lately. As he pondered this apparent oddity, a realization swept over him. It occurred to him that thus far, his conversation with Mick had served as a reminder of something very important—that separation from loved ones who know Christ and have passed-on, is only a temporary thing. Keeping an eternal perspective on the events of your life is the only way to live successfully, without being dragged down by the inevitable tribulations, suffering, and losses which occur. Based on his latest experiences, he knew that he had to keep his eyes squarely focused on God's plan of redemption. For Wyatt, looking backwards only brought a visit from the pain brigade. Instinctively, he knew that he must keep his eyes fixed forward, where there was only true joy to be found with the Lord in His eternal kingdom.

As Mick and Wyatt moved past Cutters, Tully's appeared on their left. There was a large, open paved area in-between two tall office buildings which faced Elliott Bay. At the bottom of one of those buildings was their destination. They quickly covered the short distance along Western Avenue and entered into the java version of the Promised Land.

When they arrived at the counter, there was a young lady in front of them who ordered a really girly sounding frapa-something or other. This greatly amused Mick. When it was their turn to order, Wyatt spoke first and said, "Okay, my *father* here will have a grande double mocha. I'll just have a regular coffee."

Mick looked at Wyatt with false amazement and let out a quick chuckle, saying, "Darlin', throw a shot of honey into my mocha, would you please? And by the way, I don't look old enough to be this guy's father, do I?"

"An older uncle, perhaps?" she replied, smiling.

"That's a *little* better," Mick said. Wyatt remained quiet, holding back a laugh.

After paying for their drinks, Wyatt was handed his coffee. He then proceeded to put some honey, Splenda, and a little half-and-half into his cup as they waited. When Mick's sweet beverage was ready, they both took a seat in adjoining puffy-looking chairs in the far corner of the cafe. There were a few other people scattered throughout the store, but they were several tables away. Since it was still a little cool outside, the fireplaces were on, providing a very comfortable setting.

They both silently sipped on their coffees for a few minutes before Mick broke the relaxed atmosphere with his opening comment, "Wyatt, my friend, I'm afraid the time has come to delve into some of the details about the evil ones."

"Hmmm . . . I really liked our discussion at breakfast this morning about angels," Wyatt said. "I suppose today's agenda wouldn't be complete unless we talked about your evil counterparts."

"This won't be so bad, so relax and take it easy. Actually at some time down the road, we'll do a more in-depth study of Satan and his demons. But for now, I have a few Scriptures to review with you. After that, we're gonna discuss the Three Little Pigs."

"You've *got* to be kidding me . . . The Three Little Pigs fairy tale?"

"The very one."

"Don't even try to sell me some baloney about that story being more of your, *art imitating life* stuff," Wyatt said.

"Hold on to your knickers—remember, I'm good at this. Now pull out your Bible, whilst I take another sip of this delicious coffee."

"Fine." Wyatt pulled out his Bible and declared his readiness, "Shoot."

"Mmmm, that's good," Mick said, obviously happy with his very sweet beverage. "Okay, first turn over to *2 Corinthians 4:4.*"

"Alright, here we go . . . *The god of this age has blinded the minds of unbelievers, so that they cannot see the light of the gospel of the glory of Christ, who is the image of God . . .* That's a good one. What else do you have?"

"*Ephesians 2:2.*"

"Okay." Wyatt quickly found the verse . . ."*In which you used to live when you followed the ways of this world and the ruler of the kingdom of the air, the spirit who is now at work in those who are disobedient . . .* Do you have any others?"

"Nope. That'll do for now. Okay, the Lord has permitted Satan to be in charge of the current, fallen Earth. He's clearly evil, and Jesus calls him the *evil one* in *Matthew 13:19* in the parable of the sower."

"So, Satan's a baddie who tries to corrupt people. I'm with you so far."

"Now then, how can a human overcome demons and their evil influence?"

"By calling on a tough group of angels who specialize in demon butt-whooping?"

Mick grinned at this, "Well, that won't hurt either, but no. We're actually not permitted to do all of the work for you."

"Okay then, how???"

"By knowing, outsmarting, and staying one step ahead of the enemy. The best way to defeat the evil ones is to both understand their tendencies, *and* to take proactive action against them. Sadly, there are far too many Christians who believe that demons are only mythical, and therefore not real."

"Okay, I'm with you on all of that. But again, where are you going with this?"

"Patience, Luke."

"Oh, so you're a *Star Wars* fan too, huh?"

"Isn't everybody?"

"Yes, Mick. But will you *please* tell me where you're going with all of this? You have my curiosity piqued."

"This is where the Three Little Pigs comes in."

Wyatt let out a long sigh, "I'm not even sure I remember that story."

"Well my dear chap, fortunately for you, *I* do!" Mick said, trying to sound British. He failed.

"Wonderful," Wyatt bemoaned.

"Now, before we get started, let me first tell you that I'm going to tell you this story based on the original tale, which is a lot more violent than the subsequent versions you may have heard. Is that okay with you?"

"Do I have a choice?" Wyatt asked.

"No, I suppose not. Anyway, here goes . . . the three little pigs ventured out to seek their fortunes. The first little pig built a house of straw. When the big, bad wolf comes along, he says that he'll 'huff and puff and blooooow your house down!' Well, he did, and ate the first little pig."

"How touching."

Ignoring Wyatt's sarcasm, Mick continued. "The second little pig tried the same house building deal, but this time with sticks. The wolf had to blow a little harder, but he achieved the same result—a blown down house, and pork chops for supper. Oh, by the way, I forgot to say that the little pigs declared, 'not by the hair on my chinny chin chin' when the wolf asked them to let him in.'"

"Lovely."

"Okay now, listen closely. The *third* little pig was smarter than the first two, and he built his house with bricks—so it was nice and sturdy. Soooo, when the big bad wolf came-a-calling, he couldn't blow the brick house down. At this point, the third little pig was in charge, and began psyching out the dumb ole wolf."

"I'm not even sure what happens after this part of the story."

"After that, the third little pig outsmarted the wolf three times. First, the wolf tried to meet the pig in a turnip field at a certain time, but before escaping back home, the pig got there an hour early and got what he wanted. Then, the wolf tried a second time to meet the pig to trick him, but this time it was at an apple tree. The pig pulled the same deal, getting there early. This time, the wolf got there while the pig was still in the tree, but the pig threw an apple and the wolf went after it. So, the pig escaped and once again, and got home safely."

"My-oh-my—how gripping," Wyatt chided.

"The third time—smarty pants—the pig agreed to meet the wolf at the Fair. As usual, the pig got there early. But this time, he bought a butter churn."

"I sure hope that the payoff for this is good," Wyatt said.

"It is dude, so *dummy up!* Anyways, the third little pig saw the wolf coming, so he got into the butter churn. He then rolled down the hill towards the wolf. Well, this macho, *big bad wolf* got scared, and once again, the pig got away."

"Whew, I'm sure glad of that."

"Okay now, this big bad wolf is pretty ticked off, so he goes to the pig's brick house and climbs up on the roof—because he knows he can't blow the pig's house down. However, he still thinks he can get inside to eat that pig, just as if he were at a Shoney's breakfast buffet back in your home state of Georgia."

"Yes Mick. The Shoney's breakfast buffet is a bacon bonanza. How's that for alliteration? Please, continue with this *riveting* story." Wyatt was obviously enjoying his own smart aleck retorts.

"Well, this ole wolf drops down the chimney, clearly ready to chow down. However, the third little pig had a pot of boiling water waiting for him. When the wolf drops into the water, the pig pops on the lid and kills the big bad wolf. You see, he actually had *the wolf* for dinner."

"Geez, I didn't know that pigs were omnivores," Wyatt chided.

"Anyways smarty, in the end, the third little pig wins and lives happily ever after. The End."

"Mick, on that note, I have to use the restroom. No offense intended." Wyatt excused himself. When he returned, Mick did the same routine while Wyatt watched their seats. Tully's was in a mid-afternoon business lull, and the store remained relatively quiet.

When they settled back into their seats, Mick asked, "Okay dude, have you had a chance to think about the moral of the story?"

"Actually, no. I'm just kind of hanging back and waiting for your *sage* words of wisdom."

"Okay then, here we go." Mick's formerly playful voice turned back to serious. "The big bad wolf in this allegory is Satan, and humans are the three little pigs. The wolf is stronger than any pigs who don't have Christ, so the pigs are considered vulnerable creatures. However, pigs who have the Holy Spirit are actually stronger than the wolf. Are you with me?"

Wyatt quickly snapped back into a serious listening mode. "Yes, I certainly am."

"Okay. The houses represent each of the pigs' respective faith in God; or rather, each of their own, Church of One."

"Hmmm . . . I'm still with you, Mick."

"Well, the first two pigs didn't have a strong Church of One, so their houses blew down. The first pig had a very weak house of straw, and although the second pig had a little bit stronger house of sticks, the wolf still ate both of them after destroying their houses. You see, the wolf was being a wolf, and sought out to devour them—that's what wolves do, you know. Are you tracking with me?"

Wyatt nodded, "I am."

"Okay, so the third little pig built his house—or rather, his *Church of One*—with brick. The bricks in the third pig's house represent the strength of Jesus Christ. Did you notice the big bad wolf knew that he couldn't blow down the third pig's house?"

"I sure did."

"That's because Christ cannot be defeated by Satan, regardless of how hard Satan may want to."

"Oh my gosh Mick, this is actually starting to come together," Wyatt said, clearly surprised.

"Well, since the wolf can't blow down the third pig's house, he tries to trick him. Do you also remember what we spoke of earlier regarding Satan's *Trifecta of Tricks?*"

"I do."

"You must always remember that Satan is a liar and a deceiver. Anyways, three times the wolf tries his tricks, and each time the wise pig outsmarts the predictable wolf. The first time, the pig just plain ole outsmarts the wolf by showing up early. The second time, getting there early wasn't enough, so the pig threw the apple as a decoy, thereby tricking the wolf again. The third time, the pig rolls down the hill in the butter churn, and actually scares the wolf. You see, at this point, the third little pig went on the *offensive!*"

"Yeah, it seems like that chubby little bloke has been in charge since the start of their ordeal."

"That's correct. He's in charge because he has Christ. But that's not all. The third pig anticipates another assault from the enemy, so he prepares a boiling pot and gets the lid ready. The pig knows that the wolf will try to come in through the chimney, because he's a liar, a trickster, and a deceiver—just like I said. But, the pig is both smart *and* prepared. Additionally, he knows his enemy very well. Okay, so when the wolf did what a wolf does—whammo! He lands in the boiling water, which in this case represents the Word of God. All the pig has to do is put on the lid, which he does. The wolf is history, and actually becomes food for the pig."

After a few stunned moments, Wyatt was humbled and asked, "Well, are you going to bottom-line the rest of the metaphor for me?"

"No, I don't think so, this time," Mick said.

"Why not?"

"It's because I've given you all of this up until now. Why don't you finish this up for me instead?"

"Okaaay . . . I think I'm up to it." Wyatt took a long sip of his coffee. After a few moments, he was ready. "Well, the conclusions that I can draw are as follows . . . first, you can always expect Satan to try to blow your house down, because he has consumed countless people over the ages. Second, even when you use the power of Jesus to fend him off, Satan will come at you in a more covert way; so you can never let your guard down. Third, having Christ is more than sufficient, but whether we like it or not, the battle with Satan has been thrust upon each of us. It seems that all humans are born into this battle. We should not live in fear, but should expect the unexpected, and use the Word of God against any and all wolves. Fourth, it's time to go on offense and take the battle to the enemy, because the best defense is a good offense. Fifth, the enemy is defeat-able, because he's predictable, and because he has no power against Christ . . . well, how's that?"

"Not too bad," Mick said, sounding impressed. "We're really making some nice progress here, dude. Good work."

"Well, did you have anything else to add, Mick?"

"Yes—sixth, I'm almost ready for my mid-afternoon snack."

"For real? You must be the biggest angel-foodie of them all . . . so what do you have a hankering for, now?"

"How about some of that mac and cheese from Beecher's?"

"Nice choice. Let's finish our coffee first, though. Oh, and I want to stop by that park next door for a few minutes. The views are really nice."

"Okay, my friend. But before we move on, I have a couple more verses to look at before we depart our Three Little Pigs story."

Wyatt shrugged, "You're the boss. Geez, I never thought that you'd pull off that last one about the pigs. I sure didn't see that coming."

Mick nodded, "Remember, I've been at this for a long time. Anyways, let's look up *Job 1:12.*"

"Okay, here it is . . . *The* LORD *said to Satan, Very well, then, everything he has is in your hands, but on the man himself do not lay a finger. Then Satan went out from the presence of the* LORD . . . Of course, we're speaking here of Job. This is obviously a chat between God and Satan."

"That's right. The point here is for you to look at *Who* is in charge and *Who* has the power. We've already touched on this today, but the primary point here is that Satan is both predictable, *and* has no power over God. These are two very important things to remember when waging war against those demonic scumbags. However, all people would be best advised to not underestimate them."

"I understand. Do you have any other Scriptures?"

"There are plenty, but I'm going to defer some of them to your second mission."

"What!?! You haven't even given me my *first* mission."

"I know," Mick winked. "Anyways, I saw something on a bus back in Minneapolis that really made me angry," he said, changing the subject.

"I'll bite, what was that?"

"It was a slogan from some misguided atheist group that said something like, 'You can be good without God'. I mean, *come on!* Do those folks really think the moral code embedded in people actually developed from miscellaneous spores in some primordial soup? Talk about science fiction."

"Well Mick, it seems to me, maybe that campaign was inspired by the *big bad wolf* himself. What do you think about that?"

"Wyatt my friend, nothing surprises me with the evil ones."

"I agree."

"Anyways, why don't we head outside to finish up this lesson?"

"I'm good with that." Wyatt donned his backpack, and they both made their way out of Tully's. After arriving outside, they turned right, walking the short distance on the pavement between two large office buildings. The buildings created a partial shade, and it was mostly overcast. Walking between these buildings was very much like walking through a steep canyon, in that there was an echo to every sound. It was cooler there, than back out on the street.

When they arrived at the end of the open space, they looked out over Highway 99, just below. The views of Elliott Bay were beautiful, causing Wyatt to think about his next trip on the ferry across to the Olympic Peninsula. He had been planning an overnight trip to the Lake Crescent Lodge for several months now, and he wanted to take some pictures along the long road down to Sol Duc Hot Springs in the Olympic National Park.

Mick interrupted his thoughts. "Dude-ster, all I really want to say about what we've discussed here is this—people often try to sit on the fence when it comes to really important spiritual issues, because they don't want conflict, and that's understandable. With smaller issues in life, you can sometimes pull that off. However, with bigger issues like Heaven, Hell, eternity, and God, I'm afraid that sitting on the fence isn't an option. In other words, the battle is thrust upon you, whether you like it or not. Do you know what I mean?"

"I do."

"So, if you have to engage in battle, you might as well *win,* dontcha think?"

"Yes, absolutely."

"Well then, everyone is best advised to follow the example of the third little pig, right?"

"Yes indeed, Mick. The first two pigs were not prepared for the battle, because they didn't build their houses with the proper material; which is Christ. The inference with the apparently wise third pig was that he *was* prepared, mostly because he had the Lord in his heart. Not only that, but he took several counter-offensive maneuvers to answer the wolf's attempts at subterfuge. In the end he knew how to draw in the enemy and destroy him with the Word of God. How's that for a thesis?"

"My boy, I almost have a tear in my eye," Mick joked. "But seriously, the whole moral to this story is that you can do either one of two things— either become food for the devil and let him devour you, or you can conquer him with the help of Jesus Christ, who is *brick solid*. I'm afraid those are the only two available choices."

"That makes sense to me. Do you have anything else to add about wolves?" Wyatt asked.

"Actually, I do. *Acts 20:29* says . . . *I know that after I leave, savage wolves will come in among you and will not spare the flock.*"

Wyatt nodded, enjoying the angel's substantial knowledge of Scripture, "Mick, I'm beginning to see why you like our various art forms so much— many biblical truths can be found in them. In the case of those three little pigs, I'm quite sure I never considered discerning allegory out of that seemingly innocent little fairy tale. I'll have to pay more attention."

"Actually, that was the whole point of this exercise," Mick said. "I wasn't trying to re-write the story—only show you how to look at things from a more biblical perspective. That's kind of my thing, you know."

"Yeah, that really seems to be your specialty," Wyatt agreed.

Mick winked and declared, "10-4, Wyatt. You're catching on, my man."

14

HEAVEN AND HELL

As if hearing a subtle beckoning from an irresistible siren's song, Mick and Wyatt turned right on Western Avenue, heading back towards the north end of the market. The instinctive allure to return to the main body of the shopping bazaar was both invisible and enchanting. However, after passing by Cutters once again, they temporarily abandoned the market's invitation, detouring into Victor Steinbrueck Park, to pay homage to that very unique and eclectic downtown space.

As usual, the park contained numerous people of all shapes, sizes and economic standing. Directly in front of them was a big pentagonal area, where several small clusters of people were chilling out. One bohemian-looking young man with a scraggly beard was playing a folksy sounding song on his acoustic guitar. Another group was sitting in a circle reading something together—*probably poetry,* Wyatt thought. Within view was a large grassy area where several people had out blankets, relaxing in Seattle's beautiful downtown atmosphere; they began to move in that direction.

As they continued along the grassy area, they spotted people tossing Frisbees, playing with their dogs, and otherwise enjoying the day. Mick and Wyatt walked mostly in silence until the angel asked, "Hey, how does that spot over there, look?" He pointed to a vacant bench facing the waterfront.

"Sure. It looks good to me," Wyatt said, and they went over and sat down. Wyatt sat sideways and unhooked his backpack, placing it on the seat in between them. They both then proceeded to sit back and soak in their newfound repose.

A slight breeze gave the entire park an almost idyllic feel. The softly pleasant sounds of activity nearby accentuated the beautiful view of the bay. After sitting quietly for a few minutes and taking in the relaxing atmosphere, Mick broke their comfortable silence. "So Wyatt, tell me about that song that you and your music buddies were working on. What was it called, *'Who Will You See'*—right?" Wyatt had played the bass guitar on-and-off for several years since he got out of high school, and used to sit in with some local rock bands in the late eighties.

"It sure is, Mick. But I'm not a song writer. Me and some buds actually dinked and dunked around with that and several other tunes. However, it seems to me that *Time* often robs people of the many things we dream about doing—like writing and playing music for me."

"That's interesting—go on."

"You know this equation for humans . . . life happens, and it seems like you just can't get around to doing everything you want to do. The results often equal huge disappointment."

"Okay my friend, I understand. I really do. Listen—down here, many people don't always get to completely follow their innermost dreams. However, no one should ever feel robbed, because in Heaven, it's a completely different story."

"So, tell me . . . what's it really like up there?"

"My friend, it's absolutely incredible; *especially* compared to this place." Mick opened his hands as if to say "everything that you see." He continued, "However, contrary to what many people say, it's really *not* beyond your imagination—at least not completely."

"For real???"

"Absolutely. You know, the Bible indicates that the desire for a happy eternity is built into the hearts of every person who God creates. The problem for many people is that their tribulations sometimes get in the way, and this often creates a discontented heart. As a result, people often develop some hugely misplaced hostility towards their Creator."

"I won't even ask you how you knew about it . . . but why did you bring up that song we used to work on?"

"Because, the impetus behind the song is your desire to have a conversation with the Lord, coupled with His prospective question to you, *'when you walk into Heaven, who will you see?'* Right?"

"Right, it sure is."

"Well, have you considered that my showing up today might be more than just to hang out, shoot the breeze, and drink coffee?"

"No, I suppose not. Actually, I haven't really had a chance to think about it too much."

"Wyatt, after Jesus ascended to Heaven, doesn't it seem like He answered everything, directly for mankind?"

"Well, now that you mention it, it does seem that way," Wyatt said. "So tell me; has Jesus showed up on Earth to talk to anyone since his ascension?"

"No, not in the in-person sense. His death and resurrection was sufficient until He returns to reclaim His world. However, doesn't it make sense that God would send messengers like me, instead?"

"Yeah, I suppose so—"

"Think about it," Mick interrupted. "God's great and complete grace was made perfect by Christ's sacrifice on the cross at Calvary—period. So many of the Old Testament prophecies pointed to that fateful day. But, let's not forget the fact that God historically used intermediaries like the prophets to speak with His people—*until* Jesus was born, which completed the prophecies. After that, *Christ* became your intermediary. Remember, no one comes to the Father but through Him."

"Okay, I'm with you on all of that. So, what's your point?" Wyatt asked.

"Your song idea is a good one, and it contains an important and appropriate message from the King. It's something He would likely say to you—or anyone else for that matter—who asked Him the question, *who will be in Heaven when I get there?*"

"Yeah, we wanted to write a song that looked at eternity from the heavenly side. We figured that all too often, people only think about Heaven from their own perspective, and they rarely think of things from the Lord's point of view."

"That's true," Mick agreed. "They only see the world as if it revolved around themselves, right?"

"Right. That song essentially looks at it from God's perspective—a loving Father who only wants for us to do our jobs by being ambassadors of His Gospel."

"So, the moral of the song is—?"

"If you want someone in Heaven with you for eternity, you need to wake up and try to show them the way to Paradise by introducing Christ to them; that is, if He's not already a part of their life. That's what the basic message is."

"That's an awesome concept, dude. You and your buddies keep at it, and just maybe God will do something with that idea."

"Perhaps so. Anyway, what's the topic of our next lesson?"

Mick gently sighed, his gaze focusing on the beautiful waters of Elliott Bay and the Olympic Mountains in the distance. As a gentle wisp of wind blew through his hair, he said, "This next lesson will center on the glory of Heaven and the agony of Hell. We'll spend most of this chat on Heaven, because we'll be delving more into Hell during your second and third missions."

"There you go again . . . you haven't even hinted to me yet as to what my *first* mission is."

"Listen my friend, once you've joined the King's army, you're in for good, so just relax," Mick said. "We've got you covered."

Wyatt nodded, "Actually, I'm just busting your chops, Mick. I'm good here—no worries."

"Good deal. Anyways, I want for us to look at a couple of passages of Scripture that'll open your mind to God's greatness. The enemy has done an excellent job of dulling the senses of both Christians and non-believers out there, and we absolutely must turn that around."

"Geez, this sounds interesting. So what shall we start with?" Wyatt asked, pulling out his Bible.

"Psalm 150:6."

"Okay . . . *Let everything that has breath praise the* LORD. *Praise the* LORD . . . Hey, that's in a Christian song that gets played in a lot of churches."

"Yep, it sure is. Also, please look up *Romans 8:19-21."*

"There's a little more to that one. Okay . . .

> *"The creation waits in eager expectation for the sons of God to be revealed. For the creation was subjected to frustration, not by its own choice, but by the will of the one who subjected it, in hope that the creation itself will be liberated from its bondage to decay and brought into the glorious freedom of the children of God."*

Mick nodded, "Nicely done, dude."

"You know, I absolutely love that passage of Scripture."

"Yep, *Romans 8* is da bomb."

"Very cute Mr. Angel," Wyatt said dryly. "So, what's up with these two passages?"

"Once again, Satan's deceitful ways."

"What do you mean by that?"

"Well, let's see if I can tee this one up for you. First off, let me make an overall statement that some Christians have taken on a potentially unscriptural—and likely inaccurate position—on animals in Heaven . . . and I really think it needs correcting."

Wyatt quickly nodded, "I'm with you, but what else do you want to discuss? I think we already touched on this subject earlier today."

"Simply this—it seems that one of Satan's favorite tricks is to sucker people into believing that Heaven is boring, and that their passed away pets couldn't possibly be there. When you stop and think about it, that's a really brilliant tactical maneuver."

"How so?"

"Because if people aren't looking forward to God's promise of Heaven, they'll spend more time on their earthly desires. In other words, sin. In that flawed way of thinking, people tend to think they'd better *party while they can*. Of course, if people would simply RYB on a regular basis, then they'd begin to understand just how wonderful Heaven really is."

"I'm with you on this, Mick—big time. Like we touched on earlier this morning, when Scout died last year, I was really frustrated with some fellow Christians who shared with me the flawed-but-prevalent opinion that my little buddy ceased to exist when he died. They actually said that he was *gone forever,* because allegedly, animals don't have 'souls'. Although the meaning of souls or spirits is an often debated position, the truth is, I believe it's totally irrelevant as it relates to animals in Heaven."

"I see," Mick said. "Go on."

"I'm very familiar with the passages you just had me read, and I think they illustrate a couple of critically important things concerning this subject."

Mick chuckled, *"Of course.* That's why I had you read them."

"I see. Well, the passage in *Psalm 150* clearly says, *'everything that has breath praise the* LORD'. To me, that covers a whole lot of God's creation."

"It sure does . . . and the last time I checked, animals do have breath. Please continue."

"The passage in *Romans 8* is quite powerful. I feel like it indicates that all of creation was subjected to God's curse on mankind. It continues by saying the creation eagerly awaits for the sons of God to be revealed. Of course, the Lord's animals are an integral part of His creation."

"I see where you're going. Although there's some disagreement over this, I think you're right on track, dude-ster."

"Cool. Well, after I studied the many Scriptures regarding the Lord and *His* relationship with *His* creation, including *His* animals, I found that God is obviously very fond of His own handiwork. Furthermore, it seems like we're ultimately heading back to an Eden-like existence, with no more pain, suffering, or death."

"I like it! Keep on chugging, big daddy."

"Well . . . and I know that some Christians won't easily buy into what I'm about to say . . . but I feel like God's enormous creation is heading for some kind of restoration or redemption, because unlike mankind, the creation is without sin. That passage in *Romans 8* states that it was subjected to frustration and God's curse—*against its will.*"

"Seriously, using Scripture to back up your point is the right thing to do. What else do you have to say?"

"Also, mankind's arrogance about being a *higher creation* than animals comes into play, here. Many people—even the most devout Christians—don't read their Bibles often enough. Yes, mankind *is* God's crowning achievement in creation. However, that title also carries with it a lot more responsibility—and I mean a *lot* more."

"So, why is the animal kingdom bound by mankind's sin, and why do animals die?" Mick challenged.

"Well, here it is . . . animals didn't originally sin; their world was corrupted by *mankind's* sin. As stewards of Eden, Adam and Eve clearly made a humongous mistake which negatively affected God's entire perfect world."

"I agree," Mick said. "Go on."

"So truthfully, people who are worried about their beloved pets getting into Heaven would be best advised to look in the mirror."

"What exactly do you mean by that?"

"In my opinion, I believe the creation will be redeemed or restored, but *not* all of mankind will be with Jesus in Heaven . . . and ultimately, on the new Earth."

"Hmmm. This is really getting interesting," the angel said.

"And according to *Romans 8:21,* the creation will be redeemed. Since *Romans 8:22* says *all* of creation groans, and *Romans 8:23* says only the *redeemed* groan, it seems reasonable that all of creation will be redeemed."

"That's a reasonable interpretation," Mick agreed.

"Okay Mick, tell me what you know!" Wyatt said.

"DP, dude—sorry."

Unfazed, Wyatt continued, "Anyway, it stands to reason that when someone has a pet die, they should be much more concerned about getting their own tail end into Heaven by surrendering to Christ. That's what I meant when I said that people should, *look in the mirror.*"

"Don't stop now, dude."

"Essentially, I believe that our pets are already there! That's the ironic thing about the whole animals or pets in Heaven issue, because it's really not an issue at all. It's more about mankind's arrogance, and in my opinion, biblical ignorance."

Mick grinned, "So, you understand that your position is not specifically addressed in the Bible—right?"

"That's correct. The Bible is actually silent on whether our pets are in Heaven. However, I think the Lord expects us to examine His character, and to perhaps give Him a little more credit for being a loving, compassionate, and giving Father."

"I can't argue with that," Mick agreed.

"I also believe that my opinion is very consistent with biblical teaching," Wyatt said.

Mick nodded in agreement, "Outstanding—nice work Wyatt. Much of your reasoning is biblically sound. It's absolutely true that people have a higher calling, and therefore, a higher *responsibility* as heirs of Christ."

"That's my whole point in a nutshell," Wyatt agreed.

"Actually, it *astounds* me that any Christian would think their little buddies wouldn't be waiting for them in Heaven. That goes directly against the whole idea of a loving God and Father who described His entire creation as *very good.*"

"Geez, we sure have talked a lot about pets in Heaven today."

"That's because this topic is perhaps the most under ministered-to area in all of Christianity," Mick said. "And a lot of people would really like to know what the Bible says or indicates about this subject. However, it seems to be hard for an 'average Joe' to find a consistent opinion from among the theological experts."

"How true. I know that from my own investigation."

"You know," Mick continued, "convincing people that God really doesn't care enough about your feelings that He would neglect to restore your pets, is really symptomatic of the campaign by the evil ones to convince people that the Lord is uncaring, not very powerful, and aloof. I'm afraid that Satan has laid his filthy fingerprints all over this subject with his treachery, deceit, and lies."

"Well Mick, I sure can't argue with that. I used to wonder why the Bible didn't speak directly of this. But then I remembered two really important things. The first thing is the passage in *Romans 1:20,* which we've discussed a few times already today, regarding God's invisible qualities being apparent. The other is the notion that the Bible is a *survival manual*—it tells us what we *need* to know—not everything there is to know."

"Right. The King expects for you to love Him enough to examine His holy character. The pets-not-in-Heaven thing is actually an evil trick intended to drive people away from their Lord."

"You know, I've actually heard Christians say they don't want to go to a place where their pets won't be, when they die. That's a pretty sad statement, but all they really have to do is open their Bibles—they just may find some important clues there."

"You're absolutely right, my friend."

"I'm really surprised that so many people of faith neglect to do the one thing that'll give them answers to what they seek. God's Holy Word is awesome, but it can't be read without willing participants . . . I'm sure the evil ones really love it when Christians don't read their Bibles."

"Yep. Satan, Damon, and all their evil buddies are very pleased when folks don't read God's Holy Word. Regarding animals in Heaven, once again, that's them doing their evil thing. They'll actually do anything they can to separate God's children from their maker. That's what those *wolves* do, you know."

"You just can't get away from the story of the Three Little Pigs, can you?"

"No, I suppose not," Mick agreed, grinning.

"Anyway," Wyatt said. "Please tell me something . . . if you can."

"Sure thing."

"In pondering God's character and greatness, I've been wondering about a couple of things. However, I'm not sure if they fall under Divine Privilege or not."

"Well if they do, I'll certainly let you know—so out with it."

"Can animals speak in Heaven?"

"Actually, the *animals* module in your orientation program up there is one of the more interesting programs that you'll learn about. Let me ask you an important question—do you think that what you're suggesting is beyond the Lord's greatness to accomplish?"

"Of course not. Although I do feel like many people tend to sell God short."

"Narrow minded Christians would think that your question is ridiculous, but I don't. The one and only true God—the One who created *all* things—can accomplish much more than He's given credit for by many people. Also, you'll often hear people say that Heaven is *beyond our imaginations;* but again, that's not entirely true. If you'll simply RYB, you'll find out that God is immense and can do all things. Ultimately, if it can bring praise to Him, animals speaking in Heaven is certainly a possibility. That's all I can say on that hypothesis. DP kicks in here." Wyatt nodded his understanding. "So what's your other question?" the angel asked.

"Okay, when God's Word indicates that 'the creation' will be redeemed, is it possible that may cover every living thing which has ever existed—except those people who reject Christ's sacrifice?"

"*Now* you're thinking correctly about God's character. As usual, I'll give you the answer first. None of the angels or saints in Heaven knows either the day or the magnitude of God's final redemption. However, I can definitely tell you that there are animals in Heaven—there are plenty of biblical passages to back that up."

"Indeed there are."

"Anyway, all God has ever wanted for any of His creation to do is to worship Him. So in examining the loving part of His character, I expect the Lord strongly desires for His people *and* His creation to be awestruck by His greatness. Essentially, God wants all of us to love Him as our Father."

"So, what about my second theory?"

"Essentially, I'm saying I don't know. However, think about what *the* creation, or *all* of creation being redeemed means. Have you ever considered the incredible ramifications of that?"

"Actually, I have."

"Well, let me ask you a few questions next."

"Be my guest."

"Is the entire, gigantic physical universe part of God's original creation?"

"Genesis 1 clearly states that it is."

"Is it reasonable to think that the physical, redeemed universe will be similarly big?"

"Absolutely."

"Is it also within the realm of possibility that God may need umpteen gazillion animals, as well as a whole lot of His people, to enjoy His new universe—the *redeemed* universe?"

"Of course it is."

"Now then, do you realize that scientific estimates in the past have indicated that the projected number of stars in the universe is over seventy-sextillion?"

"Nope—how many did you say?"

"Seventy-sextillion! That's a seven, followed by twenty-two zeros."

Wyatt whistled, "Wow! You know, that doesn't even take into consideration the number of planets circling those stars. I suppose you can say with confidence that the possibilities are absolutely staggering."

"They sure are—at least to the human mind. So sit back my boy, and eagerly await the revelation of God's majesty when His plan of redemption takes place. Again, I don't know His ultimate plan or when it'll occur. But considering the infinite power of the Lord, it's certainly possible that *everything* will be redeemed. It's plausible that God will want to reclaim everything He made in creation that Satan has tried to take away from Him, except those folks who reject Christ's sacrifice."

"I trust the Lord, Mick, I really do. It'll be very cool to watch this whole thing unfold."

"Dudemeister, I'm actually glad to see that your mind is expanding towards God's greatness. I'd strongly encourage you to continue doing that, because I don't think the Lord appreciates being stuffed into a narrow minded little box."

"I'm not planning on being the dummy who does that."

"And I have one important caveat here, Wyatt. The Bible is God-breathed and without error. Anything or anyone who contradicts His Holy Word is absolutely *false.* Now then, you can certainly speculate on things which are not specifically mentioned in the Bible—like animals in Heaven—but you must be very careful when it comes to anyone who directly contradicts God's Holy Word."

"Of course, Mick. I understand, completely."

"And one more thing. Anyone foolish enough to put their pets ahead of God will do so at their own peril. Loving your pets as an important part of your life is tantamount to enjoyment of His bounty. Putting your pets—or any other false idols for that matter—ahead of the Lord is very risky business, indeed. I strongly recommend against it."

"I agree and I understand," Wyatt said humbly.

"Anyways, you kind of stole my thunder in the first part of this lesson on Heaven and Hell, but I'm actually glad that you did."

"How did I steal your thunder?"

"It's just another part of the important message that you need to know."

"Important message?"

"Yep—the important message is that Heaven is incredible and *can* be imagined—at least partially—if you'll simply examine the character of God and His Holy Word."

"Oh, I get it now. That's actually the best part of my personal walk with the Lord; anticipation of Heaven that is."

They both sat for a minute, looking out on the busy Seattle waterfront. Several smaller boats were slowly gliding out on Elliott Bay, adding a tranquil layer to the backdrop of their discussion. The pleasure boats were soon joined by another Washington State ferry, which had just pulled away from the dock, beginning its journey across Puget Sound. Mick was apparently deep in thought, so Wyatt decided not to bother him. After a minute or so, the angel spoke up again. "Okay dude, let's talk about Hell for a minute."

"Hmmm. You seem to be a little bothered over this subject."

"I'm not really bothered—I'm perplexed."

"Why is that?"

"If the people who reject Christ only knew what awaits them, they'd surely be singing another tune. Hell is an unbelievably *awful* place."

"So I hear," Wyatt agreed.

"And the worst thing about Hell is that people who go there are forever separated from their Creator, who truly loves them."

"Yeah, well those arrogant atheists will ultimately get what they asked for—eternal separation from the Lord."

"That's not something anyone should ever be happy about . . . and I'm afraid it's not just the atheists who'll be disappointed," Mick said sadly.

"Who else then?"

"Well, how about all those folks who try to water down Christ's sacrifice by claiming that all people get into Heaven? If that were true, then why proclaim the Gospel?"

"Good point."

"I'm afraid those people will be shocked when they discover that it's only a portion who actually makes it to Heaven."

"I'm sure they will . . . I also believe that type of thinking stems from their own desire to play God."

Mick raised an eyebrow with curiosity, "That's interesting. Please, explain to me what you mean by that."

"Sure thing. Well, let's start off with asking the question—why do people try so hard to explain the unexplainable?"

Mick chuckled, "Now *you're* getting cryptic, my friend. I'm afraid you're gonna have to *bring-it* a little better than that."

"Okay, it's really quite simple. Essentially, people should just let God handle *God-business*. Instead of trying to reconcile how a loving God can let anyone go to Hell, they should be more concerned about spreading the good news about Jesus, and that He offers eternal life in Heaven."

"That's true," Mick agreed.

"Yes, there are several definitive answers for why everyone doesn't make it to Heaven. However, it's really not any person's job to reconcile the universe—except the Lord."

"They're not getting the big picture about God, are they?"

"I agree, Mick. But oddly, I can also understand their concern."

"How's that?"

"I think it stems from people concentrating on only one aspect of God's personality—that is, His great love and grace. People who don't really know God, only—"

"Correct!" Mick interrupted. "Their error is that God is also a *God of judgment.*"

"Yes. Deep down, people tend to want to avoid having to answer for their own sins."

"Christ's death on the Cross wiped all of that away and atoned for all sins. However, people are still required to accept His sacrifice. If you ask me—*that really isn't asking too much!* Instead of trying to interrogate the Lord about why He does things the way He does, people would be well-advised to concentrate on using their gifts and talents to help others. In other words, let God be God; let Him handle the big things."

"I've often heard the question, *what about the tribesman in Botswana who has never had the opportunity to know Jesus?*"

"Again, let God be God, and let Him handle the big things."

Wyatt nodded, "I see what you're saying—quit trying to answer all the mysteries of God and the universe, and stay on track with trying to help others towards Christ."

"That's correct. People should not look upwards, trying to completely figure out the mysterious ways of the Lord and His universe. But rather, they should consider looking at the people around them who may need their help."

"Are you saying that people who pose these types of questions are actually trying to—?"

"Yes. They're ultimately trying to play God—just like we discussed."

"That's interesting," Wyatt said.

"Listen, there's nothing wrong with discussing difficult questions for humans to understand. It's when someone goes too far by putting God on trial—that's when it goes wrong."

"I'm with you on this," Wyatt said.

"Listen, each person's mission is simple—spread the Gospel of Christ and help others towards the Cross."

"Mick, you keep saying that, over-and-over."

"That's because it's critically important, *over—and-over.*"

"I gotcha—so what about Hell?"

"Hell is actually pretty simple—it's the place where God doesn't live. Being in Hell is all about eternal separation from the Lord . . . and I'm afraid that only a *fool* would want that."

"I agree. But where is Hell—or at least, what people often refer to as Hell?"

"DP dude—the Bible doesn't say. I can tell you that a bunch of unsaved people and a boatload of dirtbag demons live there."

"Isn't the final resting place for Satan and company in the eternal lake of fire?"

"It is. Please read *Matthew 25:41* for us," Mick said.

Wyatt quickly flipped to the passage, *"Then he will say to those on his left, Depart from me, you who are cursed, into the eternal fire prepared for the devil and his angels."*

"Now, let's compare that verse with *Philippians 3:20-21.*"

"Alright . . . *But our citizenship is in heaven. And we eagerly await a Savior from there, the Lord Jesus Christ, who, by the power that enables him* to bring everything under his control, will transform our lowly bodies so that they will be like his glorious body . . . I especially like that last part."

"It basically all boils down to this, Wyatt. Which would you rather have—Heaven or Hell; the lake of fire with demons, or the glorious and perfect body with Christ?"

"That's obviously a rhetorical question. I'll take Christ."

"Of course you will! But isn't it shocking how many people don't?"

"Yes it is," Wyatt said sadly.

"Well, I don't have much left on Heaven and Hell for now, and I'm also ready for my mac and cheese."

"You and all this comfort food, Mick. Well, I guess I can't blame you."

Mick nodded, "Okay then, I do have a couple of quick things left on the agenda for this little chat."

"Like what?"

"Let's next talk about *glimpses.*"

"No problem. What's on your mind?"

"Well, while humans are still here on Earth, you get glimpses of eternity. If you are heading towards Heaven, you get a glimpse of Hell; if you are heading towards Hell, you get a glimpse of Heaven."

"That actually sounds like a future song, Mick."

"Maybe it should be. Anyways, while you're here on Earth, you can accumulate the data which can lead you to take the direction you want to take when you die—it's up to each of you to make your own decision. I do hope that more people choose Heaven over Hell—that'll just add to the great celebrations we have up there."

"That sounds pretty good to me."

"Hey, do you mind if we get up and start walking, again?" Mick asked. Wyatt nodded as they both stood up and stretched their legs. The angel continued, "Dude, will you please look up *Proverbs 12:10* for me once again, before we go?"

"Sure thing." After a moment, he said . . ."*A righteous man cares for the needs of his animal, but the kindest acts of the wicked are cruel* . . . Do you have another point to make?"

"Nope, I sure don't. But don't you think it's high-time to call Miss Charlene to see how Baby is doing?"

Wyatt was stunned, "Wow . . . I feel like a *real* knucklehead."

"I agree," Mick chuckled.

"I've been so engrossed in our discussions that I forgot to check in on Miss Charlene and Baby." Wyatt pulled out his phone and called Charlene's cell phone. As he waited for her to answer, Wyatt ruminated over the immense lack of masculinity in his dog's name . . . .

Charlene greeted him, "Well hello dear! How're you doing up there in the market?" Her voice was as comforting and engaging as ever.

"Great, Miss Charlene. How's the little stinker doing?"

"Oh, she's fine. I've taken her for another walk, and now she's napping again."

"If you ask me, that sure sounds like a great life."

"Are you and Mr. Mick having a good chat today?" Charlene's question surprised Wyatt. He felt like he was perhaps the last person in the world to know that he was going to have a visit from an angel that day.

"Actually, we're getting to know each other quite well. I'm learning a lot from him."

"Good, dear!"

"Miss Charlene, how long did you know—?"

"Oh hush up sweetheart. We'll get all caught up after dinner when you two get home, tonight."

Wyatt shook his head and realized that continuing to press Charlene would be fruitless. "Okay. So I guess you know that our dinner on your terrace is being postponed?"

"I've known for some time now that you wouldn't be home until after dinner with Mr. Mick. But don't fret over me. I have plenty here, and so does Baby."

"But—"

"Now you two finish up your business, and I'll see you later."

Wyatt sighed, "Okay. I'll see you a little bit later, then."

"Everything is okay at home, sweetheart. Don't you worry about a thing . . . bye-bye now." Charlene hung up.

Wyatt was quiet for a few moments, then said, "Alright Mick, I suppose it's time to go get you some *serious* comfort food."

"I thought you'd never ask—please lead on."

Everything was now falling into place for Wyatt. Although their ultimate destination and purposes continued to be a mystery, his discussions with Mick were most certainly significant. Still though, he remained unconcerned about what was next, because he knew that when God sends an invitation to follow Him into a mighty work, then the wisest thing to do is to simply follow His lead.

Human instinct will often tell you it's too difficult to follow an uncomfortable or unplanned path. However, after a little practice, you come to realize that it's actually harder for you to carry out your own will, instead of what you instinctively know is the Lord's plan for you.

Once again, Mick and Wyatt headed back over the grassy area of the park towards Western Avenue. They were returning to the hustle and bustle of the ancient market; a place that now contained a brand new history for Wyatt Hunter. Although he already loved Pike Place Market more than anywhere else in the world, the developments that day would only serve to strengthen its special place in Wyatt's heart.

15

TROUBLED WATERS

Mick and Wyatt walked in silence as they continued to work their way back towards the market. By this time, Wyatt was now quite sure that his unorthodox angelic visitor had been methodically teaching him spiritual lessons, one by one. He found himself marveling at the love and knowledge that Mick had for their heavenly Father, and it made him yearn to know more about the Creator of all things.

The copious amount of biblical wisdom which Mick had been imparting to Wyatt, was curiously incongruent with their sometimes comedic banter. However, the level playing field which the angel had presented as the forum for their discussions, had somehow been a very effective way for him to build their now, mutual trust.

Wyatt was sure that the effectiveness of their interactions would have been greatly diminished, if it weren't for the wonderful combination of Mick being so easy-to-identify with, coupled with his informal approach to their dialogue. He wondered if Mick had always used such a casual approach to his duties, and for some reason, he just couldn't help but to wonder what the Aramaic word for "dude" was . . . .

As they continued their short trek back to the market, Wyatt pondered the progressive nature of their discussions that day. He very much realized that they weren't random in the least bit. He also found it ironic that the day had started out as a primarily biblical discussion between two complete strangers, but it later evolved into a student-teacher discourse.

What at first seemed to be an innocuous chat over coffee between two guys about the Lord, had inevitably revealed itself to be an invisible curriculum. Wyatt could almost now see the angel checking off topics on a mental clipboard as they progressed throughout the day. All-in-all, this was definitely the most interesting day Wyatt had ever experienced—and it wasn't over quite yet. Actually, not by a long shot.

They crossed back over Western Avenue and returned to its intersection near Pike Place. Wyatt looked south on the descending street and saw the skybridge. This was location where he and Mick had engaged in their discussion about the Church of One. It was also where Damon had spoken those chilling words, "*. . . there's another side to the story*". He instinctively knew those haunting words would lurk around the back of his mind, and that ultimately, he would have to deal with it. After standing on the corner for a few moments, they crossed back over Pike Place, making a beeline towards the Turkish Delight sign on the east side of the street.

The aroma wafting from the restaurant was enough to make your mouth water. The windows were open wide, and Wyatt looked in and pointed out to Mick where the alluring smell was coming from. "You see that stack of chicken on a vertical spit over there, Mick?"

"I sure do—*man, that smells good.*"

"That chicken sandwich-thingy they serve here is really good . . ." Wyatt trailed off as Mick unceremoniously proceeded into the restaurant. The angel immediately began quizzing the lady behind the counter about the Turkish Delight candy. Wyatt followed behind.

"So ma'am, can you tell me what flavors the Turkish Delight comes in?" She gave Mick the rundown. He ordered a few pieces of several different flavors, putting them all in a little white bag for him.

"You're becoming quite the expensive date, Mick," Wyatt bemoaned, paying for the candy.

"Hey, this candy was featured in some C.S. Lewis books," Mick said. "He and I have spent time having afternoon tea, talking about his writing experiences . . . oops, never mind. I'm not supposed to talk about him."

"So, you know C.S. Lewis, huh?"

"DP, dude. Sorry, I got a little carried away."

"Will you and I spend time in Heaven talking about my own writing experiences one day?" Wyatt asked.

"Perhaps, but nothing you've written thus far."

Wyatt had a quick adrenaline rush. Although he was speaking about his infrequent magazine articles, was his "Hail Mary pass" on the possibility of writing something else a part of this *mission* Mick kept speaking of? The angel's reaction sure indicated that maybe he was on track. However, he decided to let it go and not push it any further. It was past mid-afternoon by then, and they would likely be heading down towards the waterfront before too long.

After leaving the Turkish Delight restaurant, they stood on the sidewalk for a few moments, before proceeding south on Pike Place. After some general chit-chat, Mick declared that school was back in session. "Dude, let's take a moment to look at the keynote passage for our next lesson." It seemed as though Mick was now fully embracing the fact that he was clearly teaching Wyatt via some unseen curriculum.

"Sure. What do you have for me?" Wyatt asked.

"Romans 8:17."

"Didn't we just—?"

"No. This is the passage before all of the stuff we talked about earlier, starting in verse 19."

"Oh, okay. Here we go . . . *Now if we are children, then we are heirs — heirs of God and co-heirs with Christ, if indeed we share in his sufferings in order that we may also share in his glory* . . . Mick, this is a very illuminating passage."

"Yep, it sure is. So, this lesson will center on suffering, trials, and tribulations."

"I see, Sensei. So, what's your take on this Scripture?"

Grinning, Mick said, "I think we're now past the training wheels part of your agenda. Why don't you give me *your* take?"

They continued slowly walking south towards Beecher's Handmade Cheese, which was a block or so from where they were. "Well," Wyatt began, "this one seems pretty straight forward. However, I don't want to go through the whole Adam and Eve—plus original sin—causing all of this human suffering again. We've already covered that enough times today."

"No problem—you don't have to."

"So let me ask you this . . . isn't it the goal of all Christians to be *Christ-like?*"

"It is, if a Christian knows what's good for them," Mick agreed.

"Well, Christ endured pain, suffering, and death for all of mankind's sins. Without even getting into the magnitude of His sacrifice for us, if Jesus suffered like that, who are we to complain about some suffering as well? This passage says that we're 'co-heirs with Christ'. If you ask me, that's pretty good news."

"Very good," Mick said. "Now then; we'll come back to suffering in a minute, so don't forget this passage of Scripture. Let's now switch over and talk about a GPS."

"GPS? What's that an acronym for, *good people suffering?*"

"No. But that's actually a pretty good guess," Mick said. "The GPS I'm talking about is global positioning satellites."

"Oh. You mean like the ones I see people using—sometimes on their phones—to get them to their destination?"

"Yep, the very ones."

"Okay, so where are you going with this analogy?"

"To truly live a fruitful life, God has to be your GPS."

"Okay, I'll buy that . . . but is there more to your point?"

"Yep, but I have a few more things to cover before I return to this. I'll then tie it all together for you."

"It sounds to me like you're getting cryptic, again."

"Nope, I'm just building a case. For the next point, a little birdie told me that you once heard a good sermon concerning Moses and the Red Sea."

"A little birdie, huh? Now *there's* a credible source," Wyatt teased.

"Whatever, dude. Anyways, the Lord was there for His people, and directed them through the leadership of Moses; ultimately God delivered His people from bondage . . . that's the point, here."

Wyatt nodded, "As I recall, the preacher was talking about the importance of not standing still in your walk of faith, and that the Lord can't bless you if you're not moving forward—towards His will."

"Yes. He said that if you want for the Lord to part the Red Sea for you, it's an absolute necessity that you must first move *towards* it. In other words, you can't expect for God to take action to either help or bless you, unless you're charging ahead—right?"

"Yes, absolutely. As a matter of fact, the boys and I were actually working on another up-tempo song titled, 'Keep Moving'. Both the prospective song and the sermon have a similar message."

"You're on the right track here, dude. *Keep moving!*"

"Cute, Mick. Anyway, the whole idea is that Christians can't just sit around and expect for God to do everything for them. Now, I'm not talking about the concept that God helps those who help themselves, which is not in the Bible; I'm actually talking about something much *bigger* than that. What I'm really saying is that Christians shouldn't just sit on their duffs and wait for God to give them what they want—then curse Him if they don't get it."

"You're getting there," Mick said.

"Well, based on the aforementioned items, I would say that in order for us to be properly prepared for our life in eternity with Christ, we'll have to endure some suffering during our brief lives here on Earth. Actually, some Christians have to endure a lot of suffering in their life, just like Christ did."

"How true," Mick agreed.

"However, I believe it's important to not let this suffering prevent us from seeking out His will, not our own. Too often, people stop moving towards God once they don't get what they want; or, if they don't get what they want fast enough. This is where I'm out of gas. How does the GPS thing fit in?"

"Dude-ster, I'll be glad to bring this home for you. So listen up. To properly serve the Lord, what you just said is all very true. The one thing that'll be helpful for all people to know is that once you understand where the Lord wants you to go, by letting Him lead you, a person will reach that goal. However, if you don't pay attention to what His desired path is for you, you're sure to get off track."

"I'm with you so far. Please go on," Wyatt said.

"Well, you know how those GPS thingy's work, right?"

"I do—although I actually don't have one myself. Anyway, I'm still not onboard with your analogy yet."

"Then keep your ears on. Okay, those GPS navigators take you from where you are, to a specified destination. Once you program in a destination, the nice sounding lady inside the device tells you your next step in the programmed set of directions. Now then, have you ever noticed what happens if you go off route; or if you stray off of those pre-determined directions?"

"Yes," Wyatt said. "I understand that the GPS reprograms your route if you don't stay within the original directions."

"Yep. The GPS still gets you to your destination by reprogramming itself after you get off of the original route; that is, of course, if you listen to it. In the case of a saved Christian who has the Lord as their GPS, you still end up in Heaven with the King, no matter how far off the original route you stray. You see, sometimes God has to deal with re-routing His people when they wander off of His specified path. The destination doesn't change, only the *route* changes. See what I mean?"

"I do see it now. But what does that have to do with suffering and tribulations?"

"Suffering happens because it's part of living in a fallen world. Still other times, it happens because you stray off of His GPS directions. However, once you're part of His kingdom, He'll always step in and re-route your path so that you can still end up doing His will. Of course, you still have the ability to ignore God, which means you won't be of any real use to Him while you're still here on Earth."

"Interesting. I like the analogy. But still, what does this have to do with tribulations?"

"Once again, tribulations happen because of the fallen territory you live in. Remember, you all live in a corrupted world that was not part of God's original plan."

"You're right, Mick. There's no doubt that both Christians and non-Christians experience troubles."

"Yep. But sometimes, Christians experience troubles because the Lord wants you to be able to relate to your unsaved brothers and sisters."

"That seems kind of ironic, doesn't it?"

"It does, but only from the human perspective."

"I keep getting that from you," Wyatt said. "But what about those times when troubles are not by God's design?"

"Well, tribulations sometimes happen because you stray off of His course, and sometimes they happen because of the mayhem caused by Satan and company. Either way, suffering and tribulations do happen on this fallen Earth, and God does sometimes allow troubles to happen to you. However, they should ultimately bring you closer to Him, not further away. That's why you have to keep your GPS tuned to God and follow Him, so that you can hear his instructions. Either way, once you've accepted His Son, you still end up at your same destination with Him."

"So what about the *keep moving* part?"

"No matter what tribulations happen, you absolutely must keep moving towards the Red Sea—or whatever destination God has you pointed in. Think about it, dude. What would've happened if you had stopped moving forward in both your life and your faith, and had emotionally shut down after the accident that took Vanessa last year?"

Wyatt thought for a few moments. "Well, I sure wouldn't have moved all the way out here. Honestly, I probably would have fallen into complete despair; and perhaps, I would have shut down on an emotional level."

"Exactly! How can you live a fulfilled life for God if you're sitting still, mourning every night about the painful events that beset so many others as well? Dude, you kept moving forward in your life, even after losing your wife, your mother, and your dog—all in the same year. That doesn't even take into consideration the estrangement of your only son. That's enough to put most people over the edge."

"Well, I have to admit," Wyatt said. "It taught me that in the end, the Lord is all I really have."

"Amen!"

"I find it incredible that the Lord won't reject me because I understand that *He* is the only one who I can always count on. Basically, the Lord is my only real option."

"He is, indeed. God created you and loves you more than anyone else can. That's what the Lord often tries to accomplish by allowing some suffering—to bring you desperately closer to Him."

"Well Mick, you'll have me pondering this for some time. Thanks."

"No charge, dude."

By this time, they arrived at the entrance to Beecher's on Pike Place. The shop was crowded, so Mick and Wyatt quickly got in line to get their snack. In Wyatt's opinion, that was the enjoyable thing about dining at the market. There were so many wonderful choices for different kinds of food, he felt like the best way to approach meals was to eat a little here, and a little there.

They each ordered some of Beecher's famous mac and cheese, which is renowned to be the best anywhere. Mick got a small cup, but Wyatt got a larger size, because he didn't expect to eat much later on at Ivar's, which specializes in seafood—his nemesis.

After they seated themselves at the bench facing the cheese making tubs, Mick started back into their lesson as they dug into their snacks. "Anyways, let's switch over and talk about folks who seem to get picked on with tribulations."

"This'll be interesting. What's on your mind?" They watched as a young man gently stirred the cheese curds by running a rake through the gigantic tub.

"Well, since we're talking about pain, suffering, and tribulations, let me point out something that you may not have ever considered before."

"I'm all ears . . . man—this is good grub, huh?"

"It sure is. Anyways, it's important to remember that perhaps the biggest irony of life on the current Earth, is that God will often test His favorite people to see how strong their faith is. Oftentimes, that draws people closer to Him . . . and sometimes, it drives them further away. Either way, it's important to remember that Jesus is always there."

"What's that got to do with folks who seem to get picked on with suffering and tribulations?" Wyatt asked.

"Okay, let me answer your question with a question."

"Oh brother—go ahead."

"Regarding your travels in the trucking business . . . although you travelled all over the country, you primarily worked in the southeast, right?"

"Yes, I sure did."

"Well, based on the folks who you met over the years, would you say it was a diverse cross-section of people?"

"Absolutely. I enjoy the fact that many of the people who I've met in the trucking business are very down to Earth. In general, I mean."

"Right. That's why the King chose that profession for you. You see, He knew the kind of person who you would evolve into, and that you'd rather deal with more of a down-home person, than a starched shirt, dark suit, and red-tie finance type."

Wyatt nodded, "You know, the latter group is probably the kind of people who Danny deals with in the finance area of business."

"It is, but that's because Danny is wired differently than you . . . and that's also by God's design. Anyways, in all of your travels, and with all of the people who you've met over the years, who do you think depends more on God—folks with a lot of stuff, or folks with very little?"

"Hmmm . . . folks with very little, I suppose . . . what's your point?"

"I'm getting there, dude-ster. Now then, poor folks generally have less earthly possessions than other people, right?"

"Right."

"And, you're well aware of the financial plight of several groups of people, like those who live in small towns, and in poor urban areas of big cities, right?"

"Sure. As it relates to material possessions, some groups of people seem to have a harder go of it."

"Well, in general, who do you think is closer to God—people who have had to struggle, or people who have lots of stuff?"

"That's a pretty big generalization, but people who have had to struggle seem to be more apt to cling to God, because of—"

"Because of their *tribulations!* Think about it. A person who has had very few tribulations in life, is often less inclined to depend on Jesus Christ—unless they've already gone through a bunch of troubles."

"I see where you're going with this. Are you saying that people who struggle are more likely to have a stronger relationship with God?"

"In general, yes. Now, please read me *James 2:5.*"

"Okay . . . *Listen to me, dear brothers and sisters. Hasn't God chosen the poor in this world to be rich in faith? Aren't they the ones who will inherit the Kingdom he promised to those who love him?*"

"So what does that passage say to you?" Mick asked.

Wyatt had a quizzical look pass across his face, "That God blesses some groups of people with suffering because He loves them?"

"Yes. Why do you think the Lord has allowed tribulations with so many different kinds of people? Every single era of human history is replete with oppressed and poor people. Like I said, one of life's great ironies is that the Lord sometimes allows suffering and tribulations to bring His people closer to Him. Admittedly though, suffering and tribulations are also sometimes God's way of getting your attention."

"Hmmm . . . so, are you going to get into the *love of money is the root of all evil,* thing?"

"No, not now," Mick said. "But clearly, we're sniffing around the perimeter of that issue. Yes, money and affluence can dull your senses to God—*but they don't have to.*"

"I agree."

"You know, the truest measure of financial success before the Throne of God, is when a person can have money and possessions, but still passionately love the Lord by keeping Him ahead of those things. If you've experienced any financial success, using that affluence to enjoy your lives and promote the Kingdom of God is the way to go . . . but let's not forget this—the Lord doesn't choose for everyone on the current Earth to have material wealth."

"I understand. But, let's also not forget that folks who do have material wealth should embrace the genuine joy at giving back to God and His people. All of the stuff on Earth is going to be replaced one day by the New Heaven and New Earth anyway."

"You're right on track with that," Mick agreed. They remained quiet for a few moments.

"Do you have any good examples of people who have endured a lot of troubles, yet still maintained their faith by continuing to forge ahead?"

"I do," Mick said. "How about King David and Abraham Lincoln?"

"This sounds interesting."

Mick finished chewing a bite of mac-and-cheese before beginning his explanation. "King David did a lot of bad stuff during his life, but God still loved him so much—because David loved God so much. However, every time David fell, it was because he lusted after his own way at that moment, rather than loving God's way."

"I believe that a lot of people do that."

"I agree . . . and . . . have you ever looked at how many times that Abraham Lincoln failed before he became arguably the most important President in American history?"

"Yes, ole Abe had a ton of bad things happen to him, including when he was assassinated not long after the end of the War Between the States."

"In reality, sometimes you get your reward in Heaven, instead of down here," Mick said.

Wyatt nodded, "So, tribulations in this temporary life are a way of building a Christian's character?"

"If you're wise and look at them that way, then yes. Not only that, but tribulations can also help you build a stronger love for God. Listen Wyatt, there are only two kinds of people in this world—members of the kingdom of light, and members of the kingdom of darkness. That's it. You are either of the Lord, or you're against Him."

"I can't argue that point."

"And another thing, your true family is not necessarily the people who you're related to. If you really examine it, you're going to spend eternity with your fellow Christian brothers and sisters—those folks are your *real* family. When you get to Heaven, your genetic blood lines won't matter anymore, because all of you will be heirs with Christ."

"So you're saying—what?" Wyatt asked.

"That your real family in Christ is not necessarily the people who you're actually related to. Your real family is the body of Christ."

Wyatt took a sip of his lemon soda, pondering Mick's latest revelation. "I think I understand you now. However, that's not the general sentiment most people have about who their family is."

"My friend, being a follower of Christ is counter-intuitive to many prevalent thoughts in your society. That's just one of the many things that don't seem to make any sense to people, until they begin to look at things from the Lord's perspective, instead of their own."

"That's interesting. Now I understand why one of my friends considers me far more a part of his family than his own father," Wyatt said.

"I know who you're talking about, Wyatt. Sadly, his father was a deceiver," Mick said.

"I suppose you're right . . . so anyway, what else do you have?"

"Please turn to *1 Peter 4:13,* and I'll lay some more angelic words of wisdom on you."

Wyatt looked up to see if anyone else heard Mick's comment. However, the other patrons in the restaurant seemed to be more interested in the incredible aroma of panini sandwiches and baked cheese. "I take it this angel stuff is a secret, right?"

"Of course it is. And don't worry—no one's paying any attention to us," Mick said coolly.

"Whew. Good deal . . . anyway, here's your verse . . . *But rejoice that you participate in the sufferings of Christ, so that you may be overjoyed when his glory is revealed . . .* Mick, for most people, this concept just doesn't make any sense."

"Yeah, it goes directly against your sinful, self-centered human nature. It's just like when some new Christians get all jacked up about becoming a *new person* when they first get saved—then start judging others. You and I both know that being a solid citizen of the kingdom *clearly* doesn't include the judging of others. Quite to the contrary, it does mean being Christ-like and always loving, which is often at odds with your natural, human instincts . . . no offense."

Wyatt sighed, "I see. Perhaps churches should emphasize this and teach each person to work on themselves, so they can be a better example for others. Instead, sometimes you see some new Christians getting a little sanctimonious."

"Yep, that happens sometimes. However, many church leaders have begun to teach a far more appropriate brand of evangelism."

"How's that?"

"Speak the truth and live it, but don't try to cram Jesus down people's throats—that's exactly what the enemy, Satan, wants. Basically, I think you need to stay balanced in your witness to the world."

"Go on," Wyatt said.

"Well, what I mean is—don't try to scare people with too much hellfire and brimstone, but also don't preach that people won't ever have tribulations. People are going to have troubles, since that's part of your current life; even the Apostles suffered greatly for their faith. Balancing God's grace and His judgment—which is the *whole* Gospel—that's what a basic understanding of the Bible is all about."

As they were finishing up their snacks, they continued to enjoy the cheese making show from behind the glass directly in front of them. Although the market was still at full tilt, it was also beginning to have that general feeling that it was in the early stages of winding down. When they were finished, Wyatt asked, "Mick, do you mind if we start walking again? My legs are getting stiff."

"Sure thing, dude." They got up and promptly exited Beecher's. Once outside, they turned east on Pine Street, heading up the hill towards First Avenue. The Seattle's Best cafe was on their right, and both Sur La Table and The Inn at the Market were on their left. As they walked, Wyatt asked, "Do you have anything more to add on suffering?"

"Yep, we need to look at one more passage. Let's take a look at *1 Peter 1:6-7.*"

"No problem," Wyatt said. By this time, they had reached the top of the hill at the corner of Pine and First Avenue. They stood there for a moment as Wyatt read aloud, "Okay . . .

"In this you greatly rejoice, though now for a little while you may have had to suffer grief in all kinds of trials. These have come so that your faith – of greater worth than gold, which perishes even though refined by fire – may be proved genuine and may result in praise, glory and honor when Jesus Christ is revealed.

"Well, it appears this passage really sums up what we've been talking about."

"It's funny how it works out that way, huh?" Mick asked, grinning. "Anyways, I only have a couple of more items on tap for this lesson." They continued to walk south along First Avenue until they reached the corner of First and Pike Place. From there, the view into the market was quite famous, with the large "Public Market Center" sign in clear view.

"So what's left Mick? I wouldn't mind heading down to the waterfront."

"Just a few bullet points. How about if I start firing away?"

"Sure thing—shoot . . . oops, no pun intended."

"Whatever, dude," Mick said, grinning. "Anyway, regarding the whole God as your GPS thing, remember that setting goals can be a very productive thing to do. However, it can also go too far."

"How so?"

"Well, in the secular world, many people have written books all about the importance of setting goals—blah, blah, blah! That often goes too far, and heads people towards their own goals—to the exclusion of the Lord."

"Do you have any Scripture to back that up?" Wyatt asked.

"I do. *James 4:15* says . . . *Instead, you ought to say, 'If it is the Lord's will, we will live and do this or that' . . .*"

"I see," Wyatt said.

"Just remember," Mick began, "it's okay to set goals like where to go to college, what technical trade to train for, and what kind of job to go after, etc. However, too many of those business books forget to mention—*or intentionally don't tell people*—that sometimes God intervenes and changes your GPS route towards Him. Listen—God has a right to change your goals, if He knows that it's best for you."

"That seems like good advice. So what else do you have?"

"Sometimes, events happen in your life like a series of stepping stones, and sometimes He plants you in one place for a long time. Either way, God's will is what's important."

"Okay, but I'm going to need a little more than that."

"Fine, let's look at professional athletes. Take the example of a highly paid rookie who signs a big contract, and then blows out his knee during his first season and can't play anymore. Is his life over? Of course not! In this scenario, a professional sport was only a *stepping stone* for him—or her, for that matter. Now, take that same rookie who plays for twenty years and ends up going to the hall of fame. Is that person leading a better life than the one in the first scenario? No—it's only *different*. The second scenario basically had a different path for the rookie—one that God kept him or her on. Am I making any sense here?"

"You're getting there."

"Just remember, things happen in God's time, not yours. You folks don't always know what's best for you, but the Lord does. It's essential that you always stay faithful to Him."

"Of course."

"No, dude. Everyone agrees with that, but they don't necessarily walk the walk."

"Why do you say that?"

"I think that we're past the point where I'm going to have you read the verses we're discussing. I'll now recite to you *Matthew 25:21 . . . His master replied, Well done, good and faithful servant! You have been faithful with a few things; I will put you in charge of many things. Come and share your master's happiness! . . .* Do you know that passage?"

"I do," Wyatt said. "Are you saying that God will entrust people with bigger things after they've done well with smaller things?"

"That's it!"

"Like turning to Him during suffering and tribulations?"

"Once again, spoken like a true prodigy. Are you about ready to head down to the waterfront?"

"Sure thing, Mick."

And with that, it was time to for Mick and Wyatt to venture beyond the fringes of the market once again and move into the next phase of their eventful day. The engaging confines of the Pike Place Market would have to temporarily take a back seat, as the coffee-loving angel and his newest student moved towards the culmination of their very interesting day.

PART 3

MISSION . . . POSSIBLE

16

TWO FATHERS

Moving westward along Pike Place towards the Public Market Center sign and the hub of activity once again, Mick and Wyatt quietly enjoyed a little bit of afternoon sun peeking through the clouds. Like a steady bloodstream flowing steadily throughout the market's vibrant body, they always seemed to end up back at the heart of the ancient emporium. The late afternoon brought with it some slightly cooler temperatures, and because it was October, it would soon turn chilly.

"Well Mick, don't keep me in the dark for too long," Wyatt said. "So tell me—what's the next learning module?"

Mick smiled, slightly nodding his head. *My newest pupil is advancing through his lessons quite well,* the angel thought. "Okie-dokie . . . since we talked about two sons and two mothers earlier today, we're now gonna talk about *two fathers.*"

"It sounds to me like we're covering all the bases."

"Yep, we sure are. Anyways, let's head inside for a minute."

They walked back into the market and past the flying fish once again, before heading down the stairs towards the Pike Place hill climb. Mick had to make a quick restroom stop, so Wyatt reclaimed his spot along the railing where he had waited for the angel after lunch.

What happened next was one of the more bone chilling moments in Wyatt Hunter's life. After living a life full of watching countless scary movies, he began to feel like he was about to play a role in one. Seemingly out of nowhere, a menacing voice asked, "Have you given any thought to what I said earlier today on the skybridge?" The male voice was deep and confident, yet cold and disingenuous, as if feigning courtesy.

Wyatt spun around and found himself staring straight into the baby blue eyes of Damon. Being the proverbial "handsome devil," Damon was smiling and trying to appear friendly. Wyatt's goose bumps must have looked like mountains on his neck and forearms, but he was a fast thinker. Without hesitation, Wyatt pulled up the left sleeve on his Steelers sweatshirt and showed off his cross tattoo.

"Yes I did, Damon. But what I really want to know is—*how do you like this?*" As Damon scanned his arm, Wyatt looked carefully into the demon's eyes.

Surprisingly, Damon nodded his head with approval, "Well Wyatt, that's an impressive looking bicep. However, I'm afraid I've seen guys in better shape than you . . . no offense."

Leave it to a demon, Wyatt thought, *to give an insulting compliment.* "I'm talking about the *Cross* pretty boy. What do you think about that?" Although Damon continued to smile, Wyatt sensed that it had become a little more difficult for him to maintain his put-on manners.

"Jesus Christ was no stranger to me, my friend," Damon said. "If you ask me, he was a pretty incredible guy."

"Is that a fact?"

"Sure it is. Historically, Jesus did a lot of good things around the Middle East. In truth, during his day, Jesus helped to care for a lot of people. I'll have to give him credit for that."

"I thought you guys didn't like Jesus," Wyatt said.

Like a cracked dam getting ready to burst, Damon replied, "Yeah well, like I said. He was an okay guy I suppose . . . but I'm afraid that's all he was—*a regular man!*"

Before Wyatt could respond, a thundering command came from their right, *"Move along jackass!!!"* They both turned and saw Mick stomping right towards them.

Damon immediately began back peddling. As a parting shot, the demon sneered, "Just remember *this* Wyatt Hunter—the divinity of Jesus Christ was a myth. *My master and commander has the true power in this world!* Look around! Your god is nowhere to be found down here, *because he doesn't care about any of you!*" The reverb from the demon's voice sounded a haunting echo in the semi-enclosed space.

"I'm fixing to stomp you, boy!" Mick bellowed, and Damon quickly made his retreat up the stairs; back into the main level of the market. A few passers-by heard Mick's loud comments, but they quickly went back to their own business as soon as Damon disappeared.

After a few stunned moments Wyatt said, *"My hero."* He used a falsetto voice in an attempt to provide some levity.

"No charge, dude."

Wyatt was surprised at the lack of anger in Mick. "Mr. G.Q. seemed to back away from you pretty quickly—I'm actually impressed," he said.

Mick's next comment jolted Wyatt quickly back into a serious mode. "One of the underlying reasons why I'm here today is to help prepare you for battle. You see, it's of paramount importance that you learn how to fight and survive against those demonic scumbags, because I may not always be present to get your back."

Wyatt strongly sensed that Mick was preparing him to survive the spiritual warfare that was on his horizon. "You've done a great job, Mick," he said.

"As much as it may pain you to hear this, Wyatt, I still have much more to teach you after today. I suppose you're kinda stuck with me for this marathon we're fixin' to run in together."

Wyatt had a huge sense of relief pass through him. Although he didn't had very much time to think about it so far, he would sure hate to never see his brand new friend again. "I'll do whatever you want me to, Mick."

"This is not about what I want; it's about what the Lord wants."

Wyatt looked directly into Mick's eyes for a moment and they exchanged an unspoken communication of mutual appreciation that was special. Then Wyatt broke up what he thought was a semi-girly moment with, "Anyway, let's get moving." They continued with some idle chit-chat as they descended down the Pike Place hill climb. After a few minutes, Wyatt snapped them back on course. "Mick, which 'father' do you wanna talk about first?"

"During this session, the two fathers that we'll discuss are your own father, Earl Hunter, and *Our* Father, Who art in Heaven. Oh, and, as an extra special bonus, I even have a few comments about your country's founding fathers . . . it's *padre time,* dude."

Wyatt chuckled, "Alrighty then. You know, I guess I kind of expected that we'd talk about my dad, today. He and I haven't spoken in quite some time now . . . and you don't seem to wanna leave any of my emotional stones unturned."

"You should've been a brain surgeon," Mick said. "Anyways, your father Earl is a very lonely, distrustful, and cynical man. But, the Lord truly loves him, just like all of His children . . . check that, since Earl is one of His proverbial lost sheep, God loves him even more."

After he left Wyatt's mother Abbie, Earl Hunter moved from Georgia to his home state of Massachusetts. He ultimately ended up in Edgartown on Martha's Vineyard. The divorce happened when Wyatt was very young, and Earl had only made time for a dozen or so visits with his son over the years. Unfortunately, he rarely ever called Wyatt anymore. These days, he wasn't getting any younger, and he lived the life of a recluse.

Directly after leaving Jefferson, Georgia, Earl moved back to his hometown of Peabody, Massachusetts. Several years after that, he moved to Martha's Vineyard. For many years, he owned a boat charter company on the Vineyard, among many other businesses throughout his varied careers in business. However, no one in his small family really knew what he did with his time anymore.

"I gave up a long time ago trying to have a relationship with dad," Wyatt said sadly. "He's actually only seen Danny two or three times . . . if that often," he mused.

"Right. I understand. Well, you never know what might happen. Maybe that'll change."

"If it does, then it does. If not . . . well, I guess I should continue praying for dad. What I'm most concerned about is that he somehow never reached the point of salvation, and he won't ever talk about it. I do believe that he abandoned the pursuit of the Lord many years ago, and he's now in his seventies. It's sad, because he won't live forever on this Earth."

"I understand," Mick said, "and yes, you should continue to pray for Earl, as well as for the salvation of all of those who don't know our heavenly Father."

"You know, dad even seems to feel some hostility towards the Lord. To be honest, I'm not really sure where all of that anger at God comes from."

Although Mick knew the answer to that perplexing question, he was unable to explain it to Wyatt at this time. He generalized, "That sometimes happens when people can't seem to reconcile why they're seemingly bound in an earthly prison, with no direct contact with their Creator and Savior. They feel a misplaced sense of unrighteousness in the Lord, because they think, *hey, I didn't personally do anything to deserve this.* From a human perspective, I can understand that. However, everyone should remember that all of you are here, *only* because the Lord wanted it to be so."

"Meaning—?"

"Earl wouldn't have been in existence without the Lord's desire for it to happen. As you well know, things don't happen randomly in this world. But rather, all things have the guiding hand of the Lord behind them."

"True. Anyway, my dad is apparently angry with God, and seems to resent anyone who has a relationship with Him. I think he may even think that people of faith are actually stupid."

"Well Wyatt, like I said, maybe we'll be doing something about that before too long."

"You know something Mick? It seems to me that many people like to criticize Christians for when they fall off the path and make mistakes. I understand that sometimes the Lord is teaching the sanctimonious Christians to be humble and not condescending in presenting a witness for Christ, but—"

"Whoa there, dude! Don't get sucked into that demon marketing vacuum," Mick said. "Every one of you makes mistakes. But, it's the Christians who are usually under a microscope. Much of that is plain old smart marketing from Satan and company. In fact, that's one of their absolute favorite anti-God marketing campaigns."

"What, the old, *hey look at those hypocritical Christians screwing up thing?*"

"You got it." They walked in silence for a few moments.

"It's not a real fair assessment, is it?" Wyatt asked.

"Nope, it sure isn't. You need to remember this—you're not necessarily a hypocrite because you set your bar high and try to achieve lofty goals— only to fail once in a while. That's hogwash. Hey, is the overweight person who tries to lose weight, but caves in and eats a pack of Twinkies; is that person a *hypocrite* just because they failed?"

"No, I suppose they're not. I see what you're saying."

"Actually, all of you should adhere to *Romans 12:1-2* by making your bodies a living sacrifice to the Lord," Mick said.

"I know that passage . . . and that makes sense. Anyway, getting back to the subject of hypocrites," Wyatt said. "Isn't it also true that there are some hypocrites in Christianity? It seems that we've already touched on this a couple of times today, but I'm not sure about—"

"Yes," Mick interrupted, "but just because an occasional Christian is a hypocrite, doesn't mean they *all* are. A great example to support this would be the subject of giving to your church. On the rare occasions when a church has someone abuse their finances, you can't logically assume that all—most—or even several churches have the same problem. That should never be used as an excuse for someone not to give to the church. In the same way, when someone presents a bad example and makes a mistake, it should also never be used to classify Christians as hypocrites."

"It seems that the enemy has sold an incorrect bill of goods to the world, that if someone openly prays, then they're likely a zealot and a hypocrite," Wyatt said. "That same, flawed line of thinking would say that if you give to your church or Christian charities, then some evil hypocrite is stealing the money so they can go buy themselves a new Cadillac."

"That's correct, dude. You should always give to the Lord and allow Him to worry about the rest. God definitely knows a giving heart, and He does indeed see everything. Not only that, but following Christ is really all about letting God do the heavy lifting. Don't forget what *Matthew 11:30* says . . . *For my yoke is easy and my burden is light."*

By this time, they had worked their way through a maze of ramps, steps, and a skybridge across Western Avenue, continuing their descent towards the waterfront. Mick continued, "Okay buddy, to stay on topic, I'm now gonna read *John 20:17* to you."

"Do I have a choice?" Wyatt asked.

Mick shot him a *dummy up* look . . . *"Jesus said, Do not hold on to me, for I have not yet returned to the Father. Go instead to my brothers and tell them, I am returning to my Father and your Father, to my God and your God* . . . How do you like that one?"

"That's pretty topical, which is no surprise from you. Hey, can you recite that in Aramaic?"

"Sure thing. How about if I—?"

"Never mind," Wyatt interrupted. "I was just checking."

Mick chuckled before continuing, "Anyways, that passage says a lot about your relationship with God, doesn't it?" They finally arrived at the bottom of the hill climb and proceeded towards the walkway which crossed Alaskan Way. To the right, a block or so away, was Wyatt's place; he looked over towards his condo and wondered how things were at home. They stood for a moment at the crosswalk, waiting for the "Walk" light to come on. Mick then snapped Wyatt back to reality. "Earth to Wyatt . . . ."

"Sorry, Mick. Where were we?"

"You were going to tell me what you thought about that passage in the book of John."

"Oh yeah . . . I think it reveals some significant things about our relationship with God as our Father."

"Like what, for instance?"

"Well, like the reference to *my father and your father*. To me, that means that God is the Father to all of us."

When the walk light came on, they crossed over Alaskan Way and took an immediate left. They quickly passed the Seattle Aquarium on their right, continuing with their southerly walk along the busy waterfront road.

"Right you are my friend, God is the father to all of us, including us angels."

"Mick, it's astounding to me that anyone can be so blind that they can't see the Lord's awesome majesty, and honor Him accordingly. You know, I remember something interesting from back in high school, when a good buddy of mine and I were watching one of those court TV type shows."

"You mean like, *Judge Whoever?*"

"Yeah. I can't remember the name of the show. Anyway, as I recall, some Elvis impersonating guy was getting a divorce, and the judge was trying to figure out what to do. So believe it or not, this guy had on full Elvis gear, including sideburns—*in court!* Well, when someone made a slightly disparaging comment about Elvis, this idiot actually piped up and said, *you can't talk about the King that way!* Of course, my buddy and I were shocked, and we laughed our butts off."

"I see," Mick said. "So . . . are you wondering why someone would impersonate a celebrity?"

"No. I'm now wondering why a celebrity would be defended so passionately by someone, and why God typically gets ignored by so many others. Since God is the Creator of everything and died for our sins, the Lord should be our hero—not any person, place, or animal."

"Ahhh," Mick said. "So, you're saying that TV show snippet is a microcosm of the overall lack of respect for our heavenly Father?"

"Yes Mick . . . and don't think I haven't noticed that you're doing less-and-less talking, and drawing more-and-more out of me."

The angel chuckled, "It's just part of your basic training, my good man."

"Yes sir, drill instructor," Wyatt joked. "But please, don't ask me to drop and give you fifty. I'm not sure that I can do more than two." Mick grinned and nodded at this.

As they walked, they passed by several piers with many different types of shops. There were places to get everything from smoked salmon, ice cream, boat tour charters, a sports shop, a bakery, souvenirs, and many more things, including good coffee.

"Isn't that the place where you and Charlene met recently?" Wyatt asked, passing a Starbucks on their right.

"It was. However, I'm afraid that wasn't our first meeting."

Wyatt shrugged, "Why doesn't that surprise me?"

"Listen, we'll get into all of that back at your place after dinner, my friend. Trust me; everything will then fall into place for you. Don't forget—we need to call Danny when we get there."

At hearing this, Wyatt felt a warm wave of joy. "So, do you have any other Scriptures that are relevant to our chat about fathers?" he asked.

Mick nodded, "I do—*Psalm 89:26 . . . He will call out to me, You are my Father, my God, the Rock my Savior . . .* I must say, that sure is a great way to speak about the Lord. Just like King David."

After walking a little way further, they finally arrived at Ivar's. The whiff of fried seafood and french fries suddenly hit their noses with an assault-like efficiency. It was a little early for dinner, so there weren't many people standing in line at the outside, quick serve restaurant. Wyatt strongly preferred casual dining over a more formal atmosphere, and he was quite sure that Mick didn't care where they ate—just as long as he got his chowder

Along with Mick's clam chowder and a three piece fish and chips, Wyatt ordered three servings of french fries and a cole slaw.

"Geez dude, I don't think eating that many fries is real healthy," Mick chided. "At least down here on Earth, it's not."

"Very cute. Actually—*wise guy*—most of them are for tossing to the sea gulls." When their order was ready, they proceeded to their left and walked down to the covered patio area. Finding a nice table off on its own, they sat down, said thanks to the Lord for His provision, and proceeded to enjoy the good food and pleasant atmosphere.

After a few minutes of intermittent silence and idle chit chat, Mick said, "We need to get back into something we touched on earlier."

"Which is—?"

"Your old job of salesman in the trucking business. I do know that you spent a lot of time on the road. But I've been wondering if you ever felt cheated out of time at home because of this?"

"Yes and no."

"Whaddaya mean?"

"Well, I made a nice living by going out into the world and seeing customers and independent contractors. While I'm basically a *home body,* I worked hard at keeping a good balance between success at work and success at home. In other words, I didn't travel too much—or too little."

Mick nodded, "Balance between the two is like walking a tight rope in your society. For what it's worth, it seems to me like you did a good job of producing for your employers, while still being an involved father and a good husband."

"Thanks, Mick. I guess the important thing for any traveling professional is to not go too far in either direction; to stay on the tight rope and keep your balance, so to speak."

"It is. You certainly could've taken non-travelling jobs, but because of your personal work experience, you wouldn't have been able to provide as much for your family. But more importantly, the Lord was preparing you for something by sending you out into the world."

"Well, I suppose that each man or woman ultimately needs to make their own decision regarding this issue," Wyatt said. "Allowing God to direct your path on this subject is critical to making the right decision. The Holy Spirit will absolutely show you the right way."

"Good point . . . and speaking of the Lord, have you come to realize that all along, He's been guiding your path by sending you to see people all over the country for a reason? I've been dropping hints on you all day about this particular point."

"Oh, I've been hearing you, but I'm not real sure what you mean."

"Well, it's no accident that God had you do what you did for a living. That's what I mean. Like I said before, He made you to be exactly who you are for a reason, just like He does for all of His children. Folks get all discombobulated when they try to be someone other than who God designed you to be."

Wyatt dipped a french fry in ketchup before tossing it in his mouth. "For example?"

"Well for one, how about your cousin Frank?" Frank Hunter was the only son of Billy Hunter, Wyatt's uncle. Billy Hunter was the younger brother of Wyatt's father, Earl. Wyatt loved his uncle Billy, who had a strong heart for the Lord. So did Frank.

"So what about him?"

"Well, I know that Frank and his wife Nadine have had trouble conceiving, haven't they?"

"Sadly, yes. What's your point?"

"My point is this—yielding to God's will. Frank and Nadine have tortured themselves with trying to have a child, and have almost crossed the line of being angry at God for Him not giving them one. Unfortunately, this kind of thing happens to a lot of couples."

"Are you saying that people shouldn't keep trying to have children when they're having difficulty?"

"No. Of course not. Your own mother, Miss Abbie, had a heckuva time having you, didn't she?"

That's true, Wyatt thought. When he was growing up, Abbie told Wyatt on several occasions that she had to do several odd, doctor-prescribed exercises during her pregnancy, just to be able to have him. Sadly, she had lost a child during pregnancy two years before him, and that had really broken her heart.

"Yes, I suppose she did have a hard time," Wyatt said.

"The point is this—when you keep running into brick walls in any situation—whether it's trying to get pregnant, find a job, or decide what to do with your life, all too often, people blame God and turn away from Him. Remember, the Lord will always give you an answer; but it may not always be the one you want to hear. As you well know, sometimes, God's answer is a plain old *no*. All of you would be well advised to accept the fact that the Lord always knows what's best for you."

"Although that's very difficult to do, I know you're right," Wyatt said.

Nodding, Mick continued, "Miss Abbie never questioned God about having you. She completely surrendered to Him, and went about doing all that she could to bring you into this world. Amazingly, she even prayed that you would go directly to the Lord, if it was His will that you go straight to Heaven—just like the child she lost before you."

"Geez, that's really heavy . . . but what does that have to do with my old travelling job?"

"It doesn't really; it has more to do with the frustrations of Frank and Nadine. At some point they need to at least consider the possibility that God has a different plan for them. If they do that, they just may get what they asked for."

"Hmmm," Wyatt mumbled slowly. "I guess I never thought about it like that."

"Once again—*no charge, dude.*"

Wyatt shook his head, "By the way, what do you mean by this thing you keep saying—*no charge?* You're becoming quite an expensive date, you know. I'm pretty sure that none of these businesses are willing to accept a good-will payment from me—*they want real money!*"

"I understand, my friend. However, I sure am worth it, huh?!?!?"

After a few moments, "Yes Mick, you're worth it," Wyatt said.

They continued with their meal. Slowly but surely, both of them began to toss french fries to the dozens of sea gulls around the area. When they were through with eating all of their food—except the fries—they stood up and leaned on the railing, which ran along the inlet of water from Elliott Bay. Several sea gulls were perched on the various railings in the L-shaped seating areas, while many others had landed in the water, eagerly awaiting any scraps.

"Wyatt my good man, that was some excellent chowder," Mick said.

"I'm sure *you* think so."

"By the way, the whole point I was trying to make a few minutes ago is that God has a special plan for each and every one of you. For all of your life up until now, He's been preparing you for what's next."

"So tell me . . . what *is* next?"

"Actually, I'll give you the full breadth of your mission after we call Danny and visit with Miss Charlene. I've already told you, the stakes in the cultural battles here in America have greatly increased, and the God-haters are really coming after people of faith. You've been chosen to play a relatively small, but important, role in this battle. Chill out, and let me lead you through this thing. I promise that it'll all turn out well."

"If you say so . . . ." They continued to toss fries to the birds. Mick became amused when a particularly bold and portly bird approached him from the railing to his left. The gull continued to move closer to the angel as he continued luring him closer with food. Mick started laughing heartily when the chubby bird was almost up to within reach of his fry tossing hand. The child-like innocence of the angel's personality was very apparent, and it was at once surprising and enjoyable for Wyatt to witness.

When they were out of food to give to the "poor little birds," they worked their way back up to the sidewalk on Alaskan Way, heading north, towards Wyatt's condo.

By this time, the sun was beginning to set in the western sky, just above the waterfront. Balanced between the purple-colored clouds and Elliott Bay, were the stunningly beautiful Olympic Mountains, which stood as rugged sentinels in the darkening landscape. The temperature continued to slowly decline, but it was not uncomfortable at all. As they walked north along the waterfront, angel and human basked in the beautiful October sunset on their left.

Mick and Wyatt continued to chat as they soaked in the festive atmosphere of the lively-but-not-intrusive commerce on Alaskan Way. This only accentuated the unique combination of God's beautiful creation, coupled with mankind's development of the downtown waterfront. Wyatt remained very relaxed as they walked, blissfully unaware that their day-long saga was about to hit its crescendo.

They walked for a few blocks and continued with their idle chit-chat. At this point, they were approaching the aquarium, when Mick said, "Okay, we only have one more subject to cover before we get back to your place."

"Geez, what we haven't covered yet?"

"Do the 'founding fathers' ring any bells?"

"That's it. Well, what do you have for me?"

"Are you familiar with those folks at Wallbuilders and their DVD titled, *America's Godly Heritage?*"

"I sure am. When I first watched that video, I was quite angry about the pack of lies it exposed regarding our founding fathers, and their real intentions towards the separation of church and state issue."

"Well then, as you already know, the founding fathers of the United States were largely men of faith. And the country which they fought so hard to establish was one based on freedom *of* religion, not freedom *from* religion."

"True enough. It seems to me, the truth needs to be more heavily emphasized in our society. I often hear of many misconceptions and untruths about the founding fathers' beliefs towards faith and religion."

"How true," Mick agreed.

They arrived at the entrance to the Seattle Aquarium, just as it was turning 5:30 pm. Usually, admission was stopped at five, but the aquarium was still open until around six. The exhibits were still open, and since Wyatt was both a regular attendee and an infrequent volunteer, the staff allowed Mick and Wyatt inside for a few minutes.

After walking into the massive entry hall, they bee-lined over to the "Window on Washington Waters" exhibit. The massive aquarium was huge—20 feet high by 40 feet wide. Ambient sounds were coming from the exhibits further into the aquarium, as well as the voices of the workers and volunteers beginning their shut down process for the day. Again, it was just the angel and his student.

"Wyatt, I believe that it's high-time for Christians take your country back for the Lord. Correctly reporting on what the founding fathers thought about their faith in Christ is only one of the many battles in this huge cultural war. Truthfully, there's still much work to be done. To accomplish this, the Lord will need devoted warriors who'll fight against the evil demagoguery in the various media sources, which have clearly been influenced by Satan."

"I see. Can I assume that telling the truth about our founding fathers is just one of the many things that need to be clarified and reported correctly?"

"Exactly! Well, that's actually all that I have on this for now," Mick said abruptly. "Are you about ready to roll?"

Wyatt shrugged, "Sure." They stood looking at the various swimming fish in the beautiful exhibit for a few moments in silence. Then he said, "Okay Mick, let's head on home."

"Sounds like a plan."

Wyatt thanked the aquarium staff and they made their exit. Mick and Wyatt crossed back over to the east side of Alaskan Way, turning north towards Wyatt's condo. As the sun continued its retreat into the mouth of the mountains, Wyatt thought about getting a fire started in the cozy fireplace at Charlene's condo. He missed his dog Baby, and was looking forward to going home after an unbelievable day. Although he wasn't exactly sure what was going to happen next, he did feel an odd sense of anticipation. Unbeknownst to him, a big surprise was waiting for him at Charlene's, and it wasn't just the adulation of his loving dog.

17

THE AMERICAN DREAM?

As they continued their stroll towards home, Mick proceeded to describe to Wyatt the exact way that he liked his coffee, which differed at certain times of the day. He explained how he fixed his afternoon cup differently than he fixed his morning cup, and several other variations. Wyatt was unsure of when he was speaking about coffee in Heaven, and when he was referring to coffee on Earth. He thought that Mick almost seemed to be distracting him for some reason. It was either that, or Mick simply loved to talk about coffee. *Perhaps it's both,* he thought.

They passed several joggers along the way. Many of them were decked out in sweat pants and comfortable looking fleece sweatshirts. Several other people were out walking their dogs, trying to gobble up some of the remaining daylight, which was quickly disappearing.

When they arrived at the condo's security entrance, Wyatt used his key to get them inside. Before they headed up the stairs to the second floor, Mick suggested, "Hey, why don't you give Danny a quick call to see if he's home yet. If so, then we'll call him back when we get inside. We might need to take Baby for a walk, and we don't want to miss the kid."

Wyatt sighed, nervously, "Okay. What's his cell number?" Mick gave it to him. Wyatt dialed the number as they began to make their way upstairs. The connection took a few moments to start ringing, and by that time, Mick and Wyatt arrived on the second floor landing. They then proceeded into the hallway, towards Charlene's place. The phone was on its third ring by the time they arrived at her doorway. Noticeably, Wyatt could hear the distant ringing of another phone as he knocked on Charlene's front door.

What happened next became an emotional blur to Wyatt Hunter. Charlene answered the door with her usual glowing smile, and Baby quickly started jumping on Wyatt. With his cell phone still on his ear, Wyatt could now hear the loud ringing of another cell phone in the living room. He looked over towards the couch, and with complete and utter shock, he saw his son Danny standing there, wearing a warm smile.

"You can hang up now, dad," Danny said, holding up his cell phone. Wyatt fumbled to hang up his own phone. Before a shock wave of the unexpected sight of his son hit him, Charlene gently took the phone out of Wyatt's hands. Baby instinctively and immediately bounced over to Mick and jumped up into his arms.

"Son? I thought—?"

"You can thank Mick for this, dad."

Wyatt whirled around and looked deeply in to Mick's gentle eyes. The expression staring back at him was one of a quiet, cowboy-like strength, coupled with the expression of joy that only a true giver has when they're able to help others. After a few stunned moments, Wyatt said, "I thought you said we were only going to call—?"

"What I *said* was this—that *Danny was expecting a call from us,* and I didn't lie. I just left out that little part about him being in Seattle to see you tonight . . . no charge, dude."

"*You tricked me, you long-haired, angel hippie!*" Wyatt said. Tears of joy began to run down his face.

"Instead of standing here jawing with me, why don't you go over and give your boy a big hug," Mick said. "He's come a long way to see you here tonight."

Wyatt quickly moved over towards Danny, who was already moving towards him. When they embraced, it was the kind of moment that releases pent up emotions, so desperate to find emancipation after being jailed below layers of pain. Father and son clung to each other for several moments, neither one wanting to release the other. Both were now weeping and mumbling apologies to each other. Mick cradled Baby as he continued to scratch her freckled belly. He then closed the door and walked over towards Charlene. They both stood beaming at the reunion, which had been so long overdue.

After a minute or so, Wyatt and Danny both pulled back, as the elder Hunter looked at his handsome son, holding him by the shoulders. Danny was six feet, two inches tall—a good two inches taller than Wyatt. Unlike his Pop, Danny had a full head of sandy brown hair, which he kept fairly close cropped. He wore no facial hair, and had a good, clean, all-American look.

Fortunately for him, Danny had never struggled with his weight like his father had. He was consistently between 185 and 195 pounds, and had a lean, athletic type of body. Danny didn't have any problems meeting girls, but he spent most of his time pursuing loftier things—like school, studies, and ultimately, a job. He was mature beyond his years, and he had taken a big leap forward in his personal growth by flying to Seattle to reunite with his father.

Figuring that neither Wyatt nor Danny knew exactly what to say, Charlene interrupted their reunion, "Now you boys need to come and sit down at the dining room table with me and Mr. Mick. I baked a fresh huckleberry pie today, and I also have some delicious vanilla ice cream to go along with it. Let's go sit down and have some dessert."

"What about giving Baby her walk?" Wyatt asked.

"Miss Charlene already took care of that," Mick said.

"Geez Mick, it seems like you had everything all planned out." Wyatt said.

"Yep—*I'm the man*, ain't I?" Mick said, and everyone shook their heads and chuckled.

Mick stepped into the kitchen with Miss Charlene, and they both started preparing the pie, ice cream, and a fresh pot of coffee. Wyatt and Danny sat down at the big, round, wooden table which adorned Charlene's great room/dining area. The kitchen was adjacent to the dining room, and looked out into both of the other rooms.

They engaged in some small talk for a couple of minutes before getting down to business. "So Danny, when did you get in—today?"

"Yeah, dad. I flew in from Minneapolis this morning. Miss Charlene actually picked me up at the airport after lunchtime."

"But son, you've never met Miss Charlene before," Wyatt said. "What's up with that?"

"Actually, Mick visited me yesterday at the Mall of America, and we spent almost half a day getting to know each other. He told me all about Miss Charlene and what was going on in your life. He also told me that I needed to come here to Seattle to see you, and I agreed. At first I was resistant to his advances for a discussion. But ultimately, he convinced me that he was for real."

"Yeah, he has that special way of cutting through the baloney and getting your attention. That old guy knows his stuff pretty well . . . ." Wyatt said it loud enough so they could hear him in the kitchen.

"Dude, I *heard* that," Mick said, walking into the dining room with a tray containing coffee cups, a large carafe, and all of the coffee fixings that someone could possibly want.

"Now you boys need to be *nice,*" Miss Charlene said, in a sweet-but-stern voice. "I've been waiting all day for this meeting, and we're going to get along—no matter what."

"With all due respect Miss Charlene," Mick said. "Actually you've been waiting for this meeting for nearly a year now."

"Right you are, Mr. Mick," Charlene said.

"I've done asked you before, Miss Charlene; it's just plain ole *Mick . . .* or if you prefer, you can call me, *dude.*"

"That's perfectly fine with me dear," Charlene said. "But since I'm not a surfer, I'll call you by your proper name." Wyatt chuckled at this. Charlene brought out four large pie plates on a tray, each containing a huge hunk of warm huckleberry pie, topped with a heaping scoop of vanilla ice cream. "Here we are, boys. Let's dig in."

After a few minutes of small talk, Mick said, "Okay, it's time to bring this meeting to order." Although he tried to sound very officious, he couldn't help but to sound like he usually did—casual, approachable, and very strong.

"Hey Mick—you have some ice cream in your goatee," Danny said.

"Right, little dude." Mick wiped the ice cream away with a napkin.

"Little dude?"

"Well, what else am I gonna do with both you and your Pop here at the same time? He's *big dude* and you're *little dude.*"

Danny grinned, "Whatever, Mick."

The angel continued, "Not to get too serious, but we need to clear up a few things, right up front. I've been promising Wyatt all day that I'd explain everything to him when we got back here."

"Let me guess," Wyatt said. "Danny being here is the gift that you promised me—right?"

"Yep. But, that's only one of three separate parts to your gift. I'm fixing to explain the second part to you right now. You'll then get the third part later on, when you and I take our after-dessert walk."

"Okay, but before you go any further, what did you mean when you said that Miss Charlene has been waiting to have this meeting for the past year?"

"Mick first visited me around this time last year," Charlene said. "It was only a short time after Vanessa passed."

"Why did he come to see you so long ago?" Wyatt asked.

"He actually came to prepare me for your arrival in Seattle," Charlene said, "and to fill me in on my mission. Of course, at the time, you may not have even been aware that you were going to move out here yet."

"And *oh-by-the-way,* it didn't take her *all day* to figure out that I was the real-deal," Mick quipped. "She actually figured it out within a couple of minutes. I suppose you could say that she isn't quite the knucklehead that *you* are."

"Sorry, Mick—my instincts aren't quite as clear and discerning as Miss Charlene's." Charlene just smiled and took a sip of her coffee. She had a strong sense of self-awareness, and an almost "sixth sense" about matters of God and the Holy Spirit. Her's was a pure soul.

"Dad, for what it's worth, I thought that Mick was a complete crackpot at first," Danny said. "But he kind of fascinated me, so I decided to listen to him."

"Where again did you and Mick meet?" Wyatt asked.

"At the Mall of America in Bloomington," Mick chimed in. "But we can go into all of that later. Right now, we need to talk about a few things."

Danny quickly added, "Dad, my apartment is in downtown Minneapolis . . . I often take the train down to the mall for a good walk and a wander—just like the old days."

"Okay . . . ." Mick said. "Let's talk about that dark cloud of evil, also known as Damon, for a minute. I know that all of you have met him by now—right?" Everyone nodded. "Well, let me give you a little background on him. Essentially, he's the demon who is assigned to attack the Hunter family, among others. Now then, I don't have time to go into all of the history of this right now, but believe it or not, he's been on this job for quite some time."

"He has?" Danny asked.

"Yep. He's gotten away with some ill-deeds in the past, but I'm here to put the clamps down on that little jerk. Now Wyatt, I know that you met Damon for the first time up in the market today, right?"

"Right."

"And Danny, he rolled up on you yesterday at the mall, after our little chat. Right?"

"Yes. He and I spoke, but only briefly."

"And Miss Charlene?"

"Yes indeed," Charlene said. "I'm afraid that old *brimstone britches* has approached me twice since our initial meeting last year." Wyatt could hardly contain a laugh. She continued, "I told him about his sorry self and shooed him away both times. He actually didn't bother me at all. I've been onto those demons and their evil ways since I was a young girl."

"Okay, that's enough about butt-head's history for right now. Next, we need to clarify what happened with Vanessa . . . and Danny, I'm mostly talking to you about your mama."

"Okay Mick. What's up?"

"Well, I'm not exactly sure how to say this to you, so I'll just say it straight out." Mick paused as the dining room became pin-drop quiet. "Damon is the one who intentionally crashed into your folk's car last year."

"What?!?!?" Danny asked.

"It was Damon who killed your mama."

"But—?" Danny began.

"Let me also tell you," Mick added, "that the man whose body that Damon indwells right now is different than the one who he inhabited last year, when he sent Vanessa to see her Lord. You see, demons have a way to move between certain people, and sometimes do. However, I'll explain all of the particulars of that process to you guys at another time."

"Son, they actually never caught the driver who crashed into us," Wyatt said. "Your mom and I each had only one glass of wine at supper that night. Based on what Mick has been teaching me today, I can now see that the evil forces tried to work things behind the scenes to allege that I was at fault for the accident, because I was drunk. Of course, they were wrong."

"Why would they do something like that?" Danny asked. "We can't be all that important, can we?"

Mick remained quiet, so Wyatt shrugged and said, "I suppose they wanted to try to create a guilty conscience for me, and a chasm of separation between us."

Danny shook his head, "Listen dad, I didn't know what to do when mom died—I've never had a parent die on me before. Deep down, I knew that you weren't drunk, but I needed someone to blame for—"

"Look son," Wyatt interrupted. "It's all in the rearview mirror now. You and I have landed squarely in the middle of a battle, and from what I can tell, Mick has already given you your mission." Wyatt looked squarely into Mick's eyes for confirmation. He was correct.

"Listen guys," the angel said. "It's actually pretty simple. We've been observing both of you for quite some time now. And I'm happy to say, you've both grown with your own, spiritual gifts. But somehow, the bad guys got wind of it. So, Damon steps in and goes to down to Georgia—"

So the devil went down to Georgia?" Danny interrupted, referencing the famous Charlie Daniels song.

"Actually, yes Danny," Mick nodded. "Damon went to Georgia and possessed an unsaved person. He then committed this heinous act on your mother. That's the bad news. Now, here's the good news, and I've been given permission by our Lord to tell you this." Wyatt and Danny were both riveted to Mick's every word. Charlene remained quiet.

"Vanessa's doing well, and of course, she's ecstatic about being in Heaven. From the very moment the accident happened and she was killed, she was instantly transported into God's holy presence. Actually, it wasn't long after her arrival that I met Vanessa; but it wasn't until later that we had a chance to talk and visit. Anyways, she now has a glorious, new, and perfect spiritual body, and no longer has any of the various physical maladies that used to plague her when she was still on Earth."

"Do you mean that she isn't having any more back problems?" Wyatt asked.

"None whatsoever. You name the affliction, and I'm gonna tell you that it's gone for good . . . and remember this; a spiritual body is still a *real* body." Wyatt and Danny both had tears in their eyes as the angel continued. "Now then . . . both of you boys are being offered positions in the King's army, and you've been chosen for the assignments that He's developed specifically for each of you. However, it's very important to remember that Vanessa is happy, and she's with all of her family and friends who've passed away in Christ—both before and after her entrance into Paradise."

"Do you mean that mom is with grandma right now?" Danny asked.

Mick winked at Wyatt, then said to Danny, "I'm afraid I can only tell you about your mama . . . but it's all good, little dude."

"I'm not sure I understand this," Wyatt said. "Did Vanessa have to die because God wants Danny and me to carry out His missions?"

"No! *Don't be a dummy*—that's an incorrect, man-centered view, Wyatt. It breaks down like this . . . Damon killed your wife, because he's in constant warfare against your family. Now then, God allowed the murder to happen; not because He wanted to see Vanessa die, but because He's always several steps ahead of the evil ones. The Lord has allowed them to rule the fallen Earth for a while now, but that's only for a finite period of time. Even when the demonic forces commit evil crimes against His people—as was the case with Vanessa—the Lord adjusts things to ultimately serve Himself and His kingdom."

"I see," Wyatt said.

"Although Vanessa's route took a different path than either you or she expected, God made sure she got home to Him, nonetheless. That's the important thing here. You need to remember that God prevented you, Wyatt, from being harmed in the accident. Damon was actually coming after *both of you.*"

"Hmmm," Wyatt mused. "I never thought about that."

"Fortunately for our missions, God wouldn't allow that to happen," Mick said.

"Why do you think that is?" Danny asked. "I mean, why would he try to take out both of my parents?"

"Because Damon was ultimately trying to derail *your* mission Danny," Mick said. They all sat in silence for another few moments. "He figured that if he nailed both of your parents, he might be able to send you into despair, thereby eliminating your threat to their evil plans."

"You mean that Danny's mission is to . . . what?" Wyatt asked.

"Danny's mission is completely different than yours. No offense dude, but Danny is much younger than you, and he has many more productive years of battle ahead."

"No offense taken, Mick. However, this doesn't sound like the typical *American Dream* scenario," Wyatt said.

"Actually it's not—*not at all*. However, I'd say that it's much *better* than the American Dream, Wyatt."

"How's that?"

"The Lord wants for you to serve a higher purpose for Him by carrying out your duties. Believe me, that's a whole lot better than just living in a house with a white picket fence, isn't it?"

"I suppose it is," Wyatt admitted. "But it sure hurt losing the love of my life."

"Mom is okay," Danny added. "We didn't lose her at all. That's all we need to know for now. Mick, I'm ready for whatever you and the Lord want me to do."

"Danny, you need to remember this—I'm only a messenger and a warrior; all good things come from the Father. I'm not empowered to decide these types of things, only carry them out. Oh, and sometimes I get to stomp on a few demons in the process."

"So that's it, Mick? Danny and I are now going to serve in the Lord's army?" Wyatt asked.

"Yes dear." Charlene added. "Vanessa is home with our Father, safe and sound. You boys now have a very important job to do, and I'll be right here to help you in any way I can. We'll all be home with our Savior soon enough, but for right now, we have some things that we need to accomplish."

Wyatt nodded, "So Mick, what is Miss Charlene's mission in all of this?"

"Her initial job was simple. We needed for someone to watch over you during the critical first phase of your move out here to Seattle. She was here to help you with Baby, and to minister to your spiritual and emotional needs. Basically, you needed a spiritual companion who you could lean on during the post-turmoil period."

"Really? And I thought she liked me for who I am," Wyatt joked.

"Sweetheart, trust me when I tell you this." Charlene looked deeply into Wyatt's eyes as she took his hand. "Having you around has been as big a blessing to me, as it's been to you. *Oh, how I have enjoyed our meals,* going to church, Bible study, and just simply being together. In no way has this been a one way street. This *mission,* as Mick calls it, has been my pleasure." *There she was again, making you feel like a million bucks,* Wyatt thought. *If she could bottle and sell that talent, she would be richer than Bill Gates.*

"Wyatt, you'll get the last part of your gift later on, along with the details of your mission. Danny has his, and Miss Charlene has her's. We need to move on, now."

Charlene began to clear the table and said, "You boys go ahead and move out to the terrace. Wyatt honey, please light the candles out there like we usually do, and I'll just get this all cleaned up. Oh and Mick, can you please cite the Scripture that we discussed earlier? I just love that passage."

"Sure thing, milady. Gentlemen, your mission's keynote passage is from *Luke 9:62 . . . Jesus replied, No one who puts his hand to the plow and looks back is fit for service in the kingdom of God* . . . Boys, now it don't get any plainer than that."

"We're good, Mick." Danny said, and Wyatt nodded his approval. The three guys all moved out onto the terrace. The nighttime air was chilly, and Wyatt lit the candles, per Charlene's request. After they chatted for a few minutes, Charlene rejoined the group. This time, she sported a warm jacket. The patio chairs were comfortable, and Baby seemed to really enjoy her spot on Mick's lap.

"Now boys, please listen to me," Mick said. "I have a movie assignment for you to watch tomorrow or the next day. It highlights an important concept for you to understand in your battles with the enemy, and I think you'll both get a lot out of it."

"What is it, Mick?" Danny asked.

"It's Ben Stein's film, *Expelled – No Intelligence Allowed.* The film is really important, because it goes into some of the Intelligent Design stuff that I've discussed with each of you during our initial meetings."

"Hey dad, from what I've heard, it's mostly about the evolution argument," Danny said. "It's also about the closed-minded intellectual atheists in the scientific community. For some strange reason, they're fighting hard against scientists who're simply saying that Darwin's theory has been scientifically disproven."

"Was it any good?" Wyatt asked.

"Yes—from what I've heard. I've actually seen a few snippets of it. A few of my friends who have seen it, say it's outstanding. I must say; I'm looking forward to watching the whole thing."

"Danny, there's an old expression about atheists," Mick said. "Arguing with an atheist is like wrestling with a pig in the mud; after a while, you realize the pig is enjoying himself." They all had a chuckle. "But seriously, you guys will need to brace yourself for the onslaught of hatred and cruelty that you'll endure by standing up to the God-haters and fighting for the Lord . . . and you won't be able to sit on the fence with this issue. Remember, this war in imbedded in your culture, and the enemy won't give up without a humongous fight."

"Now boys, Mick is absolutely right," Charlene said. "I'm afraid that I've seen some hateful things that many people haven't. Back in the sixties, I was cursed at, spat at, and called racist names I wouldn't even say to an evil demon. In other words, evil has many faces."

"Hear, hear," Mick agreed.

"Now then," Charlene continued, "what you're really embarking on is a battle against an enemy who doesn't care about who they take down with them. This whole thing is basically a battle for the hearts, minds, and souls of millions of our countrymen, as well as people all over the face of this planet . . . by the way, would anyone else like any more coffee or pie?"

Mick smiled and nodded, "Yes ma'am. I'll have another shot of coffee, please."

"So Mick, how long are you going to stick around on your mission, here?" Wyatt asked.

"I'll explain all of that to you when we resume our walk. Anyways, I have one last thing. Let's get back into the American Dream reference which you made a little while ago, Wyatt."

"Okay, be my guest," Wyatt said.

"Be *our* guest," Danny added. Wyatt smiled, feeling a sense of relief to have his son by his side for the first time in over a year.

"Okay dudes, here goes," Mick said. "The *American Dream* is a phrase coined by a writer back in the early thirties named James Truslow Adams. He felt that in your society, even with all of its flaws, that with enough hard work and luck, anyone can achieve what they wanted to in life. He acknowledged that during this process there would be material gain with regard to possessions, but he also said that, *'It is not a dream of motor cars and high wages merely, but a dream of social order in which each man and each woman shall be able to attain to the fullest stature of which they are innately capable'.* So, are there any thoughts on this?"

"Someone has corrupted the whole thing, dear," Charlene said.

"I agree," Danny added.

"We're with you, Mick. Please continue," Wyatt said.

"Well, let's take another look at the American Dream—this time with our *God glasses* on. What do you see now? How about you, Wyatt?"

"Well, I see a modern society that's completely lost track of that whole ideal. I see a former free-thinking society that is now steeped in political correctness versus Christ-correctness; one that sees you as a failure if you drive a Toyota Camry instead of a Cadillac Escalade; one that hears issues like 'separation of church and state', and doesn't know where it came from—and is too lazy to look it up; one that doesn't want to reward hard work, but rather, feels like each individual is entitled to equal benefits without equal effort. Shall I continue?"

"Those are all good points. But look at it again, this time with *only* your *God glasses* on."

"It's one that sells a bogus bill of goods that keeping God out of our society is doing the fair thing," Danny added. "And, that only religious whackos believe that prayer should be allowed in schools . . . and in government public places."

"Bingo, little dude. However, there's still one thing that you're both missing. Can anyone guess what it is?"

"The boys are missing the main point," Charlene began, "that Satan is behind the corruption of the American Dream. His nasty fingerprints are all over our society now. Just look at all of the greed that's out there, and it's being sold as *good!* Yes-sir-ree, the devil, his demons, and his hellhounds are out there creating all sorts of troubles. And sadly, folks have turned away from their only true weapon, which is Christ's power in the Bible."

"Right you are, ma'am," Mick agreed.

"No charge, Mick," Charlene said, stepping out of her humble persona for a moment. They all had a chuckle. "Mick dear, I'll go get your coffee now."

"If you don't mind, please put it in a to-go cup for me."

"No problem. I know that you and Wyatt need to go and finish up your one-on-one talk." She got up and headed towards the kitchen. Baby got down from Mick's lap and followed Charlene inside.

The three guys sat for several minutes, idly discussing Danny's flight and Mick and Wyatt's interesting walk through the market. Danny told them from the moment that he met Miss Charlene at the airport, he felt like he had known her for all of his life. Mick proceeded to comment on how good honey tastes in coffee, and Wyatt just looked at his son, who he had missed so much. He prayed silently, thanking God for bringing an end to the chasm of separation between them. Deep down he knew that not only would they never be estranged again, but that their renewed relationship would actually be much better than it ever had been.

"Boys, let's talk about one last thing," Mick said. Charlene returned to the terrace and handed Mick a large paper cup of coffee, topped with a white, plastic lid. "Let's close the subject on the American Dream and highlight what Miss Charlene said a minute ago about greed. Now, I'm not going to use any names here, but I think that we all know about that investment scammer guy who lost over sixty five billion dollars in bogus investments for his clients. Now I want you to think about that for a moment—*he stole over sixty five billion dollars!* What kind of person can do that kind of thing?" The others all nodded, and Mick added, "Yoo-hoo guys, that was actually a *question."* Danny raised his hand. "Danny boy—shoot."

"That guy got sucked into the greed vacuum that I see so often in the superficial world of finance and big money. However, I'm afraid he went *far* beyond the simple point of greed. I believe money that big can't be stolen without a level of greed that's beyond all human understanding."

"You're absolutely right Danny," Charlene said. "I'm sure that obviously *very* lost man had some of the dark forces encouraging him along the way. And you know what else? Like that old saying goes, 'I've never seen a hearse with a U-Haul behind it'."

"Miss Charlene takes the prize," Mick said. "Some of my reconnaissance reports tell me it's likely that demonic activity is surely behind that whole mess. For a level of theft that immense, the demon crew responsible for greed would very likely have been involved."

"The thing that I can't understand," Wyatt began, "is what would someone do with all of that money? You can only buy so many golden toilets, you know. Plus, isn't he kind of old now? I mean, did he actually think he could take all of that money with him when he dies? It's like what Miss Charlene just said about the hearse and the U-Haul."

"Wyatt my friend, the depravity and depths of the evil behind Satan and demonic influence is immense. Do you remember what we discussed earlier about Satan's Trifecta of Tricks?"

"I do," Wyatt said, "and I suppose it doesn't hurt to have regular reminders about how dangerous demons are."

"Well, that's the one thing about living in a fallen world," Mick said. "If you have the internal strength to follow Christ, the daily reminders of the evil created by the various demons can actually serve as both a reminder and a warning about them. It's sort of like jogging; it may not be the most pleasant thing to do, but it does make you stronger." Before anyone could comment any further, he added, "Wyatt, I'm afraid we need to go now; to discuss your mission. I'm armed with coffee and a good knowledge of the Bible, so I've got the tools I need to finish this thing."

Wyatt shrugged, "That'll work for me. I suppose that I could have done much worse than dealing with an unorthodox, coffee-loving angel like you, today." Mick grinned and nodded.

They both said their warm goodbyes to Danny and Charlene. Mick had an odd sense about him, and it seemed as though he was a little sad when he hugged Charlene and Danny goodbye. Wyatt played with Baby for a minute as they prepared to leave Charlene's condo. He completely missed it when Mick gave knowing looks to Charlene and Danny, as if he was affirming their previous instructions.

It was finally time to finish up their business, and Mick knew the best place to accomplish this was back up the hill in Pike Place Market. This time, there wouldn't be any more cryptic references or lessons. For Mick, it was finally time to finish up this mission.

18
BEHIND ENEMY LINES

The stage play between Mick and Wyatt entered its last scene, as the culmination of their day-long adventure approached its finale. Charlene gently closed the door behind them as they left her condo, leaving behind the fading, familial sounds of Danny's laughing and Baby's playful barking. As they moved down the hallway and quickly out of the complex, their hearts were warm and their bellies full.

It was cool outside and pitch dark by then, giving the night-time atmosphere a much calmer feel than they had experienced throughout their busy day. Wyatt had donned a light jacket to put over his sweatshirt, and Mick continued to sport his worn leather jacket. The wind was still, and the autumn evening was very pleasant.

They made their way around to the front of the complex that faced Alaskan Way. Right in front of the complex was a paved walking area, which ran parallel to the street. It was often used by joggers and dog walkers. Adjacent to this path was a light rail track used for a trolley service, but Wyatt had not seen it in use for some time. There were a few other people walking about, and the street was well lit. It was indeed, a beautiful night for a walk.

As they continued north along the paved walking area, out of nowhere, Mick asked, "Hey dude, do you like fresh cherries?"

"Sure I do," Wyatt said. "*Oh man*—you should see the fresh cherries in the market during the summertime. I especially like the Rainier cherries—they're outstanding."

"Well, have you ever thought about how a cherry tastes *sooo* good, but it's such a hassle to eat because it has that nasty ole pit?"

Wyatt shrugged, "I suppose that removing the pit is important to the enjoyment of the cherry. Why do you ask?"

"I was just thinking. Does it seem like your lives are just like the cherry? I mean, once you remove the pit of sin, the cherry tastes so much sweeter to the Lord."

"Sure, but you can just eat around the pit and still enjoy the cherry," Wyatt said, challenging the angel.

"Yeah, but the eatin's so much better when you don't have to worry about that nasty ole pit ruining one of your bites—isn't it?"

A smirk crept onto Wyatt's face, "Okay, I give in. The cherry's much better after the pit's been removed. What's your point?"

"Christ died to remove the pit of sin in each of you, so that you can become holy and acceptable to our Father. However, the problem lies with the fact that so many people won't accept His invitation of the pit's removal. Let's face it—God finds the cherry unacceptable if it still has a pit in it. After all, Christ suffered and died to permanently remove the pit of sin for all of mankind. Personally, I don't think it's an unreasonable requirement. Our Father in Heaven simply won't accept you into His holy presence if you haven't allowed Christ to remove your pit of sin. Are you tracking with me?"

Wyatt nodded, "Yeah, I'm tracking with you. So tell me; how do you want to close out this *riveting* fruit metaphor?"

"Always bear in mind that if you don't want your pit of sin removed, then you're unacceptable to God. I'm afraid His requirement isn't negotiable."

"I get that," Wyatt said, and thought about it for a few moments. "Well, have you prepared my keynote passage of Scripture for what appears to be my final lesson for today?"

"As a matter of fact, I have. It's *Ephesians 6:10-12* . . .

> *"Finally, be strong in the Lord and in his mighty power. Put on the full armor of God so that you can take your stand against the devil's schemes. For our struggle is not against flesh and blood, but against the rulers, against the authorities,*

against the powers of this dark world and against the spiritual forces of evil in the heavenly realms."

"Ah-ha," Wyatt said. "I knew it! Spiritual warfare is what we've been talking about all day."

"Indeed we have," the angel agreed. "Anyways, the next few passages after that go on to explain the different analogies of God's spiritual weapons to use against the devil, and how they relate to an ancient soldier's uniform."

"I'm very familiar with this passage, Mick."

"Good, because it's absolutely critical to study and use these weapons against our enemy. Please always remember this—you're behind enemy lines right now, and you can never let your guard down against those dirt bag demons."

"I understand. But that passage indicates that we're not fighting against *flesh-and-blood* enemies. However, doesn't it seem like we sometimes are?"

"Well . . . sort of . . . ."

"Once again, you're being vague," Wyatt said.

Mick held up his hands in a halting gesture. "Well, that's only what it appears to be. Please remember this—demons merely utilize human bodies as a weapon; the power and attacks from the evil realm actually come from *non-flesh* demons. Basically, demons are like an enemy soldier, and the human body is like a gun; the enemy soldier may shoot at you, but the gun is merely his chosen *tool.* The enemy soldier is the one who has to be stopped—in this case, a demon. Anyways, if you're able to take away his gun, the demon will merely get another weapon."

"So what are you telling me, here?" Wyatt asked.

"Essentially, this passage illustrates how to use God's *spiritual* weapons against the enemy. However, as you just touched on, demons can indeed carry out their evil missions through flesh and blood people. Have you ever heard of serial killers like Ted Bundy, Richard Ramirez, Jeffrey Dahmer, and the like?"

"Of course."

"Well, there've been many, many, more than just those few. The Scripture here tells you to use God's spiritual weapons, and I'm advising you to be prepared for any physical assaults as well. Let's face it—the evil ones use both the physical and spiritual world to carry out their evil plans.

Basically, you'll never know where evil will come from, so you need to be on constant alert. Do you hear what I'm saying?"

"I do. I promise to stay vigilant."

"Now then, I'm going to tell you one more time, just to be sure. You're about to enter a new ballgame. That's why you must be exceptionally on guard for both spiritual and physical attacks from the enemy. Keep your eyes open and expect the unexpected. Wyatt, you're moving into the big leagues now."

"I understand, coach."

They finally arrived at the end of the numerous waterfront condominium buildings. In between the condos and the Marriott hotel next door was an elevator, which went up several floors to street level. Once up there, a walkway and a short street led up to the northern fringes of the market. Mick and Wyatt walked over to the elevator and pushed the button to go up.

Wyatt began to think about his family's numerous trips to Seattle in the past, and how much they enjoyed their stays at the Marriott. Because of these memories, he was expecting a launch from the pain brigade. However, it didn't come this time.

It was then that it occurred to him that everything which Mick told him during the day had actually come true. Having Danny back in his life had released a huge amount of anxiety, and hearing Mick talk about Heaven and how happy that Vanessa was, had deflated his anxiety even more. In fact, he couldn't even muster up any kind of recognition of where the pain brigade might be. He wondered if they had finally been defeated for good.

The elevator door rang before slowly opening. Mick and Wyatt got in and prepared for the short ride up. As they continued their ascent, the angel looked out towards Elliott Bay, deep in thought. Wyatt looked backwards at the beautiful pool at the Marriott, which was half indoors and half outdoors. He had been in that pool many times before.

When they arrived at the top, they turned left out of the elevator and up the ramp towards Western Avenue. They crossed under Highway 99, then onto Lenora Street, which bisects Western. After a short-but-steep walk past some stores on their left, and a parking garage entrance on their right, they landed on Western. They turned right and began walking south towards the market, which was only a block or so away.

"As you probably expected dude, I'm not yet through with Scriptures for this lesson," Mick said.

"I'd be really disappointed if you didn't have any more for me. So what's next?"

"Let's discuss *1 Peter 1:17 . . . Since you call on a Father who judges each man's work impartially, live your lives as strangers here in reverent fear . . .* Other translations and passages indicate that Christians are indeed *foreigners* in this fallen land."

"So let's see . . . you're saying that Christians are foreigners on the current Earth, and that we're designed to be with our Father in Heaven?"

"Yep. Can you tell me why I'm pointing this out to you?" Mick asked, then took a sip of his coffee. A pleased look swept across his face as he swallowed.

"Because you don't want me to forget where I live or to underestimate the enemy?"

"Nice work, pardner. I can see that you're finally listening to me."

"Mick, this is stuff we've already covered today."

"Not the Scriptures. Anyways, why do you think that new recruits in boot camp get taught how to assemble and disassemble their weapon over and over and over again?"

"So that defending themselves and fighting with their weapon becomes second nature?"

"Exactly!"

"So, you're saying that as I head into battle, it's critical to remember that I'm behind enemy lines, fighting a powerful foe in the unseen, but real world?"

"Unseen *foes.* Trust me Wyatt; demons are some really bad guys who'll stop at nothing to destroy God's creation."

"I see."

The angel and his friend passed by Tully's, Cutters, and Victor Steinbrueck Park on their right once again, then crossed over Western at the northern tip of the market. Proceeding south, they worked their way along Pike Place, continuing at a steady pace, towards the heart of the market. Unlike earlier that day, Pike Place Market was now like a ghost town.

Neon lights glowed in the distance, joining the ambient light from several parts of downtown. This kept the market from being too dark. The intermittent voices of people not far away blended in with the occasional dog barking. The market had taken on a slightly eerie atmosphere as Mick and Wyatt walked in silence for a few minutes.

"Dude, I have one more Scripture for you now, and this will complete the setting for our discussion. But first, I wanted to tell you how proud I am of what an excellent student you've been today. And I promise you this—I'm not blowing any smoke, either. Many people would have written me off as a complete crackpot, even though I'm pretty good at getting folks to listen to me. Anyways, I just wanted to let you know how much I've enjoyed our day, today."

"Thanks Mick. You almost sound like you're fixing to give me a big ole bear hug."

"You ain't quite purdy enough for that, my friend." Mick was smiling. "Anyways, I'm going to read to you *2 Chronicles 20:15 . . . He said, Listen, all you people of Judah and Jerusalem! Listen, King Jehoshaphat! This is what the LORD says: Do not be afraid! Don't be discouraged by this mighty army, for the battle is not yours, but God's."* . . . They were quiet for a few moments.

"Well Mick, with all of this battling-demons stuff, I guess I didn't really think about the overall war. Indeed, this seems to be a war between God and his angels, against Satan and his demons. We-humans all seem to have been born into the middle of it."

"That's correct. The battle described in this Scripture was not as important as the overall war between the Lord and Satan. Also, none of your individual battles will be as important as His overall war with Satan either. When Jesus was crucified and conquered the grave, Satan's days became numbered—and the Evil One well-knows that. However, I'm afraid that we'll all be fighting these battles until the Lord returns to end this thing."

"I see."

"Well, I suppose these three Scriptures are the proper setting for you to consider as I lay out the final details of your mission. Are you about ready for that now?"

"Yes Mick. I've been eagerly waiting for this moment all day." By this time, they had arrived at the L-shaped bend on Pike Place where it turned left towards First Avenue. Once again, they had returned to the heart of the market. Rachel the pig was nearby, and so was the Pike Place Fish Market, which was now closed. The "Public Market Center" sign was lit up in neon, joined by the large clock that was part of the famous entrance. Below that, the "Farmers Market" sign was also lit up. The entire area had a kind of orange-red glow, which set the stage for the culmination of their day-long saga.

"Well dude, I'm probably not going to shock you with anything I'm about to say to you, now. I've actually done this kind of thing countless times in the past, and I've found that the best way to approach the offer of a mission is to do it periodically throughout a day or night; that is, whenever possible. In other words, a methodical discussion like we've had today really cuts down on the shock factor. Does that make any sense?"

"It does."

"Okay, then. The first part of your prospective mission was a partial setting of the table. It's a kind of preparation for what's about to occur. And we all know that you can't properly eat dinner without first setting the dinner table. Am I right?"

"Yes you are . . . did you say 'was'?"

"Yes, *was* . . . please bear with me. But, in order for everything to move forward properly, the Lord needed to give you three gifts."

"Why is that?"

"Because essentially, you had to be fully relieved of your emotional burden—and His gifts were designed for just that purpose. The Lord allowed some painful things to happen to you last year, but He's very proud of how you never turned your back on Him. Unfortunately, many people do that very thing during their times of tribulation. Gladly, you didn't do that. You've truly proven yourself to God."

"I'm sure glad to hear that," Wyatt said.

"Anyways, there was still a problem left to be dealt with. You see, the burden of your emotional injuries had been taking its toll on you, and you can't be a true warrior for the King unless you're all-in. Do you know what I mean?"

"I think so."

"So, I was first dispatched to Minneapolis to reel in Danny yesterday. Now then, we'll talk more about his role at another time. But rest assured, he was critical to today's success, because this was actually your first gift—the reunion with Danny."

"Geez Mick. That was an awesome gift, and I'm hugely grateful for it in ways you just can't know. But I'm still curious about the other two. What are they?"

"For the second gift, I had to methodically tell you about Vanessa being in Heaven. You see, like we discussed earlier today, Heaven is a place that is vastly better than here on Earth. However, it's naturally terrifying for a human to die and cross over to be with the Lord. Although it's very unusual, sometimes the King sends a message to people on Earth, through handsome angels like me."

"So, getting some info about Vanessa's activities in Heaven was actually a way to—what?"

"It was simply a way to rout that pesky little *pain brigade*; at least that's what I think you call it."

"It is. Or rather, *was.*" Wyatt grinned, nervously.

"Anyways, the first two gifts were designed to release the pain—sort of like pulling the plug in a bath tub, and draining the dirty bath water down the pipes. I believe that your tub should be just about empty by now . . . am I right?"

"Actually, I think you are," Wyatt agreed.

"Now then, the third gift is completely different than the first two."

"How so?"

"Well, the first two gifts were like going through separate surgeries to remove the painful cancers. However, the third gift is designed to promote joy. You see, the Lord will allow you to experience both joy and pain while you're still here on Earth—all in an effort to draw you closer to Him. Ironically, He even specifically allows you to sometimes experience pain for your own benefit."

"I understand. So what's this third gift all about?"

"Now Wyatt, I want you to understand something—this is a rare thing. It really doesn't happen very often, and it can only come from the Lord—and Him alone. It's not from some séance, Ouija board, tarot cards or any of that other trickery that's used by the evil ones. In fact, God rarely allows people on Earth to get a glimpse of eternity in Heaven. Like we discussed earlier, that would ruin your ability to freely choose Christ."

"I'm still with you." Wyatt's heart began to beat more rapidly as a rush of adrenaline shot through his veins. He was absolutely riveted to Mick's every word.

"Now then . . . do you remember when you and Vanessa took your honeymoon, twenty some-odd years ago in New England?"

Wyatt nodded, "Yes, we had an absolute blast. It was in October, and the leaves were beautiful. We even met dad for lunch one day; although as usual, that ended up not being very much fun."

"Right. Earl took the ferry over to Hyannis, and y'all met him for lunch. After you said your goodbyes, do you remember that Vanessa said something very memorable to you?"

"She did—I remember it well," Wyatt said, not elaborating.

"Vanessa told you she felt that someday, you would have an opportunity to help your dad and bring him closer to the Lord. She said it with so much conviction, that you were actually surprised, because of how cynical that Earl was—and still is, for that matter. What she said always stuck with you, right?"

Tears began to well-up in Wyatt's eyes. It was true. They had never spoken of it again. Wyatt had actually not spoken of that discussion with anyone. Ever. "Right," Wyatt said, clearing his throat.

"Because of the Lord's great love and concern for you, He's sent you a vision of Vanessa in Heaven—through me—your humble messenger."

Wyatt looked incredulous, "A vision?"

"Indeed, a *vision.*"

"Why a vision?"

"God did this so that you can be fully dedicated to the achievement of your mission."

"Wait a minute—doesn't the Bible warn against messages from the spiritual world?" Wyatt asked.

"Actually, it does. Are you familiar with *1 John 4:1-6?*"

"I sure am."

Mick nodded approvingly, "Well, you've had plenty of time, today to hear me tell you that Jesus came in the flesh, and is the only way to eternal life with God. Christ is my King, and I only seek to serve Him."

"Hmmm . . . I suppose that makes sense. Anyway, what can you tell me about this vision?"

"Like I said, this is at the Lord's request, and obviously with His permission. So, here we go . . . ." As Mick began speaking, his voice seemed to fade, and a mental picture opened in Wyatt's heart and mind; almost like a flip-up screen on a video camera. Wyatt found himself immediately transfixed . . .

> *"Darling . . . continue to follow the Lord, Jesus Christ in all that you do. Being in Heaven with Jesus is so much greater than we ever imagined. With all of your heart, please look after Danny as you both take on the evil forces together. I've been spared from ever experiencing evil again, due to the* LORD's *tremendous grace. One day, you'll experience this yourself.*

The King of kings desires to bless you and Danny as you fight against evil. During these battles, please go see your father Earl, because his heart is completely broken. Although you may not fully understand this right now, but your dad figures prominently into the affairs of God's kingdom.

Please continue serving the Lord, and follow Mick's leading; he is your messenger and your mentor. All good things come from our LORD, who I'm with right now. Paradise is absolutely incredible.

But for now, think of our brief separation as if it were like a long business trip for you. Whenever your work on Earth is completed, you'll come home to Heaven to be with Jesus Christ forever. When the Lord brings you to our eternal home, I'll be waiting for you with open arms. Until then, my love, fight hard. I love you."

Mick's words faded, and the brief, mental picture in Wyatt's heart and mind faded back to normal. Wyatt's heart beat furiously with excitement and joy. He had never felt something like this before.

They were both silent for a minute or so as Wyatt began to sob tears of pure and utter joy. God's mercy and greatness were beyond what he had ever imagined, and he was awestruck. The bath tub of his pain had indeed, completely emptied.

Sensing the combination of both his relief and joy, Mick embraced Wyatt, but remained quiet. There was really nothing more to say about the situation. Mick could almost see Wyatt's broken heart now being sown back together as his tears of joy continued to fall.

After a minute or so, Wyatt began to compose himself. Mick waited patiently until his student, and now friend, was ready to proceed. Three young people came from off of First Avenue and walked past them, though at a comfortable distance. The two young men and one young lady were all in their late teens; they laughed heartily, and gave each other an occasional playful shove. The youngsters were very much engrossed in their own conversation, and they didn't even notice the angel and his student. As the teenagers' voices faded into the distance, Mick asked, "Are you about ready to proceed?"

"I think so," Wyatt said, working to regain his composure.

"Okay, so to do a recap for you . . . your three gifts from God are what you needed to be prepared for battle. He had to clear your decks emotionally, so to speak. Now then, the rest of the table-setting for your prospective mission breaks down into two primary events. The first event was that the Lord didn't allow Damon to take you out in the car wreck last year."

"I'm sure glad of that," Wyatt said.

Mick nodded, "You obviously had to survive, in order to do the work He wants you to do. Based on your knowledge of the Bible, I believe you're sensible enough to realize that you shouldn't feel any guilt over Vanessa being chosen to go home to Heaven, instead of you. Her entry into Heaven was a reward, not a punishment."

Wyatt cleared his throat, "Don't worry Mick. I get that."

"Okay. So, the first event took place last year; then some time had to elapse, before you were ready for the second event, which was today."

"Today?"

"Yes, today. I had to make you battle-ready by reviewing all of the Scripture which we've covered. To accomplish that, the first thing I had to do was to get you to realize that I wasn't a crackpot. The second thing was to then draw out your painful experiences; all in an effort to help you deal with them. So . . . while all of this was going on, captain jackass from Hell showed up, and tried to interfere with our progress."

"Is Damon still around?"

"He's not real near us right now, but he's surely still in Seattle, not too far away. I'm afraid that Damon doesn't give up very easily."

"I'll sure be on the lookout."

"Good deal—make sure that you do. Anyways, we had much to talk about today, but we actually covered everything I needed to cover."

"Have you done a lot of this kind of thing in the past?" Wyatt asked.

"Yes I have; but the details are mostly under Divine Privilege, dude. I'm afraid you'll have to figure out the rest, on your own."

"That's very interesting."

"Oh, and let's not forget—I also approached Miss Charlene last year to aid in this process . . . so the wheels have been in motion for your mission for some time now."

"That's amazing when you think about it. The Lord truly knows all things."

"Indeed. So in summary, the three gifts today, the saving of your life in the car wreck last year, and today's lessons are what we needed to happen before I could give you your mission. The table has now been properly set."

"Did Miss Charlene receive any gifts?" Wyatt digressed.

"DP dude—sorry. That's between her and the Lord."

"No problem . . . so what *is* my mission?"

Mick nodded, sporting a satisfied grin. He knew the story of their day-long saga was about to hit its apex, and he always relished this moment of truth. "Well, this probably won't be any shock to you," the angel said, "but the Lord wants you to write a book. Actually, He wants you to start it right away—like tonight."

"A book?"

"Yes, a book."

"I won't bother asking 'why me'. But I suppose the Lord understands that my writing style is more geared towards newspaper and magazine article writing, right?"

"Yes, that's what you've done in the past. That's *not* what you'll do in the future. You are being requested to write a book."

"What kind of book?"

"A Christian novel."

"But there are *lots* of Christian novels," Wyatt said.

"Not like this one."

"Hmmm. So, what should I write about?"

"That's a good question. First, let me tell you about the attributes of this book."

"Okay, I'm listening."

"First and foremost, use Scripture throughout the book—and I mean *lots* of it. God's Holy Word is the sword you must use to fight the evil ones, so use Scripture often. However, don't just pontificate with the Bible. This can potentially cause some people to become uninterested if they feel that they're being preached at too hard."

"Hmmm," Wyatt mumbled.

"Listen Wyatt, you need to weave Scripture into the story so that its readers can understand the Bible's importance. However, you need to use your imagination—*and* the sword of God's Holy Word. *Ephesians 6:17* says, *Take the helmet of salvation and the sword of the Spirit, which is the word of God* . . . God's Holy Word is critical for the message in the book, so the story needs to draw the reader *towards* the Bible. However, an interesting story should be in the forefront."

"Okay. Shall I write this down?"

"No. I'm sure you'll remember what to do. You're good at that."

"Fine. What else, Mick?"

"You need to keep an appropriate balance between God's grace and His truth. Too many world view religions—and even some Christian churches—are preaching that *everybody gets into Heaven.* That idea essentially renders Christ's sacrifice on the Cross, moot. Whether people realize it or not, this is *very* unscriptural. Don't write too much about God's mercy without including His judgment of those who reject Him. Also, tell them how He had to judge your sins through His Son at Calvary. Jesus went to the Cross because there was no other way to save you."

"I've always felt like His grace is the best *lead-off batter,* so to speak, and that His truth or judgment should not be over emphasized in the beginning of a witnessing experience. Is that the right approach?" Wyatt asked.

"It's only wrong if you go too one-sided between His grace and His judgment. Both of these attributes are what make the Lord, God. Without them both, He wouldn't truly be God. Am I making any sense?"

"Yes, it makes perfect sense now. I didn't use to understand this, but I do now."

"Good. Now this book needs to be a novel with a parable-like quality. You need to remember that Jesus taught the multitudes and His disciples with parables. Think up a story and a setting, and have it play out. It needs to be friendly, and written in a way which the reader can easily relate to . . . do you understand?"

"Yes, I sure do. So what else should be in this book?"

"You should extol the benefits of remaining a humble servant while spreading the Gospel throughout the book. Sometimes, Christians become quite impressed with themselves and get on a high horse when it comes to their faith. This can even lead to them looking down on the unsaved, which obviously turns off spiritual seekers. These folks have no interest in being saved by you; they want to be saved by God. Essentially, spreading the good news about Jesus Christ and letting God be in charge of the saving miracle, is the only true goal of evangelism. The spreading of Christ's Gospel in an appropriate manner is tantamount to showing others how to get to Heaven. Trying to appear superior to unsaved people—as if *you* have all the answers—is a huge turn off. This is actually counter-productive to what you're trying to accomplish. Am I still making any sense, here?" The tempo with which Mick was delivering Wyatt's mission was quick and efficient.

"Certainly."

"Good. It's quite disturbing when Christians take that *becoming a new creature* concept too far, and we've talked about that several times today. A true experience with getting saved and baptized ignites the Holy Spirit in each person. The flame of the Spirit sometimes burns fast, and changes occur quickly; and sometimes it happens more slowly. Either way, each person who has found a personal relationship with Jesus Christ is dialed directly into Him."

"I'm with you," Wyatt agreed.

"Basically, what every person does and how they evolve is between them self and the Lord. Your responsibility is to point the way to the Cross, because you're His earthen vessel. However, the message belongs to Jesus, and it's empowered by the Holy Spirit. So, please don't ever think that *you* are actually saving anyone. Also, make sure to include the reminder that if you have the occasion to correct someone's sins, do so gently, appropriately, and with a servant's heart."

"Yeah, Mick. I was put off for many years by the sanctimony of some Christians. But, I ultimately moved past that into my own personal relationship with Jesus."

"Yep, you sure did. Anyways, you also need to try to expand people's thinking about how great the Lord really is. The idea behind all of that stuff that we discussed, about animals in Heaven and the magnitude of His redemption, was intended to combat what the enemy has done to try to make God seem unattractive, insignificant, and limited in His power. *It's high-time we change that type of thinking!* The way to accomplish the cultural changes in America that are needed, is through the various media outlets, which Satan and company have so deeply infiltrated. Telling the real truth about God's Holy Word is going to be the centerpiece of your message, in whatever you do as we move forward together . . . are we good here?"

"Yes, we're good."

"Any questions?"

"No, not right now. But I'm sure that I'll have some later. Are you—?"

"I have one last passage for you Wyatt; one that I want you to think about during your time writing this book. This time, I want you to read it to me."

"Oops—I forgot my Bible," Wyatt said.

"You did, but don't worry—I didn't." Mick pulled out Wyatt's Bible and handed it to him. *He must have gotten it out of my backpack before we left to go on our night time walk,* Wyatt thought. "Okay, what's the passage?"

"*1 Thessalonians 2:17.*"

Wyatt didn't have his reading glasses on, and the light was not very bright. He squinted hard as he looked down into his Bible. "Okay . . . *But, brothers, when we were torn away from you for a short time (in person, not in thought), out of our intense longing we made every effort to see you* . . . Hey Mick, I like—"

Wyatt looked up and was suddenly stunned. He was getting ready to tell Mick how much he really liked that passage, but after reading it, Mick was gone. *Poof—vanished!* Nowhere in sight.

19
HALLOWEEN!

O n the heels of having one of the most incredible days that anyone can ever imagine, Wyatt felt a surge of negative emotion which always accompanies a sudden disappointment. His mind raced, wondering where his new friend had gone to. *If Mick had to leave, why was he so abrupt?* Wyatt thought. He stood there for a few minutes, surveying the market.

The place that was so incredibly vibrant just a few hours before, now felt like a ghost town from the old West. The nighttime air was somber, and he could almost picture tumbleweeds blowing down the center of Pike Place. A wave of aloneness swept over Wyatt as he gazed at the reddish neon lights of the now hibernating Pike Place Market. He shook his head in disappointment.

Wyatt wondered if Mick's departure was some kind of bad joke. However, his instincts told him differently. He then remembered when he and Mick had discussed how the angel travelled, and his comments about wanting to fly "first class." He also remembered that Mick stated that he could instantly vanish into the invisible dimension. *Apparently, the wise angel wasn't kidding,* he thought.

As Wyatt ruminated over Mick's unexpected departure, he began to retrace the steps they had just taken into the market from the north. Although there was a shorter route back to his place, he wanted to have the time to think before he got home. His mind drifted . . . .

The market was quiet, and as he walked, a very light sprinkle started to fall. This was the kind of precipitation that really didn't make you feel like it was raining; but rather, misting. Although the density of the misty air made it feel cooler than it actually was, it was still fairly comfortable. Once again, Wyatt thought about cranking up the fireplace when he got home; something he had forgotten to do earlier at Charlene's place. As his thoughts naturally drifted towards Danny, his mood began to improve.

His countenance continued to brighten as he thought about the passage that Mick had given him right before his unceremonious departure. The Scripture talked about being torn away for a short time, and Wyatt quickly figured out that Mick had chosen that passage as a friendly parting message. The more he thought about it, the more relaxed he became. He then tried to put Mick's abrupt exodus out of his mind.

As the mist continued to lay a slightly damp blanket across the inky darkness, Wyatt considered getting a coffee from Tully's, which was coming up on his left. However, the coffee shop had already closed for the evening. At that point, and much to his chagrin, his thoughts gravitated back to Mick's sudden departure, and why it happened the way it did.

He and Mick had discussed on several occasions that day, the passage in *Genesis 3:24,* which cites the flaming sword and mighty cherubim, who guard the way to the tree of life. Wyatt came to the conclusion that it was likely that passing through this flaming sword must not be the most pleasant experience for an angel. He figured that angels only did so when they absolutely had to. His instincts also told him that Mick would be teaching him much more about this flaming sword in future missions. When he came to the full realization that he would indeed see Mick once again, Wyatt's anxiety began to simmer back down.

Although he knew his mission to write a unique Christian novel would undoubtedly be uncomfortable at times, deep down, his instincts told him that he would follow Mick's instructions and write the book, regardless of the experience he lacked for the endeavor.

Despite his initial doubts, Wyatt's mind began to inexorably shift into creative mode, as several concepts began to drop into his head. He had a couple of blank composition books back at his place, and he figured they would be useful tools in getting his ideas on paper. Since he was instructed to start the project that very evening, as soon as he got home, he planned to begin making notes and pulling out Scriptures for possible use in the book.

By the time he made it to the waterfront elevator, Wyatt's mind had fully shifted into his new mission. His mind raced as he became quickly absorbed with numerous concepts for the book. When he stepped on to the elevator, he suddenly felt very leery, although he was completely alone. Wyatt took the elevator down, and when he reached the bottom, he proceeded out and towards the paved walking area in front of the condominium buildings; his pathway home. Since his place was at the very end of the buildings, he still had a good little walk ahead of him. At that time, there was no one else on the walking path.

Wyatt's thoughts began to drift towards Halloween, which was only a couple of weeks away. Since Mick had advised him to view all things with *God glasses,* he decided to mull over what was an often controversial subject within Christianity.

On the one hand, although Halloween was paganistic in its origin, so were many other more readily adoptable Christian traditions. Wyatt knew from his research that it was possible—and even likely—that Christ's birthday was not actually on December 25th. Still others believe that it was on that date, Jesus was actually conceived of the Holy Spirit. Either way, he always felt like the important thing was that people celebrated the birth of the Savior of the world. He had learned that there were several other pagan elements built into many early and current Christian traditions, especially Christmas. Some people believe that the early church did this intentionally, as a way to evangelize the pagan communities.

Wyatt got curious about a passage that he knew was highlighted in his Bible, so he stopped under a street light and pulled it out. After about a minute, he found the passage, reading it silently . . . *Romans 14:5 . . . One man considers one day more sacred than another; another man considers every day alike. Each one should be fully convinced in his own mind.* He continued to think about Halloween as he began walking once again.

The one thing that Wyatt always believed about Halloween was that the Lord knows each person's heart and their inner-most thoughts. He and Vanessa always liked Halloween, because they enjoyed spooky movies and the trick-or-treating with children. Their son Danny had grown up in a Christian home, and they clearly taught him not only the difference between right and wrong, but also that matters of the occult were very dangerous, and often the playground of the evil ones.

It really disturbed Wyatt when Christians engaged in dogmatic battles over such matters as to whether to celebrate Halloween or not. Some Christians can do it without any effects, while others simply cannot. He believed that it's fine for a Christian to enjoy the festivities of the day—just as long as the festivities are wholesome. He also knew that other Christians choose to ignore the day because of its paganistic background.

Personally, Wyatt felt very strongly that Christians should not vacate October 31st to Satan, as if the day is evil, just because Satan had created an evil activity for that day. But at the same time, people needed to respect anyone who chooses not to have designated yearly activities, because of Halloween's sordid history. It never glorifies God when the day is used for battles between the two positions, since it never enhances the Christian testimony in the world. The important thing was to not let the Evil One divide God's people; something that Satan seemed to be very adept at doing.

Wyatt and Vanessa had often discussed those individuals who vehemently oppose Halloween, and strongly espoused their passionate feelings about it. The couple had agreed that turning the matter into an actual controversy, in-and-of itself, was often the most evil thing that would happen on a typical Halloween night. As he continued his walk home, Wyatt decided that he would continue to mull over this complex issue.

As he approached the end of the buildings and the entrance to his home, he opted instead to wander out towards the parking lot to walk a little while longer. Wyatt figured this would be a good way to gather his thoughts and emotions.

The parking area adjacent to his condo was mostly empty, except for an SUV similar to his on the left, and a motorcycle several yards to his right, near a building. Sitting on the bike was a surprisingly well dressed man who had on a helmet; he appeared to be texting on his cell phone. The bike was cranked up, revving a low, bear-like growl.

Wyatt continued to walk towards Alaskan Way, stopping at the rail tracks. Gazing towards his left at the Seattle Aquarium, he thought about taking Danny there in the next day or so. He very much wanted to reminisce about some of the good times their family had enjoyed on previous visits, when Danny was younger.

Through his daze, Wyatt vaguely heard the motorcycle guy rev his engine. The well-dressed bikester was closer to him this time, but Wyatt was lost deep in thought, and wasn't paying much attention. Suddenly, the motorcycle was revving much more loudly, and it seemed to moving closer towards him. His first thought was to turn and give the ole "stink eye" to the rude driver as he passed by. *He's obviously getting ready to enter onto Alaskan Way,* Wyatt thought. As he turned to his left to stare down the driver, Wyatt was shocked to find himself right in the bike's path. With the headlight shooting directly into his eyes, he thought the motorcycle looked like a dart moving towards the bull's-eye, which unfortunately, was himself.

Wyatt felt like a proverbial "deer in the headlight," frozen in his tracks. People can often do amazing things to save themselves and others in emergency situations, but that usually happened when one's mind was clear. Wyatt's mind was far from focused, and suddenly, he found himself in the path of a crazed motorcycle driver, who was racing straight towards him. The driver had to have veered off of his normal course to be aimed at Wyatt, so he knew this crazed man was not playing games.

When the motorcycle was within two feet of Wyatt, the driver reached out and thumped his head with a blunt object. Simultaneously, he felt himself being tackled towards the left, landing him on the ground. He felt someone's entire weight on top of him as a numbing pain enveloped his entire body.

With his consciousness fading, Wyatt heard the sound of his attacker speeding away, moving north on Alaskan Way. The guttural growling from the shifting gears of the motorcycle slowly faded into the distance, as the waterfront returned to quiet.

Wyatt was not exactly sure what happened, and further, who was on top of him. He did have the instinctive feeling that whoever tackled him out of the way had likely just saved his life. Wyatt was tired and his head hurt. He was dizzy as his mind faded . . . .

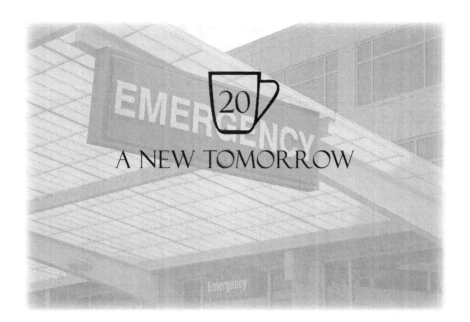

A NEW TOMORROW

W yatt fully came-to in a hospital emergency room trauma area, with curtains surrounding his bed. Through his mental haze, he vaguely heard his doctor say something about getting some rest, but he was still very disoriented and confused. As he continued his ascent towards lucidity, the doctor said, "Mr. Hunter, your father is fully awake now".

Danny quickly entered through the closed curtain with a big smile on his face; this instantly warmed Wyatt's heart. Danny thanked the doctor, who then excused himself. "Dad, you're being released now, but only because I was insistent and promised I would watch you very carefully tonight. They actually wanted to keep you overnight, but I talked them out of it."

"Nice job son—I think. By the way, where are we?"

"The hospital."

"Boy, my head hurts."

"You were lucky, Dad. You only ended up with a few cuts and bruises, and your concussion was very minor. You semi-passed out when that whacko on the bike came after you . . . do you remember any of this?"

"How can I forget? It looked like a freight train running straight towards me. Fortunately, someone tackled me out of the way at the last moment."

"I know—"

"Do you think it was Mick?"

"No Dad, it wasn't Mick. But he sure did help a whole lot."

"What do you mean—who saved me?"

"I did," Danny said quietly.

"You did? That was you who tackled me away from the psycho biker?"

"Yeah, it was me. We were pretty lucky; the driver only grazed you when he hit your head with something . . . I'll bet you wish I had been as good at tackling opposing quarterbacks at Jefferson High, huh?"

Wyatt thought for a moment. "Well now that you mention it, if you had been better and won yourself a football scholarship, I sure could've saved a few bucks," he joked. They both exhaled nervous laughs.

"Dad, I have a lot to share with you over the next few days. But about tonight . . . Mick forewarned me to be outside, and to watch for you coming along the path from the Marriott at around 8:00 pm or so. He told me that Damon would possibly try to mount a physical attack on you, by catching you by surprise."

"You were watching me as I walked past my place towards the road?"

"Yeah, I sure was. Mick said that I shouldn't interfere with you, unless I had to. Obviously, I did."

"Geez . . . ." Wyatt said.

"You know," Danny began, "I believe you'd be with mom now, if Mick hadn't instructed me to keep an eye on you. I guess he knows his enemy pretty well. Damon tried once again to take you out. *He was the psycho biker."*

"I wonder why he did that?" Wyatt thought out loud. Then he wondered if Mick's sudden departure had something to do with the saving of his life by Danny. However, if that were true, he wondered why Mick hadn't done it himself.

"I'm sure that it probably had to do with your new mission, dad. Demons don't like it when God's people try to fight back."

"Yeah, but I wonder why Mick didn't stick around to help me, himself." Wyatt said.

"It's probably because the role of angels is to be messengers—not to do everything for us. Mick told me the other day that it was his job to mentor and oversee our efforts. He also said that the role of humans was different than that of the angels; their job is to basically follow God's instructions. We're actually the ones who are playing out this drama down here."

"I suppose that makes sense. Did Mick tell you what was going to happen?"

"No. He only told me that he was taking you back to the market so he could give you your mission. I really think that once he reunited you and me, he figured that we were big boys, and we could catch each other up with everything. I'm just glad that we could do it in this awesome place where we came so often when I was a kid."

"The hospital?"

"Of course not! I'm talking about Seattle."

"Oh," Wyatt grinned. "Yeah, well, I knew that if we ever got back together, you'd be happy with my move out here."

"Dad, you and I are reunited forever. Nothing will ever come between us again, no matter what." Danny hesitated for a moment as he looked down. When he looked up once again, he continued, "I've missed you so much dad. My life really hasn't been the same without you around to talk to. I'm really sorry about—"

"We've moved past that Danny," Wyatt interrupted. "It's in the rearview mirror now, so let's leave it there, okay?"

"Agreed," Danny said after a few moments. "Now, let's get you home."

"How did I get here in the first place? Did you call an ambulance?"

"No, I had your car out of the garage and was sitting in it, right outside of your condo . . . per Mick's instructions."

"How did you—?"

"Miss Charlene let me into your place to get your keys. When I saw the guy on the motorcycle revving up and acting fishy, I got out of the car and started jogging in your direction—to warn you. Unfortunately, Damon must've seen me, and quickly sped up, so I started running as fast as I could. The problem was, the bike was so darned loud, you didn't hear any of my yelling. Fortunately though, it seems that I got there just in the nick of time."

"You certainly did. Was I awake on the way to the hospital?"

"You were in-and-out. It didn't take me long to get you here; then I helped you inside."

"By the way, how do you like my new car?"

"It's great, dad. Hey, unless you're having a lot of fun right now, why don't we get out of here?"

"Good idea."

When they first arrived at the hospital, Danny was unsure if his dad would be admitted or not. After checking Wyatt in at the emergency room, Danny realized that calling law enforcement regarding the attack would be of no value, so he concentrated on getting his father's head injury checked out. When his concussion was diagnosed as being very minor, the ER staff allowed Wyatt to be released. Danny now took the time to jump through the necessary hoops to secure Wyatt's emancipation. It took them a couple of hours after Wyatt was cleared, before they were in the car and heading home. Danny drove.

It was a dark and drizzly early Seattle Thursday morning, and both of them were exhausted; they had been in the hospital for several hours. They drove silently for a little while, taking in the peace and quiet of the night. Both Wyatt and Danny were ecstatic about being together once again, as they proceeded through the darkened drizzle towards home.

Danny finally broke their silence, "Hey Dad, do you want to go see the Trans Siberian Orchestra this winter? If so, I really don't care if we see them here in Seattle, or back in Minneapolis. You decide."

"Sure son. Good idea. Let's check their touring schedule when we get home." Wyatt often wondered why more of the evangelical community hadn't caught on to the incredible fusion of God praising Christmas music that the Trans Siberian Orchestra performed on their winter tours each year. Their music certainly didn't resemble any kind of secular version of "Jingle Bells." But rather, it was about the birth of God's Son, and the celebration of the real meaning of Christmas.

Wyatt was one of a growing population of newer Christians who couldn't be put into the stereotypical "suit and tie on Sunday" type of classification—not that there was anything wrong with dressing up for church. How someone dressed for church was unimportant to him, because he knew that Christians came in all shapes and sizes, and from many different cultures and backgrounds. To Wyatt, it was all a matter of preference.

As it related to music, if it praised God, Wyatt didn't care if it was heavy metal, rock and roll, country, hip hop, gospel, or any other genre. Truly loving and praising the Lord was the critically important thing; the style of music wasn't. He also felt that music was simply a matter of taste, and it was strictly up to each person to praise God in whatever way that brought them closer to Christ.

"Hey dad, I need to ask you another question."

"Sure Danny, what's up?"

"Well . . . what actually happened that night of the accident with mom? I never really took the time to listen to what you had to say about it; probably because I was in complete shock and utter despair."

Wyatt looked over at his son for a few moments, then said, "It's still tough for me to talk about, Danny." Wyatt hesitated for a few more moments to compose himself. "But basically, we were pulling out of the restaurant's parking lot and onto Atlanta Highway in Athens, when whammo! Some idiot crashed right into the passenger side of the car. I was knocked silly, and when I came to my senses, I was sitting on the sidewalk with an icepack on my head. It was then that I saw the most horrible thing that I've ever seen—a gurney with the sheet pulled over the body going into the ambulance. I almost threw up when I realized that your mom was gone. Later on, after the scene was cleared, a policeman took me home, *and poof*—I was suddenly all alone."

"So they never found the guy who Damon inhabited when he did this?"

"I'm afraid not. The owner of the car was some old man out in Watkinsville, but he had an alibi. I suppose that Damon possessed some poor soul, stole the car, then disappeared after the crash."

"I feel so terrible," Danny said. "The news insinuated that you might've even been at fault, and I wasn't strong enough to want to find out the real truth. Even if you had been at fault, I should've never abandoned you during your time of need. I guess that I just needed someone tangible to be mad at."

"That's enough, son! I already told you that we're past that now. I'm only interested in looking forward, just like the passage which Mick read to us in *Luke 9:62.*"

After a few moments Danny said, "Thanks, dad."

Wyatt smiled at his son, "Hey, if the Lord can forgive us for our sins, we can certainly forgive each other, can't we?"

"You're right—you're absolutely right," Danny agreed.

They wound their way through several empty streets until landing on Alaskan Way. Turning into the complex, Danny found their way into the condo's parking garage. They drove inside and parked, then made their way upstairs.

"I suppose we should check in with Miss Charlene, huh?" Wyatt asked.

"We don't have to dad; I already took care of that. While they were checking you out at the ER, I called and told her what happened, and that you were okay."

"Oh really . . . what did she say?"

"She said that I was wise to listen to Mick. Still though, when I was sitting in your car wondering what I was supposed to do, an odd wave of emotion caused me to become instantly alert. The next thing I knew, I felt a sudden sense of urgency to get out of the car and move towards you. I really can't explain what—"

"It was probably one of Mick's helpers."

Danny nodded, "Yeah, probably. Anyway, Miss Charlene is watching Baby for us. She also told me to let you know that we should sleep in tomorrow—or rather, today. After we get up, we can all go get a late breakfast, if you like."

"Oh yeah—I like!"

Father and son made their way into Wyatt's new home, settling down for some well needed rest. Wyatt had a spare bedroom, and Danny was glad to see his old bedroom furniture from back home. It warmed his heart to see that his father had brought his childhood bed from Georgia to adorn his new Northwest digs.

The next morning, Wyatt awoke at 9:15 am to find Danny sitting at his combo kitchen/dining room table, enjoying a cup of coffee. He had several things spread out on the table, and appeared to be embroiled in study. Included was his Bible, which Wyatt and Vanessa had given to him when was baptized at the age of fourteen.

"Good morning, son," Wyatt said. "I see that you figured out how to use my newfangled coffee machine."

"Actually, I have my own Keurig back home in Minnesota," Danny said, only looking up briefly from his reading. Wyatt moved towards the kitchen. "Is that the Bible we gave you when you got baptized?"

"It sure is—I use it all the time. It reminds me of mom."

"So . . . what're you looking at?" Wyatt asked.

"Oh, I found a passage that touches on what we discussed last night with Mick. It's about the scientific, intellectual-wannabes. This passage really zeroes-in on what it's like trying to have a rational discussion with them."

Wyatt nodded, "Mick called them *God haters,* but I don't think he was talking about your *average Joe* who may or may not believe in God, but who really doesn't know Jesus."

"Oh, I'm quite sure he wasn't referring to all people who don't believe in God as *God-haters.* When Mick and I chatted at the mall a few days ago, he spent a lot of time talking about how it made him sad that there were so many people in academia, who not only don't believe in God, but also who go overboard in trying to disprove God's existence. That's who he was referring to."

"Their overbearing passion against God is actually their indictment," Wyatt said. "But either way, we can't get caught up in returning their hatred with our own hatred. Mick made it abundantly clear that our job is to spread the Gospel of Christ, and to let the Holy Spirit handle the rest."

"That sure sounds like good advice to me."

"So, getting back to your Scripture, what passage are you looking at?"

"Oh yeah, here it is: *Luke 16:31 . . . He said to him, If they do not listen to Moses and the Prophets, they will not be convinced even if someone rises from the dead.*"

"Unfortunately, the sentiment in that passage is accurate. But you know, I just can't figure out what makes some people so adamant about their anti-God stance. Unfortunately, the door never seems open to have any kind of a rational discussion about the Lord with them. I suspect that many of those people had too many run-ins with some judgmental, Pharisee-like religious people in their past."

"I'm with you, dad. But you can't discount how so many of the hateful unbelievers out there think that people of faith are of an inferior intelligence than theirs."

"Many of them do, Danny. But let's not forget to pray for the Lord to reveal Himself to all people who don't know Him. Whether they're hateful and arrogant or not, all people who don't know Christ need our love—not our scorn."

"It's hard sometimes, but you're right. We need to do our part to help others, and let the Lord handle the rest."

Right on cue, the doorbell rang. When Wyatt opened the door, a beautiful black and white Boston terrier jumped into his arms, with a smiling Miss Charlene right behind her. "It's a *beautiful* morning boys!"

"Good morning Miss Charlene," they both said in unison.

"Baby's been out for her walk and all is well. How are you feeling, darling?" she asked, coming over and hugging Wyatt.

"I'm fine, Miss Charlene. I've had my head thumped a couple of times in the past year or so, but I suppose that I'm doing okay."

"That's good, dear."

Wyatt perked up and asked, "Do y'all wanna go up to the market to get something to eat? I'll treat."

"Sure," Charlene said. "But let's have some coffee first."

"Good idea," Wyatt said.

They both prepared a cup of coffee and sat down with Danny at the table. The three of them then began to recount some of the details of their respective missions from Mick. Charlene started with Mick's initial visit the previous year, and didn't add much. Her mission, for the time being, was primarily one of support for Wyatt, and then ultimately, for Danny. However, Wyatt felt like there was something she wasn't telling him. He knew better than to press her, because Charlene was a very strong and determined woman.

Wyatt then recounted his and Mick's eventful walk through the market the day before. He shared in detail with Charlene and Danny how the day unfolded, where they went, and what they talked about. Towards the end of the recap Wyatt said, " . . . and he used umpteen gazillion analogies and metaphors throughout the entire day."

"It appears Mick has a real knack for doing that," Danny said.

"So Danny, what did Mick tell you about your mission?" Wyatt asked.

"Well, the long and short of it is this—he wants to ultimately use me to help fight corruption in the world of finance, as well as many other things. However, he didn't give me a strict timetable. Now that I've had a little time to think about it, he was really kind of vague. He did say there was a specialty demon crew which worked in finance and big business, and that they were especially nasty. I guess he wants me to battle against them."

"Really, how so?"

"Like I said, Mick didn't go into too much detail about it. He only said that a few things had to first happen, and that later on, some events would have to fall into place before we got into my mission full-time."

"Oh okay," Wyatt said.

"Mick really emphasized that you can be very aggressive in business and earn a fair living and return on investments, without having to become greedy and world-absorbed about it. Actually, he kind of went on-and-on about the whole point." Danny did his very best to be vague, and not fully disclose everything that Mick had told him about his exciting-though-perplexing new future.

"That's Mick," Wyatt said.

"So, it seems that you and I are going to be like Van Helsing in fighting the vampires, huh?" Danny asked.

"Now these demons and such are to be taken *very* seriously boys," Charlene warned.

"Yes ma'am," Danny said. "Seriously though, the spreading of God's Holy Word and about His Son Jesus is best handled at the grass roots level."

"I think you're right, son. But we can't forget to keep in mind that everything we do, needs to be done with the humility of a servant's heart. When people are charged with the spreading of the good news about Jesus, we can't forget to keep in mind the importance of proclaiming the Gospel to the lost in an appropriate-but-truthful manner."

"Wyatt honey, that's right," Charlene agreed. "The idea is to guide people towards salvation, not judge them. That's the Lord's job—not ours."

"Dad, it seems to me, that Satan and his demons have chosen the weapon of *science-versus-religion,* in an effort to deceive people. It's the old, *divide and conquer* tactic, and the bad guys seem to be doing everything that they can to keep the people of faith and the people of science divided."

"Do you mean like the implication in the false paradigm that, *you can't be successful in business if you're too nice of a person?"*

"Exactly," Danny agreed. "Being a nice person and being successful in business, is similar to being a good scientist and being a person of faith in God—they're not mutually exclusive."

"Danny, it's a whole new world out there these days. There are an ever-increasing number of scientists who are finding God through the massive advances in scientific research. You're absolutely right—they're not mutually exclusive subjects."

Danny sighed, "Well, it seems that we have a whole lot of work ahead of us, don't we?"

"We certainly do son," Wyatt agreed, and they all smiled. "We certainly do . . . ."

In the following minutes, Wyatt got dressed, while Charlene and Danny continued to chat. When all of them were ready, they left Baby to take a nap on the couch, while they made their way up to the market for a nice walk and an excellent meal.

All three of them were uncertain of what adventures lay ahead for their new ministry group. However, they figured that the wise course of action would be to simply take the next strides on the stepping stones which the Lord was placing in front of them. From each of their respective meetings with Mick, they now understood that if you will only allow the Lord lead the parade, then He will always illuminate His chosen path for you.

EPILOGUE

Once again, Mick sat quietly at the old wooden table in the "locker room," near the edge of Heaven. As usual, he sipped on a large cup of coffee, savoring another perfect day in Paradise; his latest assignment complete. Although he always relished the successful completion of any mission, he sometimes felt that very slight emptiness due to the separation between himself, and the people on Earth with whom he had become fond of. Wyatt, Danny, and Charlene were now his dear friends, and he missed them already.

Although friendship and fellowship between angels and humans is rarely spoken of on Earth, he knew that the Lord's ultimate plan was for both groups to live harmoniously together, joyfully serving His will. *How can we do that without becoming friends?* he wondered.

Mick continued to enjoy his coffee while reviewing some reports, when his boss Michael, the arch-angel, joined him at the table. Michael had his traditional cup of hot tea in-hand and quietly sat down.

"Good morning, boss," Mick said, not looking up. He continued to flip through his reports.

"Good morning to you, my friend," Michael said. "So how do you think your mission went?"

"We completed everything, just as planned. No hitches at all."

"Did you encounter any *unwelcomed* visitors?"

"Oh, just the usual suspects. Or shall I say, *sus-pect.*"

"Ahh, Damon . . . and I suppose you put him in his place?"

"Yep, I sure did. Due to your help, we stayed several steps ahead of him." Mick knew all-to-well that Michael checked-in periodically and watched the events on Earth unfold. However, the arch-angel had a real penchant for hearing a mission's recap directly from the front lines soldiers. Mick very much enjoyed these post-game analyses with his fellow angel.

"Good," Michael said. "So who did Damon inhabit this time?"

"Some very unfortunate, sharp dressed guy from Minneapolis. I suppose that Damon must have trailed me when I passed through the flaming sword. Usually I can ditch him, but you know how those guys are."

"Unfortunately, I do."

"Anyways, I spotted him in the market, and ultimately, I dealt with him like I normally do."

"I hope you weren't too rough on him—?"

Mick closed the folder on one report and opened another one. "Nope, I wasn't too rough. I actually didn't even have to lay a finger on him—this time. I merely used the Father's knowledge, power, and directions that you shared with me."

"As usual, you did an excellent job, Mick. I'm very pleased that you continue to learn from each new mission."

"Thank you Michael," Mick said. "By the way, *nice job to you* for sending that guardian angel to whisper in Danny's ear. It seems that it prompted him to run over and move his dad out of Damon's way— apparently just in time. For a minute, I almost thought that Wyatt was going to be joining us up here."

"Fortunately, it's not his time yet, Mick. He has much work to do; and yes, Rebecca did an excellent job of whispering to Danny. She's actually one of our most experienced angels in the guardian group."

"I heard that."

"Also, fortunately for us, Danny's heart is one that can actually hear what a guardian angel has to say. As you well know, they speak subtly, and not all humans can hear them when they speak."

After he left Wyatt at the market, Mick instantly passed through the flaming sword and rejoined several angels at Heaven's gate. Michael used another member of his forces, a guardian angel named Rebecca, to handle the covert message to Danny. Together, Michael and Mick eagerly watched when the motorcycle incident with Damon happened, and they cheered when Danny saved his dad.

"You're right, boss . . . well anyways . . . ." Mick trailed off.

"What's wrong?" Michael asked, concerned.

"Of course, nothing's wrong. It's just that these battles seem to be never-ending. Tell me; when will the Lord execute His plan and go back down there and finish this thing for good?"

"Soon Mick, soon," Michael said softly. "Your lament is the same for every angel, saint, and citizen of Heaven." Mick understood that only God knew the time of Christ's return, and that all of God's people and the angels eagerly await that fateful day.

"Well boss, what's next for me?"

Michael smiled, "As you've likely anticipated, there's much more to do with Wyatt and Danny. Of course, I'm going to keep you on this project until it's completed—which may take some time. Actually, you and the Hunter boys still have many projects and missions left to do, especially with Danny. As you well know, your work with the Hunter family goes back many centuries."

"You're right about that, chief," Mick agreed.

"You've also probably noticed that the rest of your crew has been deployed—some of them are putting things in place to help you with future missions. Not all of these events will involve the Hunters, but their involvement in kingdom affairs is very pivotal to what's about to occur."

"Michael, we've known each other for a *long* time. I guess that I kind of expected and hoped I'd continue to work with these boys. It'll be my honor to see this project through. Wyatt and Danny are good guys, and I think they'll serve our Father well."

"Excellent. Please stay on top of things until I receive your next orders for deployment."

Mick was pleased, and continued to look over his reports. "Hey, are you hungry, boss?"

"Yes . . . oh, didn't I tell you? There's a feast being prepared nearby in honor of the successful mission. I understand that it's almost ready. Will you join me?"

"Of course I will. So, where's this *shindig* gonna take place this time?"

"It's at the forest lodge . . . can you break away from your reports for a little while?"

"I sure can—let's roll." Mick put down his reports, and both he and Michael began walking towards the forest lodge. By design, it wasn't too far away. The great city of New Jerusalem, with much of the population, was a little further into Heaven.

The two angels walked along the path together, which was beset on both sides with beautiful, wooded landscape. The forest animals were everywhere to be seen, setting a tranquil panorama in Paradise. Mick saw two beautiful deer drinking in a stream down the hill on his right, and he pondered the vast difference between the fallen Earth and the perfection found in Heaven.

Down on Earth, those deer might be dinner. In Heaven, they were to be enjoyed for how beautiful God made them to be; in Paradise, there is no destruction of God's creation, and there is no death. Sometimes, newer citizens of Heaven initially found the lack of death to be a little surprising, because this concept was definitely alien to the death-ridden culture on the fallen Earth from whence they came.

"Mick, please tell me your impression of Wyatt Hunter. Will he work hard on the book you asked him to write?" Michael asked.

"Absolutely. There's no question in my mind that he will, chief. He and I made a true connection."

"I'm pleased to hear that."

"Danny and I connected, too. You know, he's really a good kid, and since he's so much younger, he actually has more potential than his old man for future battles."

"I agree. However, both of them will play a significant role in what the Lord has planned."

After a few minutes of strolling and enjoying the view, they arrived at a huge clearing, which marked the entrance to their destination. The entire area was framed by immense, ancient trees, which were folded above and around the forest lodge, forming a loving embrace. The Lord set aside areas like this in Heaven, which were softly lit by His light, because He knew that many of His children truly relish a peacefully shaded forest setting. About a hundred yards away, they could see the huge forest lodge building, distinctive because of its four chimneys. A steady stream of smoke was slowly billowing out of all four stacks, covering the area with a pleasant blanket of rustic aroma.

"Has Vanessa and her crew been cooking for long?" Mick asked.

"Actually, they have—three days and counting. Even though we've only known her for a short time, you're not surprised, are you? You know how much she loves this kind of thing."

"I do . . . and no, I'm not surprised . . . is Miss Abbie here too?"

"Of course she is. Those two did a lot of cooking down there, and even more up here."

"So who else is here?" Mick asked.

"About fifty citizens and angels. Also, many of Wyatt and Vanessa's family members are here, along with several friends. The Lord will also stop by in a little while to celebrate with us."

"Cool deal, boss." Mick's spirits were beginning to soar. Since there can be no sadness in Heaven, Mick's early morning mood could be best described as a slightly somber, due to the weariness of battle. It usually took him a day or so to re-acclimate himself to Heaven after a mission to the sinful domain on Earth.

Mick's countless missions to the other side to take on Satan and his demons made him yearn for an end to all evil. The truth was, however, that he really loved what he did. The angel very much relished the opportunity to work with the humans who he mentored.

Approaching the bottom of the wooden porch steps, Mick could now smell the pronounced aroma of the four crackling fires, coupled with the wonderful feast being prepared. By the Lord's design, it was coolish in this part of the Kingdom, and the lodge had some very comfortable rocking chairs adorning the front porch, which was six steps up.

When they arrived at the front door, the angels looked at one another, with grins on their faces. Celebrations in Heaven went on for a long time, and no one had to rush around to do menial chores. All work for the King in Heaven was a pleasure to do, and all of His children and the angels relished the opportunity to serve God. They opened the huge medieval wooden door and made their way inside.

The slightly muted light outside was a stark contrast to the brightly lit main hall of the forest lodge. Covering much of the space was rustic furniture, some of which was stationed around the blazing fireplaces. The main room was incredibly warm, inviting, and fairly loud, due to the excited conversations, which were being carried on among all of the guests. Wyatt's mom, Miss Abbie, was the first to spot the celebration's newcomers, and she came quickly over to greet them.

"Ohhhh, there you boys are! We've been waiting for your arrival," Abbie said, excitedly. She embraced Michael with a respectful hug, and then grabbed Mick and held on to him for a moment. "How're my boys doing down there, Mick?" she asked.

"Well ma'am, they're doing really well," Mick said. "I really enjoyed meeting them, and we actually became great friends." Mick stood back and marveled at Miss Abbie's new body, which suited her well. Back when she was still on Earth, she had to use a walking cane just to get around. Now that she was in Heaven and had received a perfect spiritual body, she was lively and spry.

Because it always reminded him of Christ's resurrection body, Mick always enjoyed seeing the new spiritual bodies which redeemed people receive when they pass into Heaven. He especially appreciated this process when he saw citizens who had endured difficult physical struggles when they were behind enemy lines on Earth—like Miss Abbie.

Just then, Vanessa came from out of the massive kitchen and quickly walked over to Mick, embracing him. "Please, tell me how they're doing Mick," she said. Michael smiled and nodded, deftly moving into the main hall to greet the other guests.

"Well ma'am, both of the boys are actually excited about their new missions and—"

Suddenly, a big friendly dog came bounding into the main hall towards Mick, jumping up on him. Trailing him were three other dogs, all excited and hopping around.

"Hey Scout—how're doing boy!" Mick said, getting plenty of licks on his face.

"Great . . . that is, about Wyatt and Danny," Vanessa said, giggling as she watched Scout love all over Mick. "I miss them both very much."

"Actually, so do I," the angel said.

"Well, we both know that they'll arrive here when the Lord is ready for them to join us."

"How true," Mick agreed.

"In the meantime, how would you like a great, big latte?"

"Vanessa, that would be fantastic. Hey, I'm thinking about adding a little honey to my coffee for a change. I thought I would give it a try. What do you think?"

Vanessa smiled that knowing smile. She appreciated that Mick was telling her something personal about her beloved Wyatt. "Good idea, Mick. Let's go to the kitchen to get your coffee started."

"Lead the way, milady," Mick said, grinning ear-to-ear.

And with that, the celebration began. The sounds of laughter permeated the entire forest lodge, as everyone enjoyed another wonderful day in Paradise. The feast was almost ready, and there was a great sense of anticipation in the room. The tantalizing aromas from the kitchen had everyone eager to sit down to savor in the great celebration meal.

Soon, a special guest would be joining them; One who everyone in the forest lodge was looking forward to seeing with eager anticipation. Yes, the King of kings, the Lord Jesus Christ, the Savior and redeemer of the universe would be joining them for their celebration feast. Can you imagine that, having Christ over for breakfast?

It was indeed, another spectacular day in Heaven.

ACKNOWLEDGEMENTS

I want to sincerely thank **Mike Pfeil** for his friendship and ongoing theological mentoring. His influence on my work has been profound, and his guidance in helping me to understand some of the Bible's nuances have—and will continue to have—an eternally positive effect on my life. He is a real gem.

I also want to thank **Madge Bloom**, whose excellent photography is featured on the majority of the chapter headings which take place in Pike Place Market. We both hope and pray that seeing some of the places where Mick and Wyatt met, added to your enjoyment of the book. We also hope that it blessed your walk through the market.

Many thanks to **Robert "Hobo" Chadwick** for his work on the covers, and to **Alfred Jones**, for his portrait of Mick. Both of these artists added so much to this book, and I appreciate them very much.

Additionally, I want to thank **Johnny & Tammy Ketchum**, whose encouragement in my writing during the early stages of this book truly kept me going, when common sense would have said to give up. I also want to give a shout-out to **Gordy Dixon**, whose continuing encouragement and support is so important to this ministry.

Lastly—and far from least—I want to thank **Jesus Christ**, the One who sacrificed everything for all of us. All good things come from Him . . . including this story . . . .

The Mythology Found in
A Walk Through the Market:
Angels, Demons, & The Flaming Sword

Although the Bible provides everything we need to live our lives giving glory to God, it does not tell us everything there is to know. Therefore, when one deems to write about Heaven, angels, and how angels interact with humans, there is much we cannot know until this life is over. Truly, we can only really know how this works when our *real* lives begin with the Lord in Heaven.

However, in writing these novels, even though they are fictional, it is my steadfast desire to always write story lines which are consistent with the Bible. Novels are not, by their very nature, biblical exposition. In this section, I wish to clarify where literary license has been taken, so that you will be able to separate the two things—biblical fact, and reasonable biblical speculation (fiction).

It's also important to note that I will not intentionally write anything that directly contradicts Scripture. The story in this book is only designed as a means to present the Word of God in a way which I believe is easy for readers to understand. *Deuteronomy 29:29* speaks of secret things belonging to God, which they most certainly do. However, speculating on the boundless power of our heavenly Father is an exciting endeavor, indeed. It only seems natural that we, as human beings made in the image of God, would have a natural curiosity about the things the Lord does not directly tell us in the Bible. However, we must be cautious as we explore these possibilities as being just that—possibilities.

I believe very strongly in the inerrancy, and irresistible, life-changing nature of the Bible. So, in an effort to share my love of God's Holy Word, I consider this novel to be a "biblical teaching novel," not merely entertainment. Studying and discussing the Holy Word of God is something we should all engage in every day, and I truly hope this story has drawn the reader towards the Bible. Whether you agree or disagree with my use of fictional mythology, if you are drawn towards studying the Bible because of it, I am delighted!

One more thing, before we get started. We should always keep our minds tethered to mankind's significant foundational events—Adam and Eve's fall, and Christ's atonement—when engaging in any biblical discussions outside of these two basic pillars of the Christian faith. Essentially, this—and any future stories—are attempts to reinforce these two important premises.

To that end, here are a few notes on several subjects encountered in this book:

The Flaming Sword

After Adam and Eve sinned, God placed a flaming sword at the entrance to the Garden of Eden to keep mankind out *(Genesis 3:24)*. Beginning with this book, I have used the flaming sword as a fictional portal for the angel Mick (and others) to travel between Heaven and Earth. Essentially, I treat the flaming sword as a barrier between Heaven and the sinful world mankind currently dwells on—Earth.

According to *1 Corinthians 3:10-15*, a Christian's works will be tested by fire. Those works not done to the glory of God will be burned up. The Bible does not say whether that burning is tied in with the flaming sword of *Genesis 3:24*, therefore, it must be listed as fiction. Specifically, it is strictly under "DP," which is short for "Divine Privilege." (I've coined this phrase and utilized it in the book as an attempt to avoid controversy, whenever possible) However, for this story, the two aforementioned Scriptures are indelibly intertwined.

Demonic Activity

The activities of demons written into this book may or may not be presented in the Bible in the strictest literal sense. However, these actions are quite consistent with what the Bible presents as the activities of the evil ones and their violent, rebellious, and deceitful ways.

Demons *do* exist, and demonic possessions were often written of in the gospels. However, regarding the prevalence of demon possessions today, I cannot say—I am by no means an expert on their current activities. However, evil most certainly does exist in this fallen world, and anyone or anything you encounter in life who claims to have the truth, should be tested against the Scriptures. Additionally, if you ever encounter a being claiming to be an angel or a messenger of God, who doesn't confess that Christ has come in the flesh, then they are expressly *not* from God. In that unlikely event, you would probably be talking to a demon. Please read *1 John 4:1-6*.

Invisible Dimension

I have coined the phrase "invisible dimension" for the general abode of demons (see *Ephesians 6:12*). Some of the characters, including the angel Mick, often use this term to describe the place where demons roam; one which is not visible to the human eye. The full answer for where demons dwell is under DP.

Angels

There are many passages in the Bible where an angel delivers a divine message to someone living on Earth. In fact, the word angel itself means "messenger." However, it is clearly a rare thing, and only happens when a divine message is absolutely necessary. In other words, it is very unlikely you'll ever encounter an angel during your lifetime on Earth. Please always remember this—Mick and the other angels introduced in this book are fictional, and their entire purpose as fictional characters in this series is to draw people closer towards our Savior, Jesus Christ.

The casual communication between angel and man presented in this book is fiction, since it is beyond what is found in the Bible. However, as *Hebrews 13:2* explains, there surely is much more interaction with angels than we are aware of.

The angel characters are often shown as "having fun" as they engage humans. This type of fellowship during something as common as a meal or a cup of coffee together is a prevalent theme throughout this novel. Once again, this is speculative, but not without possibility.

The angels who travel from Heaven to Earth in the story are shown to have "human-like" bodies when they are visiting people. Unlike the misperceptions of many, this is not without biblical likelihood. For example, in *Genesis 18*, the pre-incarnate Jesus appeared with two angels and had a meal with Abraham. In that same passage, the two angels then traveled to Sodom. When they arrived, their appearance was so human-like, the men of Sodom assumed they were men.

One character in this book who is an angel is given a female name; this of course is also fictional. Any time angels appear as humans in the Bible they are presented as male. However, that does *not* necessarily mean we will only meet angels in Heaven with masculine attributes. It merely means that God has chosen to present His holy angels to us as men.

Heaven

A couple of scenes in this book take place in Heaven. They are strictly fictional accounts of what I personally anticipate Heaven *might* be like. We do know that Heaven is the dwelling place which God has created for us to live in, and the Bible tells us that God chooses to dwell in Heaven.

I take the position that Heaven is a very familiar place—a real, physical place—rather than an ethereal, non-physical place, as some claim. This is a reasonable conclusion since we were created with physical attributes. This is also substantiated by the fact that the Bible speaks of Heaven in physical terms (for instance, the great multitude of *Revelation 7* are wearing white robes and are carrying palm branches in their hands).

The subject of having bodies in Heaven is a lightning rod within the Christian faith. Unfortunately, it is seldom agreed upon. I take the position that God made us to have a body, soul, and spirit (man's spirit is made in God's image). I also believe that a Christian's body in Heaven is very likely similar to Christ's resurrection body—which was indeed, a *real* body (there is no question that His body is perfect). Christ is the first fruits, and we, His redeemed children, follow Him. Although the process of how God resurrects us after death is under DP, I believe there is enough Scripture to glean that we can expect to have a perfect body in the intermediate Heaven; one that is suited to be in God's holy presence.

Please see *Genesis 2:7, 1 Corinthians 15:35-37* and *Revelation 6:9-11* for further information.

Discovering how the Lord brings His children to Heaven, what our bodies will be like, and what we'll do in Heaven, are extremely exciting subjects to speculate on. Even if you do not agree with my speculations, we should all keep our eyes focused on God's eternal kingdom; knowing that it will be a vast improvement over our lives on the current sinful, fallen Earth.

Messages From Beyond

Towards the end of this story, in chapter 18, God sent a vision of Vanessa in Heaven to Wyatt, through the angel Mick. Although this is a very unlikely scenario, it was written to illustrate the importance of *1 John 4:1-6* (once again, please read this very important passage!). Seeking messages from beyond the grave is the playground of demons, and I *strongly* advise against it. Demons are deceivers, and they will often masquerade as an angel of light. Essentially, I'm saying this—*do not expect any messages from people who have passed on!* If you know Jesus Christ as your Savior, you'll have plenty of time to talk to Jesus and His saved children for all of eternity. Remember, this novel is just a story.

About biblical visions . . . the Bible does not give us a lot of detail about how they work. Biblically speaking, sometimes, God sent messages in dreams, when someone was asleep. Other times, they were visions, when someone was awake. The bottom line is this—the presentation of the vision in this book is strictly fictional. The truth about Jesus Christ being sovereign over everything in creation is not.

Theology

To be honest, navigating the world of theology for a "regular dude" like me can be quite daunting. My personal writing is an attempt to decipher the complex world of theology, and what the experts have to say on spiritual matters and issues (this can often be a minefield, indeed!). I then attempt to present these opinions in a way that is easy for a non-theologian to understand. Essentially, that's the reason why I write novels—to draw others towards God's Holy Word in the Bible. That's truly where all the answers are.

Coffee

While I cannot unequivocally prove that coffee exists in Heaven, I sure am hoping it'll be there! Having a *cup of joe* with some friends is an often used scenario in this story, but there's a good reason for that. It's not only because of my intense love of the wonderful beverage; but also, having coffee with friends is a very common and comfortable socializing event for many people around the world. For my non-coffee-loving readers, I beg your forgiveness.

PRAYER OF SALVATION

I am excited that even seekers of biblical truth who are not yet committed to Christ would be drawn to this novel, and I pray that your heart would be open to salvation. The amount of information now available for those seeking to find answers to their questions is nothing short of amazing. Finding faith in Christ is not about acting religious or having to dress a certain way. It's about surrender to the Creator of all that we see; the One who loves us more than we can imagine; the One who died for our sins; and the One who loves you, no matter what you have done.

It's important for you to know that it's absolutely normal to have questions and objections regarding matters pertaining to life in Christ. However, failing to truly seek the answers to your questions is extremely unadvisable. I ask you to please consider going into an investigative mode, and don't let previous potentially false paradigms about matters of faith corrupt your investigation. In other words, please go into your investigation with an open mind. I believe it will not be hard for you to find the answers to what you seek. However, you must remember that only the Holy Word of God is inspired by the Holy Spirit. Therefore, even though there are tremendous ministry tools available to aid you in your quest, they must always be synchronized with the Bible. If they fail to do that, they're absolutely false.

If you find yourself ready to find true joy for the first time in your life; if you're ready to change your days from hopelessness to hope; and if you're ready to secure your future for eternity; then please consider praying this simple prayer. If you pray this prayer in earnest sincerity, please understand that it's just the *beginning* of a long and incredibly enjoyable walk with the Lord. You'll need help along the way, so finding a local, Bible-based church with strong Christian leadership to disciple you in your walk is the next step.

Jesus,
I confess that I have sinned and fallen short of your glory.
I believe that you suffered and died on the cross for me,
And when you did that,
You paid the full price for the punishment due me, for my sins.
Please forgive me for my sins,
And accept me into your kingdom.
Until right now,
I have only lived for myself.
From now on,
I will live for you.

Thank you for your incredible sacrifice,
And please also show me
How to help others.
When it is my time,
I look forward to being received
Into your glorious presence.

Please come into my life
Now,
And forever . . .

Welcome to the family! Don't stop now, there's work to be done.

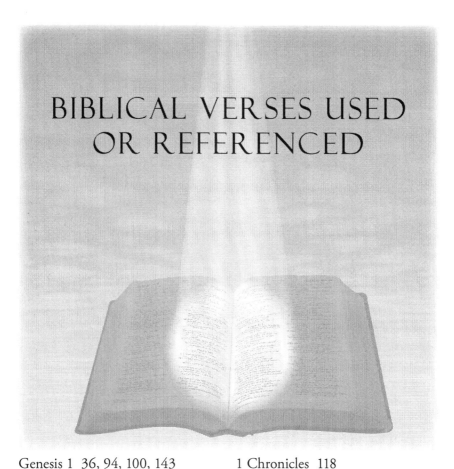

BIBLICAL VERSES USED
OR REFERENCED

19701467R00166

Made in the USA
Lexington, KY
02 January 2013